Other Books in the Jossey-Bass Nonprofit Sector Series:

Accounting and Budgeting in Public and Nonprofit Organizations,
C. William Garner

Achieving Excellence in Fund Raising, *Henry A. Rosso and Associates*

Board Leadership: A Bimonthly Workshop with John Carver

The Board Member's Guide to Fund Raising, *Fisher Howe*

The Board Member's Guide to Stategic Planning, *Fisher Howe*

Boards That Make a Difference, Second Edition, *John Carver*

The CarverGuide Series on Effective Board Governance, *John Carver*

Collaborative Leadership, *David C. Chrislip, Carl E. Larson*

Creating and Implementing Your Strategic Plan, *John M. Bryson, Farnum K. Alston*

The Drucker Foundation Self-Assessment Tool for Nonprofit Organizations,
The Peter F. Drucker Foundation for Nonprofit Management

Executive Leadership in Nonprofit Organizations, *Robert D. Herman, Richard D. Heimovics*

Governing Boards, Revised Edition, *Cyril O. Houle*

Grassroots Leaders for a New Economy, *Douglas Henton, John Melville, Kimberly Walesh*

Handbook of Practical Program Evaluation, *Joseph Wholey, Harry P. Hatry, Kathryn E. Newcomer, Editors*

Human Resources Management for Public and Nonprofit Organizations,
Joan E. Pynes

The Jossey-Bass Handbook of Nonprofit Leadership and Management,
Robert D. Herman and Associates

The Leader of the Future, *Frances Hesselbein, Marshall Goldsmith, Richard Beckhard, Editors*

Leader to Leader (quarterly), *The Peter F. Drucker Foundation for Nonprofit Mangement*

Managing for Accountability, *Kevin Kearns*

Marketing Nonprofit Programs and Services, *Douglas B. Herron*

Marketing Social Change, *Alan R. Andreasen*

Nonprofit Almanac 1996–1997, *Virginia A. Hodgkinson, Murray S. Weitzman, with John A. Abrahams, Eric A. Crutchfield, David R. Stevenson*

Nonprofit Boards and Leadership, *Miriam M. Wood, Editor*

Nonprofit Management and Leadership (quarterly)

The Organization of the Future, *Frances Hesselbein, Marshall Goldsmith, Richard Beckhard, Editors*

Powered by Coalition: The Story of INDEPENDENT SECTOR, *Brian O'Connell*

Reinventing Fundraising, *Sondra C. Shaw, Martha A. Taylor*

Rosso on Fund Raising, *Henry A. Rosso*

The Search Conference, *Merrelyn Emery, Ronald E. Purser*

Secrets of Successful Grantsmanship, *Susan L. Golden*

The Seven Faces of Philanthropy, *Russ A. Prince, Karen A. File*

Strategic Planning for Public and Nonprofit Organizations, Revised Edition,
John M. Bryson

Welcome to the Board, *Fisher Howe*

Winning Grants Step by Step, *Support Centers of America*

Changing by Design

Changing by Design

A Practical Approach to Leading Innovation in Nonprofit Organizations

Douglas C. Eadie

Jossey-Bass Publishers • San Francisco

Substantial discounts on bulk quantities of Jossey-Bass books are available to corporations, professional associations, and other organizations. For details and discount information, contact the special sales department at Jossey-Bass Inc., Publishers (415) 433–1740; Fax (800) 605–2665.

For sales outside the United States, please contact your local Simon & Schuster International Office.

Jossey-Bass Web address: http://www.josseybass.com

TCF Manufactured in the United States of America on Lyons Falls Turin Book. This paper is acid-free and 100 percent totally chlorine-free.

Library of Congress Cataloging-in-Publication Data

Eadie, Douglas C.
   Changing by design : a practical approach to leading innovation in
nonprofit organizations / Douglas C. Eadie. — 1st ed.
       p.   cm. — (The Jossey-Bass nonprofit sector series)
   Includes bibliographical references and index.
   ISBN 0-7879-0824-X
   1. Nonprofit organizations—Management.   I. Title.   II. Series.
   HD62.6.E183   1997
   658'.048—dc21   96-53567

FIRST EDITION
HB Printing 10 9 8 7 6 5 4 3 2 1

The Jossey-Bass Nonprofit Sector Series

Contents

	Preface	xi
	The Author	xxv
1	The Change Challenge for Nonprofits	1
2	Building the Capacity for Innovation	20
3	Strengthening Chief Executive Leadership	39
4	Building Boards That Lead	72
5	Nurturing Creative Capacity in Nonprofits	101
6	Strategic Management as an Engine for Innovation	126
7	Applying Strategic Management to Produce Change	144
8	Implementing Change Initiatives	170
9	Making Innovation Work	201
	References	217
	Index	221

To my wife
Barbara Krai Eadie

Preface

I doubt that the world really needs another book that focuses exclusively on how to implement change in for-profit and nonprofit organizations, and I know for certain that there is no market for another supposed all-purpose panacea purporting to deliver wonderful results at modest cost. But nonprofit leaders and managers do need detailed, practical guidance in taking firmer command of their organizations'—and their individual—change.

To provide such badly needed, down-to-earth guidance is the principal reason I have written *Changing by Design*. Although considerable attention has been given to ways that changes can be put into practice, less attention has been paid to the far more important matter that is at the heart of this book: determining the content of planned change.

Change for change's sake is as apt to cause harm as good, of course. The change that I discuss in this book is anything but random. Its intended result, and its only justification, is a nonprofit organization's realizing its vision and mission as completely as possible. In order to achieve this result, a nonprofit needs to change in ways that allow it to capitalize on opportunities to move it toward its vision and counter threats from the world outside.

Writing this book was a passionate endeavor for me for two important reasons. First, almost all of my career over a quarter-century has been spent working in or assisting nonprofit organizations, and I deeply respect the work they do. The millions of organizations populating the nonprofit sector all over the world are of critical importance to the quality of life of hundreds of millions of people, not only because they perform an amazing variety of essential tasks but also because they loom large economically, especially in the United States and other developed nations (Salamon and Anheier, 1994).

Second, personal and professional experience has intimately acquainted me with the difficulties involved in changing anything in an important way—whether it be an individual's vocation or style of management or a nonprofit's diversification into a new program area. It is critical to remember that organizational change of any magnitude is unlikely to take place unless there is also significant change in many of the individuals who work for the organization. And individual change often feels like a perilous journey through a long, dark tunnel where there is no light visible until well along the way. Knowing full well the anxiety and pain that often accompany change, and being far from a world-class change artist myself, I brought both humility and empathy to this writing task.

Choosing to Face the Challenge

Being pressured to change in response to a changing world is nothing new in human history. Life and change are intimately linked, and change has always been a staple of human affairs. Pharaoh Amenhotep III and his palace guard surely agonized over strategies for coping with change in New Kingdom Egypt over three thousand years ago, as have kings, queens, and lesser mortals from time immemorial. Still, change in the waning days of the twentieth century seems unique in its breadth, depth, complexity, and pace. As James O'Toole (1995) has observed, "There is reason to believe that in fact the depth of the alterations experienced today is more profound than ever before" (p. xii). Virtually everyone agrees that the world is growing more complex and that change is rapidly accelerating while becoming less and less predictable.

In this world of dizzying and often threatening change, nonprofit boards, chief executives, and managers must learn to design, lead, and direct their own change if they are to succeed in realizing their visions and carrying out their very important missions. Nonprofit leaders and managers face a stark choice. They can play a creative and assertive role in designing their own change—consciously planning to impact their own organizations and, sometimes, conditions in the larger environment—or they can be changed by the forces swirling around them. The middle ground of not changing is not a viable option; nostalgia for an imagined golden past is a dangerous distraction. Merely digging in, pulling the wagons into a circle, and defending the status quo is surely a high-risk course in these turbulent times.

Taking Advantage of the Change Around Us

If the pace and depth of change these days can be occasionally disconcerting and threatening, change can also bring some real blessings, even if they are well disguised. Nonprofit organizations that are committed to exercising greater self-determination in leading and managing their own change can take advantage of significant advances in knowledge and technology that have come about particularly since World War II. The several disciplines that constitute the field of management have developed dramatically, primarily through research in graduate schools of business, and nonprofit management has over the past two decades come into its own as a field that has a number of academic centers around the country. Psychoanalytical and cognitive psychology have contributed mightily to our understanding of conscious and subconscious mental processes, while our knowledge about human learning and creative capacity has grown impressively as well. The knowledge base has expanded rapidly and information is ever more quickly accessed and communicated these days, thanks to computerized databases and the wonders of the Internet.

So we now have impressive tools that can be put to good use in leading and managing change, however challenging the world may appear. I, for one, would not be the least bit tempted to trade places with the director of a settlement house on New York City's Lower East Side in 1900, or with the manager of a relief agency in Berlin in 1929, or with a hospital staff physician in London during a smallpox epidemic two hundred years ago. Never has humankind been better equipped to cope with a challenging world than it is today.

A New Approach to Designing and Leading Change

This book describes a comprehensive approach to designing and leading change in the world's huge, diverse, and growing nonprofit sector. The approach is based on the assumption that consciously designed and led change will be most beneficial to nonprofit organizations if it has the following attributes:

- It is the product of a well-established, ongoing organizational process that generates changes in response to effectively monitored environmental changes.
- It is systematic in the sense that the various changes launched at any given time are linked together in ways that take full advantage of synergies in order to produce the maximum possible benefit.
- It is rational in the sense that the highest-stakes changes are made first and involve a favorable cost-benefit ratio for the nonprofit.
- It is the product of a growthful process that contributes to organizational learning and builds the capacity to lead change in the future.

What I call the "3CAP" approach involves building—and integrating in practice—three critical, interrelated organizational capacities or competencies:

- The capacity to *lead*. This basically involves the exercise of chief executive and board leadership.
- The capacity to *innovate*. This basically involves marrying creative thinking with planning, and particularly with a variation on the broad strategic planning theme known as strategic management.
- The capacity to *implement*. This basically involves the structure and process for carrying out change and the internal culture within which change is implemented.

As suggested earlier, this book's principal intended contribution to the field is to expand the concept of change management beyond a traditionally narrow focus on implementation. The more balanced approach set forth in this book describes how the principal change leaders—nonprofit chief executives and their boards—can become actively involved in the design of change rather than merely commanding or persuading people in their organizations to change. I give much greater attention to the determination of the change targets—the *what* of change—and the role of creativity in choosing these targets than to the already well-treated subject of implementing change. I also address the critical spiritual dimensions of leadership and the innovation process.

A second intended contribution of this book is to propose how the three critical capacities that constitute a comprehensive approach to leading and managing change can, in practice not just in theory, be tied together so that they are mutually reinforcing and synergistic. I do not claim that this book presents a comprehensive system that can on its own meet all of the change leadership and management needs of a nonprofit, nor do I claim that the described system is a simple or a painless one. No single approach can guarantee success. But I have no doubt that if a nonprofit makes a serious effort to develop and use the three key capacities in a coordinated fashion, it will significantly increase the odds of realizing its vision and mission, no matter how turbulent or threatening the environment.

Sources of Knowledge

In writing this book, I drew heavily on the work of many capable and insightful students of for-profit and nonprofit leadership and management. Most notable in this respect were Peter Drucker and Lester Salamon on nonprofit management generally; Warren Bennis, John Gardner, and James O'Toole in the area of executive leadership; Chris Argyris, Nathan Grundstein, and Peter Senge on organizational learning; Margaret Boden, Joseph Campbell, Mihaly Csikszentmihalyi, Howard Gardner, Carl Jung, Soren Kierkegaard, and Rollo May on creativity; John Bryson, Rosabeth Moss-Kanter, Henry Mintzberg, and Noel Tichy on strategic planning and innovation; John Carver, Robert Herman, and Richard Heimovics on governance; and Wilkie Au, Noreen Cannon, Jay Conger, Thomas Merton, Thomas Moore, and Scott Peck on the spiritual dimension of leadership. I am indebted to many other students of leadership and management, but the foregoing influenced my thinking most powerfully.

However, my primary source of inspiration and information has been the real-life experience that I have accumulated over a quarter-century of work in nonprofits as an executive manager and for nonprofits as a consultant. The board members, chief executives, and managers of these organizations are in a very real sense my primary teachers and collaborators. Although the cases presented in this book are, strictly speaking, fictional, each one is based on the real-life experiences of these nonprofits.

A Personal Note

Writing *Changing by Design* also taught me a lot about changing and growing, and especially about the trials and tribulations involved in tapping into one's creativity and breaking away from old patterns. This is a very different book from the one that I began so optimistically and efficiently to plot out in spring 1995. As the days passed and the outline and bibliography took shape, I found myself in the grip of an unanticipated and powerful anxiety that disrupted my meticulously charted course.

Assuming, based on long experience, that I had fallen victim to that familiar demon, Fear of Failure, I willed myself to keep moving, knowing that once past the proverbial graveyard, I would soon be in full stride, whistling a happy tune. However, rather than responding to the imposition of greater discipline, the anxiety grew worse. So I called the infant effort to a temporary halt, and sat back to reflect.

Over a long weekend, I began to understand the anxiety that had disrupted my calm and to recognize it as a valuable, if taxing, ally rather than the spoiler it had earlier appeared to be. I understood that the anxiety that had momentarily paralyzed my writing effort was a valuable, if complex and somewhat contradictory, message from within. On the one hand, anxiety was goading me to be more creative and expand the envisioned book beyond the familiar and safe boundaries of managing change. On the other hand, I was terrified by the prospect of leaving a comfortable place, taking on more risk, and perhaps failing.

Indeed, I was facing the classic choice that confronts every person on the edge of change: to move forward, daring to be creative, or to retreat to a safe and comfortable place. My response was ultimately to undertake writing a broader, more passionate, and, I trust, more useful, book. The journey was anything but smooth and painless; roadblocks and potholes slowed my progress. But the valuable learning that I could put to good use in *Changing by Design* more than justified the privileged suffering I endured. Happily, what I learned while writing this book validated what I had observed in all my years of work with nonprofit leaders and managers. Above all, I learned that subconscious barriers to creative thinking can be powerful and all the more insidious for going unrecognized, that considerable courage is required to be creative, and that faith in a supreme being can be a rich—and perhaps the preeminent—source of that courage.

My Key Assumptions

Four assumptions are at the heart of my 3CAP approach to leading and managing change: strengthening nonprofit leadership and management merits serious attention; the stakes are high and getting higher; a new approach to leading and managing change is called for; and individual change is required for significant organizational change.

The Importance of Nonprofits

The millions of nonprofits at work around the world are involved in meeting an incredibly diverse range of needs—in education, social services, health care, aging, economic and community development, and the fine arts, among other areas. Hence, nonprofit leaders paying attention to their organizations' learning to lead and manage change more effectively will yield significant benefits in the United States and around the world. Their inability to cope with the challenges facing them and the nations in which they work would come at a high social and economic cost that the world can ill afford.

The Stakes

Merely coping with complex and accelerating change, particularly in the realm of technology, will tax the ingenuity, discipline, and courage of nonprofit leaders and managers. However, American society, like much of the rest of the world, is also experiencing a social transformation that is placing ever-greater demands on the nonprofit sector. The disappearance of close-knit communities and the erosion of trust in governmental, religious, and educational institutions, which seem unable or unwilling to lead change creatively, has left a vacuum that is too often filled these days with a cacophony of shrill voices that offer simplistic, black and white solutions to complex issues. Increasingly, the nonprofit sector is being called on to replace angry debate with dialogue, emotion with reason, and childish simplicity with mature complexity. The sector's success is a high-stakes matter!

The Need for a New Approach

Conventional approaches to change management will not equip nonprofit leaders and managers to meet the change challenges bombarding them. For one thing, they focus far too heavily on *how* to implement change—how to get the troops to go along—and too little on *what* to change. Traditional approaches also tend to follow particular tracks (strategic planning or total quality management, for example), failing to make practical connections that would tie the tracks together in something approaching a system.

Nonprofit leaders and managers need an approach that ties together—in practical ways that they can actually use—all the key tools that are required to lead and manage change: chief executive and board leadership; individual and organizational creative capacity; innovation through strategic and operational planning; and implementation of change. That is the aim of this book.

Individual and Organizational Change

Organizations are people working together to achieve common aims. Organizations in the abstract do not change—the people within them do. Therefore, any comprehensive approach to leading and managing organizational change must deal with individual change or it will be woefully inadequate. Unfortunately, the human factor in the change equation usually gets short shrift, especially the spiritual and psychological underpinnings of creativity and their powerful influence on innovation. When individual learning and growth are considered, it is frequently without making practical connections to organizational learning and innovation. Witness the all-too-common weekend creativity training session for senior managers, whose excitement and warm glow quickly wear off after returning to an organization whose processes are just as resistant to innovation as ever. Heightened expectations can be a disruptive force for organizations if they are ill-prepared to satisfy them. *Changing by Design* pays considerable attention to individual change and growth as the basic fuel driving organizational change.

The Audience

This book is intended to serve as a practical guidebook for all of those nonprofit actors whose participation in leading and managing change is essential for its ultimate success, including the following:

- Nonprofit chief executive officers, who are the primary "change champions" ultimately accountable for the design and execution of organizational processes to lead and manage change, and whose career development and even professional survival depend on leading change successfully in their organizations.
- The millions of volunteers, including many businesspeople, who serve on nonprofit boards of directors, in this capacity empowering the chief executive to provide strong leadership and supporting change efforts through strategic decisions, policy formulation, and resource commitment.
- The executives and managers who should be intimately involved in fashioning change targets and who inevitably do most of the work of change and experience the lion's share of the pain and suffering.

This book is also intended to serve as a resource in the education of nonprofit managers, blending developing theory and practice and suggesting areas for further study. It will prove useful to educators and students in undergraduate and graduate programs in nonprofit management, business administration, public administration, social work, and social service administration.

What Follows

The book consists of nine chapters.

Chapter One examines the nature of change external to non-profit organizations and describes the range of choices available to leaders and managers in fashioning and carrying out their own organizational change initiatives. It also describes the barriers to beginning the challenging journey of designing and managing organizational change in a nonprofit.

Chapter Two describes the deficiencies in current approaches to leading and managing change and presents an overview of the comprehensive 3CAP approach that ties together chief executive and board leadership, creative capacity, planning, and implementation.

Chapter Three describes the change leadership role of the non-profit chief executive, going beyond the traditional view of the chief executive as leader and top administrator by looking at five principal outcomes of chief executive leadership. The chapter also discusses three personal attributes that are critical to the successful leadership of change and how chief executives can develop them.

Chapter Four describes the failure of the passive, reactive style of board leadership and presents an approach to governance design that can produce greater accountability among the board members for their own performance and ensure that the resources they bring to the change process are fully tapped in leading change. The chapter also provides practical guidance to using board-staff retreats as a change vehicle.

Chapter Five explores the concept of creativity, from the "hard" scientific research on creative cognition and the use of computer simulations in understanding the creative process to the "softer" psychoanalytical and spiritual explanations. The critical role of anxiety as both goad and roadblock is also discussed and practical ways in which nonprofits can build their employees' creative capacity are proposed.

Chapter Six presents an overview of a contemporary variation on the strategic planning theme, strategic management. It describes how it can be used as a sort of engine to convert creative capacity into the practical organizational innovations that are the stuff of change. Also discussed are ways to avoid the ritualism and control bias that often take the heart out of planning, turning it into a sterile exercise that cannot foster human creativity or serve as an effective tool for innovation.

Chapter Seven describes the application of the strategic management process, from fashioning the values, vision, and mission that make up a nonprofit's strategic framework to selecting strategic issues and formulating change initiatives to address the issues. Practical guidance is provided for using task forces as an instrument for fashioning the change initiatives.

Chapter Eight looks at the implementation of change—the structure, process, and internal organizational culture—exploring ways to protect change initiatives from engulfment by day-to-day pressures and build an internal environment that is change-friendly. The chapter also discusses how chief executives can build support for the change initiatives and reduce resistance.

Chapter Nine concludes the book by summarizing the key elements of the 3CAP approach and pointing the way for nonprofit leaders who are embarking on their own change journeys.

Acknowledgments

I wrote this book, but in a very real sense I did not do it alone. Whatever creativity I brought to the writing task was—I know with certainty—a generous gift from a God who expects no repayment but calls on me to be courageous enough to exercise the gift fully. I also benefitted from contributions of knowledge, experience, and wisdom from many colleagues and friends who share a strong commitment to nonprofit leadership. While I was writing the book I became keenly aware of debts I had already incurred and acquired a number of new ones. I would like to acknowledge the more important ones here.

First, I thank my parents, Ina Mae and William Clay Eadie, who gave me much more than a life to live. In a home filled with newspapers, magazines, and books, I learned to love and respect the written word. No matter how rambunctious the table conversation among the eight of us, proper English was the rule, and it was enforced. At home I acquired the lifetime habit of taking books along with me on every trip and reading myself to sleep every night. One of my most vivid memories is of Mother's taking me by the hand and marching me to the main desk of our public library, where she informed the head librarian in no uncertain terms that her son, then eleven, could take out any book he chose with no exceptions. This caused a bit of a stir at a time when John Steinbeck's *East of Eden* had joined a number of novels on a hidden shelf under the counter. With different parents I might never have written this or any other book, and certainly not nearly as well, and I am indebted to mine for the values they instilled in me.

I am indebted to two teachers for the very different but equally important lessons they taught. Winton U. Solberg, Ph.D., emeritus professor of history at the University of Illinois at Urbana, with his meticulously crafted and eloquently presented lectures and steady stream of written assignments that were closely critiqued, provided me with invaluable guidance in organizing and clearly expressing my thoughts in writing. Nathan D. Grundstein, Ph.D., emeritus professor of management at Case Western Reserve University in Cleveland, taught me to distrust glib explanations of complex phenomena, to view with skepticism the little golden rules of conventional wisdom, and always to strive to see—to gain an "intelligence" of—the world that reveals its manifold possibilities. I can also thank Professors Solberg and Grundstein for the feeling of guilt that stays hand and mouth when I am tempted to dash out a mediocre piece of writing or parrot the conventional wisdom.

Many colleagues read and provided valuable suggestions for improving all or part of the manuscript of this book, and I am indebted to them for taking the time out of their demanding schedules to assist me. Deserving my heartfelt thanks are Goldie Alvis; Timothy Armbruster, Ph.D.; Carol Aten; Wilkie Au, Ph.D.; David Bergholz; Professor John Bryson; Will Dent; Jean Gaede; Sandra Gray; Paul Greeley; Professor Nathan Grundstein; Geneva Johnson; Ann Kent; Grace Kilbane; Robert Knight; Susan Lajoie, Ph.D.; William Laraia; Lolita McDavid, M.D.; Kenneth McLaughlin; Steven Minter; Melvin Pye; Professor David Renz; Paul Pritchard; James Richmond; Joseph Roman; Rev. Richard Tankerson; deTeel Patterson (Pat) Tiller; Fr. Robert Welsh, S.J.; and Professor John Yankey. I am also indebted to Fr. Marcel Gareau, S.J., of Loyola House in Nairobi, Kenya, whose advice and counsel over thirty years ago at Tafari Makonnen School in Addis Ababa,

Ethiopia, was a godsend to the neophyte history instructor I was then, and whose correspondence during the writing of this book never failed to inspire and hearten me.

I wrote this book while in the midst of a personal spiritual odyssey that has, I believe, deepened my understanding of the nature of creativity and leadership. Fortunately, I have not traveled alone. I deeply appreciate the strong encouragement, friendly support, and wise counsel that I have received from Fr. Carl Bonk, S.J.; Rev. Kenneth Chalker, D.Min.; Elizabeth Franklin, Ph.D.; Fr. Walter Jenne; Rev. David Kinzel; and Rev. Donald Neuendorf.

In addition to reading and commenting on all or part of the manuscript, the following colleagues arranged or hosted forums at which I presented the major themes of the book and benefitted from the stimulating dialogue that ensued: Garis Distelhorst, chief staff executive of the National Association of College Stores; Professor Norman Dolch, director of the American Humanics Program, Louisiana State University at Shreveport; Professor Bryan Downes, head of the Department of Planning, Public Policy and Management at the University of Oregon, and Matilda Deas, then a graduate student in the department; Professor Richard Edwards, dean of the School of Social Work at the University of North Carolina at Chapel Hill; Paul Greeley, president, and Eric Stowe, senior vice president, American Chamber of Commerce Executives; Professor Benjamin Hodes, dean of the Division of Continuing Education, Duquesne University; Kathy Johnson, executive vice president of the Minnesota Society of Association Executives; Robert Knight, president and CEO, and John Smith, executive vice president, of the National Association of Private Industry Councils; Professor David Luhrsen, dean of the Rinker School of Business at Palm Beach Atlantic College; Professor Peter Rea, dean, and Thomas Riemenschneider, M.D., director of Graduate Business Programs, the Division of Business Administration at Baldwin Wallace College; Maureen Robinson, director of education, National Center for Nonprofit Boards; Professor Lester Salamon, director of the Institute for Policy Studies at Johns Hopkins University; Thomas Urban, executive director, Professional Development and Regulatory Programs, American Public Transit Association; Darienne Wilson, executive director of the Mississippi Society of Association Executives; and Professor Dennis Young, governing director of the Mandel Center for Nonprofit Organizations at Case Western Reserve University.

Alan Shrader and Susan Williams at Jossey-Bass Publishers encouraged me to undertake this book, provided keen insights as I fleshed out the key concepts and drafted the manuscript, and contributed valuable suggestions for improving the first draft. Their advice and counsel relative to both content and style were always wise and helpful.

Matilda Deas provided very helpful research assistance; and I am grateful to Candy Korn for organizing a series of luncheon meetings at which I discussed the key concepts of the book with several colleagues, to Lisa McLaughlin for her careful proofreading of the manuscript and very capable assistance in assembling the references, and to Jennifer Opperman for her creative effort in developing the various figures that highlight key points.

On a more personal note, I am indebted to my children, Jennifer and William, whose love and friendship encouraged me to venture beyond familiar boundaries and to test my creativity more fully, and who have taught me many valuable lessons about human growth. My five siblings have been good friends, sympathetic listeners, and thoughtful commentators over the past year, and I am indeed fortunate to be the brother of Kay, Charles, Beth, William, and Matilda. My stepson, Kevin, gave me valuable administrative assistance this past year and, more important, inspired me by his courage during a challenging time in his young life.

Finally, I am forever grateful to my wife, best friend, and close professional colleague, Barbara Krai Eadie, whose daring to create a new business inspired me to undertake this volume, whose highly successful work in interior design introduced me to a whole new dimension of creativity, and whose love, faith in my capabilities, and unwavering support sustained me over the past year as this book evolved from broad concept to finished manuscript.

Of course, I alone am accountable for whatever shortcomings this book possesses.

Cleveland, Ohio   DOUGLAS C. EADIE
February 1997

The Author

DOUGLAS C. EADIE is the founder and president of two companies, Strategic Development Consulting, Inc., and Doug Eadie Presents! As a consultant, writer, and speaker in the field of nonprofit leadership and management, Eadie specializes in designing and implementing processes that produce innovation, strengthening chief executive and board leadership, and building executive teams. Over the past quarter-century Eadie has worked with over three hundred nonprofit organizations of all shapes and sizes. Before establishing his own companies, Eadie served as a public and nonprofit executive, holding such positions as city and state budget director, chief operating officer of a local nonprofit agency, and executive assistant to the president of a three-campus community college system.

Eadie coauthored (with John B. Olsen) one of the first books on public strategic planning, *The Game Plan: Governance with Foresight* (1982), and he is the author of a recent book on board leadership, *Boards That Work* (1994). In addition, he is the author of over one hundred published monographs, chapters, and articles on nonprofit innovation, change management, and board leadership.

Eadie is a Phi Beta Kappa graduate of the University of Illinois at Urbana. He also received a master's degree in public management science from the Weatherhead School of Case Western Reserve University. He and his wife, Barbara Krai Eadie, reside in Cleveland, Ohio.

Changing by Design

Chapter One

The Change Challenge for Nonprofits

Coming Attractions

This chapter addresses:

- Nonprofit organizations as a precious asset that must be developed and not allowed to erode
- The world that is challenging nonprofits to change and four scenarios drawn from real-life situations that bring the human dimension of change into clearer focus
- Environmental change, with special attention to troubling social changes in America
- The nature of self-generated change
- Three important barriers to self-directed change
- Some important side benefits to strengthening a nonprofit's capacity for change

Nonprofits: A Precious Resource

Salamon and Anheier (1994) have identified five common features of nonprofit organizations around the world: they are formally constituted; they maintain organizational separation from government; they do not seek a profit; they are self-governed; they are significantly voluntary in nature. Their research documents the worldwide importance of the nonprofit sector, which employs 11.8 million workers in seven of the countries the authors studied, accounting for one out of every twenty jobs in those countries and making use of the equivalent of another 4.7 million full-time volunteer workers.

1

Americans have a tremendous stake in building the capacity of nonprofit organizations to lead and manage their own change in a challenging world. Our nation's approximately one and a half million nonprofit organizations are a precious national resource that Peter Drucker (1990) has described as "central to the quality of life in America" (p. xiii) and that John Gardner (1990) has called "uniquely American in its diversity and strength" (p. 93). There is no way that government at all levels, no matter how well led and managed, could carry the whole burden of responding to the social and economic challenges that are the result of rapid change these days. Indeed, as Lester Salamon (1989) pointed out, a "central fact of life of the American welfare state as it had evolved by the 1970s was a widespread pattern of partnership between government and the voluntary sector" (p. 43).

Involved in an amazingly diverse array of activities at the national, state, and local levels in this country, nonprofits are capable of carrying—indeed, are carrying—a large share of the burden. Their reach extends to every corner of modern American life. They educate and train youth and adults, care for preschoolers and the aged, provide medical services, redevelop neighborhoods in inner cities, operate orchestras, museums, and theaters, attend to our spiritual needs, conduct research and publish reports on issues of every kind, make grants to worthy causes, represent the interests of numerous trade and professional groups, and much more.

Nonprofits are the organizations of choice to address so many of our problems and needs in today's world because they do their jobs well. One reason for their effectiveness is their focused missions: they concentrate on doing one major job well, whether it is running a museum or an orchestra, developing a particular neighborhood, or representing a professional group or constituency. Another is their flexibility. Free of the scrutiny and suspicion that constrain government these days and of the need to generate a profit, these organizations are freer to experiment with creative solutions to complex issues.

One of the greatest strengths of nonprofit organizations is the involvement of volunteers in their governance and operations. Millions of Americans serve on nonprofit governing boards, bringing different professional backgrounds, knowledge, experience, perspectives, skills, talents, and networks to the boardroom. A nonprofit board, if properly utilized, can be a rich source of information, inspiration, and creative ideas in the process of leading change. In addition, nonprofit membership organizations involve millions of volunteers in a variety of nongovernance roles, such as serving on technical advisory committees and even assisting with service delivery and administrative tasks when there are few, or perhaps no, professional staff members.

We should also keep in mind the tremendous cost of allowing a precious asset to deteriorate, or even die, and then having to reinvent or rebuild it. Nonprofits are valuable but fragile assets. They consist not only of buildings, equipment, and supplies but, far more important, of people with knowledge and experience in delivering services and in working together, expertise that has been developed and honed over the years. They consist too of complex networks of associations that are closely tied to the individuals involved. Destruction is all too easy; rebuilding never is.

I recall a community development corporation that I worked with almost twenty years ago. A dedicated board and hardworking staff had over a decade launched important economic development and employment initiatives that, although far from perfect, had a positive impact on one of the poorest neighborhoods in an ailing, aging industrial city. However, being predominately federally funded, the corporation had over time fallen out of touch with the political structure of both the neighborhood and the city. By the time we began to fashion strategies to rebuild political fences, the negative forces could not be overcome and the agency had to close its doors.

From a hard-nosed social Darwinist perspective, this development corporation wasn't able to "cut the mustard" and so it deserved to pass from the scene, making way for heartier members of the community development species to flourish. In reality, however, the community lost a precious asset that it paid a heavy price in replacing in later years.

An Increasingly Challenging Environment

These days, we read and hear a lot about human-fashioned changes and the challenges they present us with. Everyone agrees that change is growing more complex, accelerating, and becoming less and less predictable. It has been described as "a sea . . . that can twist and turn with all the power of the ocean" and as possessing "a degree of flux that often challenges the fundamental assumptions on which organizations and their managers have learned to operate" (Morgan, 1988, p. 1).

The drama of human-created change in the twentieth century offers something for everyone: inspiration, triumph, tragedy, and even comedy. The most dramatic changes—most notably a series of spectacular technological breakthroughs—have been a decidedly mixed blessing, bringing as many costs as benefits. We all know today's change litany by heart. Our economy continues to evolve away from its traditional anchor, the manufacture of durable goods, toward an economy that is service-oriented and knowledge-based. No longer standing alone, the American economy is increasingly intertwined with others and is vulnerable to economic forces in the wider world that do not respond to our direct control.

Knowledge—its acquisition, storage, analysis, and application—has, according to Peter Drucker, become the preeminent economic resource during this "age of social transformation" and our society is faced with the prospect of a growing gulf between the new class of knowledge workers and the majority of people, "who will make their living traditionally, either by manual work, whether skilled or unskilled, or by work in services, whether skilled or unskilled" (Drucker, 1994, p. 67).

The dramatic technological advances in medicine that have in this century produced longer, healthier lives also seem to have outstripped our ethical framework, foisting on us complex choices about life and death that we are ill-prepared to make and that lead to visceral debate. Instantaneous communication and an amazing expansion in information-processing capabilities may have made us, at least potentially, better informed and more capable decision makers but they also appear at times to overwhelm our analytical capabilities and foster what has been referred to as a "sound-bite mentality."

Because American nonprofits derive only 19 percent of their total revenues from private giving, compared with 30 percent from government, the 1980s were a stressful decade for them. "On the one hand, these organizations were showered with governmental attention. On the other hand, they lost significant portions of their government support as a conservative political regime sought to reduce government spending and shift a greater share of the burden for coping with social needs onto private philanthropic sources" (Salamon and Anheier, 1994, p. 89).

Nonprofits have also had to contend with the fallout from dramatic social change, including large numbers of women continuing to enter the workforce, a 50 percent divorce rate, and astounding growth in single-parent families. These are indeed, to paraphrase Dickens, the best and most challenging of times.

Oft-Told Tales

In today's and tomorrow's world, change on the outside of nonprofits forces them to fashion change initiatives themselves or risk disruption, decline, even extinction. And if changing is not easy even in relatively placid times, deciding what and how to change is no simpler. The reader will surely relate to one or more of the four fictional scenarios that follow. Based on hundreds of real-life examples, they are common enough tales of the all-is-well-*but* . . . type, tales of challenge and pain. Although the nonprofits described in the next paragraphs meet different needs, serve different markets, produce different services and products, and employ different service-delivery mechanisms and production processes, they are alike in some important respects. They are members of a diverse and increasingly important nonprofit family that deals with a wide variety of social, cultural, and economic issues. They are carrying out their missions in a complex and changing environment, and they—or their chief executives, in two instances—are picking up threatening signals from that environment. They are not sure how to interpret these messages from the wider world or how to respond to them.

All—chief executives and organizations—are faced with the same critical choice: either to pursue business as usual or to take action, to change, in response to external change. In today's wild and wonderful world, this is a choice that most nonprofits and their chief executives can expect to face with increasing frequency.

I chose to feature two chief executives along with two organizations because the failure of a chief executive to change her or his approach to the job can have profound effects on the health and welfare of a nonprofit. The reader should never forget that organizational and individual change work in tandem and cannot in real life be separated.

The Symphony Orchestra

The concert hall is electric with anticipation. Enthusiastic applause welcomes this weekend's guest conductor, a charismatic, dashing virtuoso whose recent New York triumph is the talk of musical circles. The lovely opening bars of Mozart's Jupiter Symphony announce the arrival of a familiar and comforting old friend, and perhaps even promise a revelation or two for a few discerning, fully conscious patrons.

Another full house in a season of capacity audiences points to a bright financial future for this jewel in the city's cultural crown. Or does it? Should the symphony's board and general manager lose any sleep over the sea of expensive conservative suits, grey heads, and white faces that predominate at every concert? Does it matter that this homogeneous crowd is settling down to a pleasant musical evening in the middle of a city with a majority African American population and close to the lowest per capita income in the United States? Do continuing high unemployment, population decline, job loss, and exodus of corporate headquarters from the center city in which the symphony is located signify anything for the future of such a beloved—at least to the well-heeled suburban-ites in the audience—cultural powerhouse?

The Association

The Health Product Sales Association (HPSA) has for thirty years effectively represented the interests of owners and executives nationwide who are engaged in selling health care products. Sensibly organized into professional committees representing the major markets—hospitals, home care agencies, and nursing homes and retirement communities—HPSA has been a highly successful lobbyist "on the hill," ensuring that our elected representatives are well briefed on its members' needs and on HPSA's positions on pending health care legislation, especially Medicaid and Medicare reform. HPSA also regularly publishes technical assistance manuals on subjects such as developing computerized management infor-mation systems that are especially useful to its small member firms. The association's two national conferences and numerous work-shops during the year keep members up to date on changing trends in the field and on new technologies. The HPSA volunteer

career ladder has enabled talented, public-spirited members to
move from committee service to board membership and, for the
ambitious and tenacious few, through the vice presidencies to the
top volunteer spot, board chair.

But in recent years, the field of health care has been topsy-
turvy. Hospitals have merged with each other and with home care
agencies, nursing homes, and even insurers. The traditional market
segments have become blurred and fluid. HPSA's structure of
market group committees appears increasingly out of sync with
the emerging new marketplace. And there's more to contemplate
and worry about. Managed care—whatever that means—seems
to be the wave of the future, and reform at the federal level now
appears to consist mostly of radical cost cutting. However, who
knows whether in two years' time expansion of health care coverage will become a priority again? Finally, on top of everything else,
giant firms are gobbling up the smaller firms that were traditionally
the backbone of HPSA's membership. It certainly does not seem
like a good idea to hunker down behind circled wagons, but what
action the association should take is far from obvious.

The Family Services CEO

Many nonprofit chief executives are forced to face their own
personal change in the midst of organizationwide change. For
example, let's take Will Bennett, who has become somewhat of an
institution in his own right in Pleasantville. He has for over fifteen
years served as executive director of the Family Services Agency,
which is widely seen around the state as an exemplary nonprofit
social service organization. Will is the polar opposite of the stodgy
bureaucrat. He is driven by a clear vision that focuses on quality;
he has hired and developed a top-notch staff; he has overseen a
steady expansion of effective, smoothly running programs; and
he has taken the lead in diversifying the agency's revenue base,
adding several foundation grants and a new, quite "profitable"
fee-for-service family counseling program.

Nevertheless, Will is anxious. Two weeks ago his meticulously
prepared (as always) and handsomely bound annual operational
plan and budget was kicked back by the board's planning committee—a first in Will's tenure. Actually, both Will and his trustees had
over the years become accustomed to the planning committee's
taking a couple of hours once a year to thumb through his well-
crafted annual plan and budget, raise some minor questions, and
then pass it along to the full board with only few, if any, revisions.

Never had the board in plenary session taken more than half an hour to adopt the annual plan and budget.

What does this planning committee's dramatic departure from past practice mean? How much should Will worry about the possible erosion of his working relationship with the Family Services board? Does the rejection of his recommended budget presage a rupture that might be fatal (that is, to his career, not to the board)? Is there anything Will can do to regain the board's confidence and support? Would changing his executive leadership style, if that is called for, be worth the pain? After all, Will is like the proverbial old dog whose beliefs about what a strong chief executive should be and do are deeply etched in his heart and mind. His philosophy can be summed up as follows: the chief executive does and the board blesses what he does—from a distance. Certainly, the ugly specter of the board's mucking around in the details of budgeting sends a shiver up Will's spine.

The Community Development CEO

Jenny Barclay has some serious thinking to do. As chief executive officer of one of Metropolis City's most important neighborhood development corporations, she is a technical virtuoso and consummate deal maker in the rough and tumble world of local community and economic development. Under her leadership, the Southwest Neighborhood CDC has developed two highly productive, well-managed programs: one involving the purchase, rehabilitation, and resale of single-family homes, the second involving start-up assistance to small business owners in the neighborhood. Jenny loves what she does, and she does it well. Her quiet, behind-the-scenes, and generally self-effacing approach has worked well in getting the CDC's programs off the ground and putting them on a sound operational basis.

But her board has recently made perfectly clear its desire that the CDC loom larger on the local landscape in order to acquire the greater clout that tends to accompany a higher public profile. Board members have indicated that they expect Jenny to go about the business of building a local network of professional and political leaders and to get out on the hustings, telling the CDC success story far and wide. Also, the board's executive committee at its last meeting urged Jenny to begin to explore new funding sources and promised to support her traveling to meet with foundation officials in New York and Chicago.

Jenny feels put-upon and threatened. This is not why she got into CDC work. She is technically accomplished. She loves being involved with the nitty gritty of neighborhood development, rubbing elbows with people she truly cares for. She cannot imagine spending a lot of time at the speaker's lectern or schmoozing over lunch with downtown notables. Beginning to feel like the proverbial fish stranded on the bank, she is seriously thinking about resigning. Could she grow into this expanded executive role? If she is committed to her own professional growth, how can she go about doing so?

A Never Greater Need

If the times are challenging to nonprofits themselves, the need for their services has never been greater. Whatever technological change has wrought, it is patently obvious in the waning years of the twentieth century that it has not solved our most pressing social problems in the United States. Serious poverty not only persists but has also begun growing again, despite the multitude of programs launched with the best of intentions over the past thirty years. Domestic violence, child abuse, and violent crime are rife. We cannot build jails and prisons fast enough to accommodate the increasing criminal population. Our inner cities continue to lose population and jobs. The depressing list goes on and on.

Warren Bennis (1989) has suggested that such intractable social ills are in part the result of a collective retreat from reality, observing that "today we are only semiconscious, real people living in an imaginary landscape" (p. 51). Scott Peck (1993), seeing an "illness abroad in the land," finds its source in a collective absence of "civility," which he defines as "consciously motivated organizational behavior" that values the common good above narrow self-interest (pp. 3–4). Others have seen the erosion of traditional communities as the culprit. A recent book (Conger and Associates, 1994) on the spiritual dimension of leadership makes the following comment about the workplace: "Its increased importance reflects the ebb of other communities that once served our needs for growth and connection. The extended family has been splintered by the jet age and by divorce rates. Churches and temples, which long served as important places for connection, have seriously diminished in their impact as rituals and traditions have drifted from everyday lives. The civic community that once nourished our needs for contribution has fallen prey to cynicism and apathy and to lives that are too busy" (p. 2).

John Gardner (1990) laments the erosion of shared values that were once fostered and nurtured in communities of all kinds, and he sees this values vacuum as a primary source of the more pressing social pathologies around us. He believes that a preeminent task of leadership today is to "help in restoring the face-to-face community—in the family and extended family, in schools, congregations, workplaces, neighborhoods. That is where shared values are generated, and if they decay that is where they decay" (p. x). And James O'Toole (1995) has observed that effective leadership in challenging times depends on leaders who focus "not on ephemeral details but on fundamental values" (p. 25).

Whatever the causes—disappearing communities, declining civility, eroding values, the absence of values-based leadership—as this book is being written it is all too easy to find evidence of some kind of spiritual malaise in America. Fear and the anger that often accompanies it appear widespread and growing, as do feelings of pessimism and powerlessness. There seems to be a growing reluctance to fashion or to pay for—and sometimes even to talk about—fundamental solutions to complex problems.

The symptoms are all around us. Strident, often hateful rhetoric fills the airwaves. Political discourse is often merely posturing, as wet fingers cast about for a breeze of public opinion to point the way. Bumper stickers and placards declare simple solutions to complex problems. Increasing numbers of people seem to be engaged in a search for conspiracies and demons that can be held accountable for the bad news all around us.

This may well be a transient phase in American history that will eventually give way to a renewal of optimism and social commitment and concerted community building. Time will tell. Meanwhile, these challenging times supply both the context in which nonprofits must go about their business and the issues that they must tackle as they strive to make the world a better place.

Self-Determination: Facing the Change Challenge

If change in the environment surrounding a nonprofit organization is inevitable, so is change in the nonprofit itself. The question is not *whether* a nonprofit organization will change but *how* it will go about the job of changing. A nonprofit organization's success in today's turbulent, complex, and often threatening world depends on its choosing to exercise conscious, strong, and creative leadership and management of its own change process. As noted in the preface to this book, every nonprofit has a clear choice: to exercise self-determination, taking the initiative and proactively shaping and guiding its own change, or to take a passive stance and eventually be changed by the forces around it. Be the designer and pilot of change, or merely ride along as a passenger: this is the only choice.

Taking command of its own change process is no small challenge for a nonprofit, no matter how well led and managed it has been. Indeed, this whole book is about making the proactive choice, deciding to design and direct the self-change process, rather than being dragged kicking and screaming into it. Exercising this choice requires strong chief executive and board leadership and steadfast commitment, the development of the creative capacity of the individuals comprising the nonprofit, the implementation of a planning process that translates creative capacity into practical innovations, and a structure and a process for implementing the innovations.

The real challenge facing a nonprofit board and staff who have made a commitment to take command of their own change is not how to do detailed planning or take aggressive action; these skills are common enough. Far more demanding are the twin challenges of, first, seeing and understanding realistically what is happening in the outside world and, second, creatively fashioning a range of solutions—what I call change initiatives—and selecting those that can be fed into the planning process. Seeing and understanding are hard enough to accomplish in a world of increasing unpredictability and of dim messages seen through a glass darkly. But recognizing that the human mind with all its mystery and complexity is our primary tool for seeing and understanding, as well as for generating possibilities for action, we can also anticipate a challenging journey on the road to knowing and acting.

Self-Generated Change

The purpose of consciously designing and managing a nonprofit organization's own change is, of course, to ensure that it thrives in a challenging world, doing its good work as effectively and efficiently as feasible, capitalizing on opportunities to expand and to grow, and minimizing threats that appear on the horizon. Planned organizational change usually comes in the form of diverse *change initiatives,* some looking outward toward the wider world and others focusing on internal matters. The changes that a nonprofit generates can be more or less creative and innovative, more or less dramatic in terms of impact or departure from past practice, more or less expensive, more or less risky. Changes can also be more or less opportunistic or defensive.

The challenge to a nonprofit chief executive, board, and management team, of course, is to fashion a cohesive *change agenda* that integrates and coordinates these diverse change initiatives. Otherwise, the leadership team will likely wind up telling sad tales of ambitious expectations dashed, meandering roads leading nowhere, costs far exceeding benefits, and disillusioned, exhausted staff left in the wake of the change wave.

Self-generated change can take many shapes. Changes that tend to involve more intense interaction with the outside world affect what I call the *strategic framework,* consisting of organizational values, vision, mission, and long-term goals. Also externally directed are the initiation of new programs and services, the acquisition of new customers and clients, the building of new relationships with actors outside the nonprofit, and attempts to influence directly external conditions or trends. More inner-focused changes affect board and chief executive leadership capacity, internal planning and management systems, and the organizational culture.

Alterations to a nonprofit's vision or mission are likely to have high long-term impact, to involve considerable complexity, to require the allocation of substantial financial and human resources, and to be more visible and riskier than more incremental changes. For example, a traditionally elite art museum located in a deteriorating inner city with a dominant minority population and high unemployment decides to embrace community education as a key element of an expanded mission statement. It will have a tremendous job on its hands. So will a community development corporation that decides to add housing development to its economic development mission, or a hospital that decides to merge with an insurer to create a managed care entity.

Building internal capability, such as putting a new computerized management information system in place, implementing a new board committee structure, or instituting an improved strategic and operational planning cycle, can also be very complex, require the allocation of large sums of money, and evoke strong emotions as people are forced to change established routines.

When the nonprofit's environment changes and when internal leadership and management needs change, a nonprofit should expect the balance between externally focused and internally focused change initiatives to shift over time. In the face of huge funding reductions, the whole change agenda might be externally focused on revenue generation initiatives one year. But the following year, restructuring the board and upgrading financial management might claim the lion's share of organizational time and attention. And while it is creatively shaping and balancing its evolving change agenda, a nonprofit must make sure that the change being attempted at a given time does not overwhelm its resources. We all know that moving in too many directions and trying to do too much too soon can result in disaster.

Defying the Odds

Although nonprofit organizations are continuously changing, consciously planned and systematically guided change is almost always the exception to the rule. If leading and managing organizational change can be thought of as a never-ending journey, then for most organizations it is a journey never even undertaken—in Scott Peck's words (1978), a "road less traveled." As James O'Toole (1995) has observed of planned change, "In no case does it come about readily" (p. 253).

There are a number of reasons why the road of planned and directed change is so infrequently traveled. I explore three of the most important barriers in the following paragraphs: not seeing the need for change; being afraid to change; and being too busy to change.

Failure to See the Need for Change

Crises abound in the world of nonprofit management, usually because the need to initiate and guide change is seen too late, is misinterpreted, or is not recognized at all. This is often the result of a nonprofit's being too inner-focused at the expense of information about and understanding of the world around it. But even when an organization is committed to tracking and assessing change in its external environment, important events may still be missed or misinterpreted.

I have frequently encountered variations on what might be called the emperor's-new-clothes phenomenon in my consulting work. A nonprofit board and staff become so wedded to a particular set of strategies and programs, and sometimes even to operating styles, that they block out unwelcome intelligence from the wider world that might raise the threatening specter of change. For example, I recall vividly the management team of one nonprofit employment and training agency that refused to recognize the powerful national trend toward seeing and describing training as a tool to be employed in community economic development. To this group of very competent and hardworking professionals, who had come up through the ranks in the job training field, economic development professionals were a different breed entirely. Economic development itself was a foreign country, at best a diplomatic ally, at worst a competitor threatening to poach on the training turf. The thought that training might be part of a broader economic development process was anathema to the team, principally, it seemed, because it offended their egos. As a consequence of the team's myopia and provincialism, their agency lost significant funding opportunities while clinging to the familiar and comfortable niche they had always occupied.

Think of the symphony scenario that opened this chapter, Will Bennett's eroding partnership with his board, and Jenny Barclay's anxiety over being pressured to take on a more public role in her community. The potential for being seduced by the siren song of familiarity and comfort is always substantial. Over and over again I have seen it lead to convenient misinterpretations of signals from the outside world. My readers' own experiences have surely taught them that a symphony board is quite capable of seeing more black and brown heads of hair in the audience than really exist, as a convenient antidote to the urge to venture into the community for new audience members or update a stale repertoire. We all know from experience that Will may see a wrongheaded board

intent on crossing the line into the administrative realm, its ten-
tacles grasping for bits of chief executive influence to feed its evil
appetite, rather than a well-intentioned group of dedicated volunteers who are underutilized and bored and need help in finding a more productive role. And we also know that Jenny is quite
likely to see her board's pressure to venture out into the community as an unreasonable demand rather than an opportunity to
grow professionally.

When comfort is king, illusions and delusions are likely to
flourish in the realm. When the message is threatening, an evil little imp is likely to be found whispering wishful thoughts into the
ears of otherwise capable and hardworking people.

Fear of Change

The prospect of change causes anxiety in many, if not most, human
beings, who naturally cling to the familiar. Fear is typically at the
heart of resistance to change, either consciously when vested interests are threatened or, more insidiously, unconsciously and, hence,
unrecognized. Anyone who has been involved in large-scale organizational change has confronted the power of seemingly rational
resistance fueled by unrecognized emotions that apparently reside
in the resister's unconscious. Such resistance can be the most difficult to deal with because of its largely hidden motivations.

Countless times I have witnessed this phenomenon in nonprofits that are going through a change process. One symptom of
such unconscious fear is what I call "killing change with a million
rational questions." This pathological behavior typically emerges
in a meeting called to consider possible change initiatives. The
resister wears down his or her colleagues with a succession of
detailed questions, usually of the What if? variety. The hunger for
answers cannot be appeased and the questions do not stop unless
a majority that is committed to change calls a halt to them.
Another common manifestation of unconscious fear of change is
anger, which I often see in my work with nonprofit management
teams engaged in change processes.

As I discuss in some detail in Chapter Five, unleashing creativity is often linked to overcoming fear and taking the plunge into
change, a process that often requires considerable courage. For

example, Peter Senge (1990), in his discussion of personal mastery, one of the five "disciplines" of a learning organization, suggests that maintaining the "creative tension" generated by the gap between vision and current reality is what enables human beings to engage in positive, directed change (p. 142). The prominent psychologist Rollo May (1975) sees self-directed change as a "creative confrontation" that can result in withdrawal "in anxiety and panic" or in creative change. He asks, "Shall we, as we feel our foundations shaking, withdraw in anxiety and panic? Frightened by the loss of our familiar mooring places, shall we become paralyzed and cover our inaction with apathy? . . . Or shall we seize the courage necessary to preserve our sensitivity, awareness, and responsibility in the face of radical change? Shall we consciously participate, on however small the scale, in the forming of the new society?" (p. 12).

The Danger of "Busyness"

Telephones jangle incessantly, faxes spew forth endless streams of paper, e-mail messages crowd screens, in-baskets overflow. The daily grind can be a voracious consumer of attention, time, and energy, and the time to plan and manage self-change is not often found. Over and over again, I have heard the depressingly familiar refrain, "We're up to our behinds in alligators, and there just isn't time to think about the wider world or the future beyond tomorrow. Maybe next week, when things calm down." Well, things seldom do calm down, and "next week" can often be translated as "never."

Stephen Covey, in *The Seven Habits of Highly Effective People* (1989), has probably offered the most profound advice on the prosaic subject of time management. Covey has pointed out that day-to-day operational details often fall into the urgent-but-not-important cell of his time management matrix. "They press on us; they insist on action. They're often popular with others. They're usually right in front of us. And often they are pleasant, easy, fun to do" (p. 151).

Of course, I am as guilty as anyone. For weeks after making the strategic decision to commit the amount of time and energy needed to write this book, I found a million pressing things to keep me from starting it. One night, tossing and turning, I got up, went into my study, found my copy of Covey's book, turned to his powerful matrix, found my current "busyness" in the urgent-but-unimportant cell and the book in the not-urgent-but-very-important cell, and decided that it would make the best sense to put some time and energy there. The next day, I got started—not without some pain and a hundred well-sharpened pencils—but finally started. Covey knows whereof he speaks.

A Powerful Potential Benefit

The direct and most important impact of strengthened nonprofit capacity to lead and manage change will be seen in more effective organizational performance. Society will benefit from the implementation of realistic and sophisticated strategies to address complex problems, ultimately conserving resources that would have been consumed in continuing to grapple with unmet challenges. But some less obvious results will over the years significantly increase the yield on the investment in building creative capacity among nonprofits.

Keeping in mind that organizations are basically people, and that it is a nonprofit's people who learn to lead and manage change rather than the organization in the abstract, it stands to reason that the millions of employees who staff nonprofit organizations can put their heightened capacity into play away from their places of work as well. They can lead and manage change as family members at home, as volunteers on boards and in service roles, and as voting citizens.

The American volunteer sector is huge and diverse. Thus, the potential for positive impact as a result of an infusion of creativity into volunteer activities is tremendous. The citizens armed with enhanced change management capacity who issue forth from their nonprofit organizations at the end of every day can over time become a voice of reason, realism, and civility, a force against anger, simplistic solutions, and strident rhetoric.

We should also recognize the potential impact of these nonprofit employees not just as doers but also as teachers and mentors—of family members, friends, colleagues on boards, and volunteers. Although leading and managing change has its elusive creative side, with its unconscious and spiritual dimensions, it can also in some measure be taught and learned. By direct instruction and by example, nonprofit employees can teach friends and colleagues to see the world around them more realistically and to plan and manage change more effectively.

I am convinced that our nation cannot help but benefit if growing numbers of citizens deal more proactively and creatively with the world around them. Furthermore, there is absolutely nothing to lose and everything to gain by trying. Simply expanding people's calm and spreading greater peace by reducing feelings of powerlessness and anxiety, and making inroads on the anger that we see everywhere around us would be worth the effort.

In Summary

We have a tremendous stake in our nonprofit organizations' undertaking the change journey because they play a critical role in addressing a diverse array of social and economic needs. Our society would have to pay a high price for allowing some nonprofits to fall by the wayside as victims of environmental change.

This chapter offered a brief look at two nonprofits and two chief executives whose difficult situations called for creative leadership and change management free from the paralyzing power of fear and free from delusions. Such cases are not unusual, with the rapid change in the environments around nonprofit organizations. Humans have always had to deal with change, but never has it been so complex and dizzying. The times require nonprofits to make a conscious choice to design and lead their own change, rather than merely be buffeted about by the winds of change around them.

Self-generated, self-led change can take many forms, be more or less external or internal in focus, and have more or less impact. Change can relate to vision, mission, programs, clients, customers, markets, or internal capability building. The challenge is to fashion a change agenda that is balanced, addresses the highest-priority needs of a nonprofit, and will not overwhelm the nonprofit's resources.

The barriers to undertaking the journey of self-generated, self-directed change can be daunting. Especially important hurdles are the failure to recognize the need for change, the very normal fear of change, and the inexorable demands of day-to-day life. But the benefits of learning to lead and manage change effectively can be substantial as these individuals bring their change leadership and management skills to other organizations in their communities and to their personal lives.

Chapter Two

Building the Capacity for Innovation

Coming Attractions

This chapter deals with:

- The many barriers that are typically encountered during the demanding journey of planned change
- The characteristics of an effective change process
- The key components of the 3CAP approach to leading and managing change

The Way Won't Be Easy

In Chapter One, I described three tall barriers that stand in the way of a nonprofit's undertaking the journey of self-determined, consciously directed change: failure to see the need to change; fear of changing; and the relentless grind of day-to-day operations. Anyone who has embarked on a journey of personal growth knows well how daunting these challenges can be. Changing one's life can be a monumental task; moving a whole organization in new directions is that much more so. Well-traveled paths may offer little in the way of excitement but they feel comfortable and far safer than meandering around unknown terrain, where who knows what terrors await. Doggedly working toward the never-seen bottom of the constantly filling in-basket day after day may feel productive and virtuous, but it leaves little time or energy to notice the signals from the world outside that change is needed, much less to plot a new journey.

So as individuals and as organizations, we often wait for major-league crises to jolt us out of our complacency and force us in new directions. For individuals, this may come in the form of a heart attack, a separation, a divorce. For organizations, it may be a precipitous drop in membership or revenue, an unanticipated budget deficit, or an exposé in the local press that threatens a previously stellar reputation. Fortunately, even major crises, while inevitably painful and costly, are seldom fatal. As goads to needed action they can even be blessings, although well disguised. Crises don't force most nonprofits to close up shop and lock the doors. There are often second chances, lessons that can be learned and put to good use in the future, budgets that can eventually be balanced, and good reputations that can be restored. However, the cost of waiting for a crisis to spur action can be appallingly high in dollars, pain and suffering, eroded public credibility, the consumption of precious energy, and declining internal morale. Indeed, being anticipatory and proactive is cost effectiveness at its best!

For example, alarmed by the sea of grey heads at every concert, the symphony business manager and board described in Chapter One might take action to deal with what appears to be an ominous trend before too many empty seats show up in the hall. They may plan concerts in various neighborhoods, initiate a children's concert series, or launch a direct-mail marketing campaign to new audiences. The Health Product Sales Association we also met in Chapter One might take the initiative by redefining its basic markets and aggressively seeking merger opportunities with other associations in the field. Any alert and aggressive organization can decide, before the crisis hits, to take a leading role in its own change. But in doing so, the board, chief executive, and management team need to understand that the journey of self-determined and guided change is seldom smooth and that failure is not uncommon. As Max De Pree has pointed out, "Anything truly creative results in change, and if there is one thing a well-run bureaucracy or institution or major corporation finds difficult to handle, it is change" (1989, p. 33). No matter how capable, courageous, and disciplined its people, an organization can fail in managing change for a number of important reasons: weak board and chief executive leadership; the absence of a clear strategic framework; an unsystematic, skewed approach to change; a quick-fix mentality; uncreative thinking and narrowly circumscribed strategy formulation; unrealistic implementation planning; inadequate implementation management; and staff resistance. The approach to leading and managing change that this book describes is intended to deal with all of these major "spoilers," which have limited the effectiveness of nonprofit efforts to lead and manage change in the past.

Characteristics of Effective Change Leadership and Management

Nonprofit board members, chief executives, and managers who are committed to taking command of their own organizational change should insist that, as a result of employing a particular change process, their organizations are *able to put their resources to the best feasible use in capitalizing on environmental opportunities and coping with environmental threats in order to realize fully their potential for service.*

While achieving this broad purpose, an effective approach to leading and managing change should also:

• *Be guided by a clear, detailed strategic framework.* By strategic framework I mean the values that the nonprofit most cherishes and that are its most important do's and don'ts, its vision for the future (in terms of what it aspires to be and the role it aspires to play), and its mission (in terms of its services and products, customers and clients, and key roles and functions). Without a well-defined framework addressing overall purposes, aspirations, and boundaries, organizational change cannot have any rhyme or reason; it will be just as apt to produce bad results as good ones.

Because the values that govern a nonprofit's change should serve as an ethical framework, they should include what O'Toole (1995) calls "the moral absolutes," which include "only a few moral principles based on natural law. . . . Though most of the major issues in social life are subjective and relative, not all are. There are, in short, some moral absolutes that are not contingent on circumstances" (p. 105).

• *Be guided by rational priorities.* The change initiatives that an organization selects should tackle first things first in terms of opportunities and needs. Only so much time, money, and energy can be devoted to changing things in an organization if day-to-day operations are to be managed, so careful selection of targets is imperative. Resources must not be frittered away on lesser matters while problems threaten organizational existence or one-time opportunities are lost forever. Who among us has not seen at least once a nonprofit go off on a tangent, implementing the flavor-of-the-month that ended up producing more costs than practical benefits and leaving much bad feeling behind?

• *Be humane.* Implementing change—whether personal or organizational—is taxing enough without adding to the pain by making unrealistic demands on the people who must translate change targets into practice. A humane approach takes into account the feelings and the capabilities of an organization's employees and never demands the impossible. However, the adage "No pain, no gain" applies to any serious change process, so no participant should expect a pain-free experience.

• *Be comprehensive and balanced.* As much attention should be given to the "what" of change—its content—as to the "how"—its implementation. All the forms that change can take should be comprehensively considered in determining exactly what change should be undertaken during any given year. There is outward-looking change, in revenue sources, customers and clients, and stakeholder relationships, for example, and there is internal change, in planning and management systems. The creative challenge is to choose the mix that best meets an organization's needs in the context of the changing world around it.

• *Be creative and innovative.* Creativity is at the heart of innovation, which is basically the process of bringing the new into being. In a complex, rapidly changing world, merely projecting the conventional wisdom into the future is a risky course to take. Being creative means seeing what has not yet occurred in order to envision responses that are not being made. The more open and questioning the process, the more likely that practical innovations will yield important benefits.

• *Be realistic.* Shooting high and falling short is a sure-fire recipe for disappointed expectations, lost credibility, frayed tempers, cynicism, and even organizational chaos if the failure is dramatic enough. The changes that have been planned must be implemented fully, on time and within budget, avoiding unnecessary pain and suffering.

* *Be self-sustainable.* Any process for leading and managing change will ultimately prove too expensive if a nonprofit board, chief executive, and management team cannot use it on an ongoing basis without endless consulting assistance. Only if it becomes a mainline planning and management process can it yield a return on the investment of time and energy over time.

Beware of Quick Fixes

Trying to figure out what is happening in a rambunctious world that seems to defy understanding and attempting to fashion initiatives for organizational change that will make sense is a complex process that flies in the face of an apparent widespread appetite for quick-fix solutions and low-cost panaceas. The more complex and ambitious the change being attempted, the less likely are immediate, visible results, so patience and the willingness to bear the costs for some time before reaping benefits are requisites for successful leadership of change.

Unfortunately, these attributes are often in short supply, especially when things do not go smoothly. Over the years, I have seen nonprofit after nonprofit lurch from one half-understood and inadequately implemented management innovation to another, inevitably finding the fault in the innovation rather than in its taste for a costless and painless solution. Management by objectives, program budgeting, strategic planning, participatory management, total quality—you name it, it has been tried and abandoned when the costs became clear and the pain felt, and when immediate results failed to materialize.

The instant gratification approach to change fails to achieve the desired impact, misuses and abuses the people in an organization, and damages morale. Here's an example. A little over five years ago, I was working with a task force preparing for a two-day strategic planning retreat. The specific assignment for this group of smart, hardworking managers was to assess internal capabilities. One of the issues that they focused on was how to assess the agency's experience in managing change and convey that assessment to the assembled management team at the retreat.

On the day of the retreat, the room rocked with laughter when the slide that the task force had designed appeared on the screen. It depicted a graveyard crowded with stones, each one naming a management innovation that had been attempted and abandoned and stating its years on this earth. The average life span was eighteen months. The next slide analyzed the reasons for so many premature deaths among such a large population of innovation projects and estimated both the hours and dollars wasted. It did not take long for sadness and then anger to replace humor as the assembled managers thought about the better uses to which their time and money might have been put.

Beyond Quick Fixes: The 3CAP Approach

Chapters Three through Eight deal in detail with the three broad organizational capacities that are essential for successful nonprofit leadership and management of change. These three capacities, which together form the 3CAP Approach, are the capacity to lead, the capacity to innovate, and the capacity to implement. (See Figure 2.1.) These closely related and mutually reinforcing capacities form a kind of internal infrastructure that supports the efforts of boards, chief executives, and management teams to determine and direct their organizational change. In the following paragraphs, I will describe each of the three capacities generally and contrast them with the traditional practices they are intended to replace.

Capacity One: To Lead

The preeminent leadership team of a nonprofit consists of its chief executive and the governing board. The success of a nonprofit's change efforts depends on how well these leadership roles are played and how effectively the two parties work together. A nonprofit's chief executive is without question the prime mover in any large-scale organizational change effort. No one else is in a better position to make or break the change process. No one else has comparable authority, influence, and resources (not even the board, contrary to theory). No one's words and actions are listened to as closely. Experience teaches that unless the chief executive has a deep understanding of the process of change and is strongly

Figure 2.1. The 3CAP Approach.

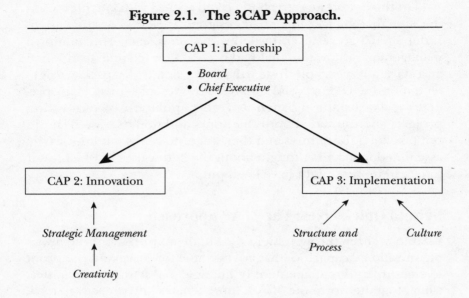

committed to developing the organization's capacity to change, little important change is likely to occur.

Chief executives can promote self-determined and managed change by articulating a clear vision that inspires employees, by building a culture that is change-friendly, by ensuring that planning and management systems promote and support change, and by ensuring that resources required to implement change initiatives—primarily money and time—are committed.

Boards can be a precious resource in the change leadership and management process too. Basically, they offer knowledge and experience during the process of creating the strategic framework (that is, the values, vision, and mission), they help generate financial and political resources, and they support the chief executive in carrying out change.

But all too often, this top leadership team does not function well. I have observed many nonprofit boards that play only the most perfunctory role—blessing vision and mission statements prepared by staff or simply signing off on plans that have already been written, edited, and bound. Such boards, which are involved only at the tail end of the planning process, naturally feel little ownership of planned change initiatives or accountability for the successful implementation of change. As a passive audience, they have the luxury of sitting back with crossed arms and judging the chief executive and the staff, and they cannot be depended on to back the chief executive when the going gets rough. There are plenty of boards at the other end of the spectrum, too, dabbling in details that are obviously operational and often having an ego investment in current operations. They too can become the enemy of planned change. For example, membership organizations that are heavily volunteer-driven, such as civic clubs, often treat board service as the top rung on the volunteer career ladder. Having worked their way up the ladder by rolling up their sleeves and dirtying their hands with the details of running programs, these volunteers-turned-board-members become wedded to these very programs and resistant to changing them. Board members with strong emotional attachments to particular organizational methodologies can also become enemies of creative change. A few years ago, I observed recovering alcoholics on the board of a center for the treatment of chemical dependency who would not allow any alternatives to the Alcoholics Anonymous twelve-step approach to be considered; they were passionately committed to the treatment process that had, they believed, saved their lives.

Many nonprofit chief executives too are ill-prepared technically and emotionally to provide strong, creative leadership for a change process that actively involves both board and staff members. They have frequently ascended the professional ladder by demonstrating technical virtuosity in specific programs or functions that do not add up to a comprehensive picture of the organization they now lead. In addition, the very competitiveness, drive, decisiveness, and rat-a-tat style that got them where they are poorly equips them to lead a creative change process.

Perhaps the most serious professional limitation that I have observed among nonprofit chief executives over the years is the need to be in control. This can stifle openness, limit organizational creativity, constrain planning, and impede meaningful involvement and partnership. Chris Argyris (1993) has written about "espoused theory" and "theory in practice," observing that it is not uncommon to find a person espousing one theory while contradicting it in practice without recognizing the inconsistency. Countless times

I have come across nonprofit chief executives who preach and apparently believe in participatory management while at the same time employing a management style worthy of Louis XIV: I pronounce, you listen and obey.

It is unrealistic to expect that every chief executive, no matter how smart or competent, can grow psychologically to the extent required to lead a change process effectively. Years of traditional management training with its control orientation, militate against easy transformation. I recall one very bright and capable chief executive I worked with some fifteen years ago. One afternoon, I found him ashen-faced at his desk, clearly shaken. When I asked him what had happened, he handed me the evaluation that his board had just completed. Every technical category was marked A+. He was judged to be top-notch over the entire management spectrum, from planning and budgeting to financial management and supervision of staff. Still wondering what could possibly have upset him in this glowing assessment, I reached the bottom of the evaluation. It concluded with the recommendation that he seek other employment because he was too difficult to work with! Knowing him well, I had to agree with the board. His need to be right in every instance, his combativeness in proving his points, and his defensiveness when challenged made him one of the most difficult people I had ever encountered. The story does not end happily. Despite advice and encouragement to deal with a character problem that was clearly deep-seated, he was not able to rehabilitate himself. Not long after this incident he lost his job, and then two others for pretty much the same reason, and he has now left the field of chief executiveship.

I am also reminded of the struggles of a nonprofit theater's managing director with whom I worked with several years ago. Bright, talented, committed to artistic quality and incredibly hard-working, this woman's need to be in command was so strong that despite her publicly announced and apparently sincere intention to involve the board and staff creatively in setting direction, she was unable to relinquish enough control to allow meaningful partnerships to develop. The one-woman show was perpetuated, and the theater's slow and steady decline continued.

Chapter Three describes a new model of chief executive leadership that is suited to the demands of leading and managing change in turbulent times. It sees the job as being far more than that of a boss at whose desk the proverbial buck stops, the program expert who understands the operational dynamics and cannot be "snowed" by managers, or the technocrat who makes sure that support systems run. The chief executive who is an effective change leader must embody the following characteristics:

- *A visionary.* Capable of thinking of the organization's long-term purposes and ends, the leader is also committed to a collaborative approach to fashioning the vision that creatively draws on the knowledge, expertise, and experience of board and staff members.
- *An architect and designer.* Eschewing the old-fashioned command approach, the leader concentrates on design, putting together the complex pieces of the organizational puzzle-board and management team roles, systems such as strategic planning and performance management, programs to enhance individual creative capacity, and more. Only through conscious organizational design can a modern chief executive ensure that creativity is transformed into innovation, that systems are compatible and integrated, and that the quick-fix solutions being peddled these days are not bought.
- *A facilitator and a coach.* The chief executive helps board and staff members perform their respective functions more effectively and grow in capability. Thus, the chief executive must not only be supportive of capability-building efforts but also teach by doing more than preaching. Such CEOs engage in personal growth strategies even though doing so might pierce their shield of chief executive infallibility.
- *An active partner with the board.* The CEO must welcome the board's substantive contribution and creative involvement and be committed to developing the board's leadership capacity. This means embracing a nontraditional model of board leadership that sees the board as both a precious asset that needs for the sake of the organization to be fully utilized, and a company within the nonprofit corporation that generates essential products.
- *A secure, nondefensive, and open individual.* The CEO must welcome and encourage wide-ranging questions and ideas, even if they challenge official positions.

In sum, chief executives aspiring to build their organizations' capacity to lead and manage change must be courageous in two major respects. First, they must develop their own creative capacity, which means taking what mythologist Joseph Campbell (1968) calls the "hero's journey" themselves, looking inward and becoming more self-aware by venturing into the subconscious sphere of the mind. I do not believe that a chief executive can lead the innovation process effectively without a deeply personal, psychological exploration of his or her own creative capacity. Second, they must be willing to promote the psychological growth of their employees despite skepticism or even opposition. Talking of the self and the subconscious will not have the rat-ta-tat-tat sound of traditional macho management. Indeed, the chief executive who dares to lead in creative capacity building must steel himself or herself to accusations of "flakiness," or even dementia from traditionalists.

In Chapter Four, I describe a new approach to leadership that goes well beyond the traditional expectation of the board as a passive audience. More effective boards will function as a kind of business within the nonprofit corporation that is guided by a clear leadership mission and focused on producing bottom-line results in active partnership with the chief executive. For example, an activist nonprofit board might every year—in a retreat with the chief executive and management team—revisit the vision and mission statements, identify new issues facing the organization (opportunities as well as challenges), and reach agreement on major change initiatives for the coming year.

The board of the future will be accountable for the quality of its membership and its own performance, setting detailed performance standards and regularly monitoring its operations. Its precise leadership roles and responsibilities will be a matter of ongoing discussion. The division of labor between the board and the chief executive will go beyond the old-fashioned policy-administration dichotomy and be guided by the nonprofit's current needs and circumstances. For example, a small, young organization might want its board to play a hands-on role in securing the financial resources to fund growth, make telephone calls to donors, visit foundations, and so on. A more removed stance, involving monitoring rather than doing, may make sense when the nonprofit is well established and revenue streams are more secure.

Capacity Two: To Innovate

The second critical organizational capacity for successful leadership and management of change is innovation. The concepts and techniques comprising what is popularly known as "change management" are for the most part aimed at figuring out how to implement change. Lots of attention is given to securing the buy-in of participants who must do much of the work of changing. Yet figuring out how to implement change is distinctly subordinate to a more fundamental question that ultimately determines success or failure: what will the content of change be? Determining the *what* of change rather than merely the *how-to* of it inevitably leads a nonprofit into the realm of innovation. Innovation is the process of putting something new into practice, whether it is a service, a product, a relationship, or a management system. In a complex, rapidly changing environment, systematic innovation is a survival tool rather than a luxury, and the greater the complexity and faster the external change, the more pressing the need for innovation.

Innovation means going beyond the tried and true and transcending the conventional wisdom in responding to challenges. Innovative solutions are not found in slogans or on bumper stickers. Being innovative requires being open, listening, and learning; it means recognizing complexities and subtle distinctions and taking them into account in fashioning effective solutions. Being innovative means seeing through the shell game of no-cost solutions and having the courage to bear the costs.

Innovation is a challenging process. Innovative solutions to complex problems can be difficult to explain and sell to the people in the street who elect our public officials and more or less directly provide the resources to implement them. In contrast, simplicity is seductive. Sound bites, if not ultimately nourishing, are easily swallowed. Stereotypes save time. Demons are fun to hate. Over forty years ago, I did a research paper on the Lincoln-Douglas debates. It is unimaginable today that an audience might listen intently for three or four hours as they did then—in the hot prairie sun, no less—to a complex discussion of the fundamental nature of the union and of the pros and cons of extending slavery into the new territories.

But no matter how stiff the challenge, innovative leadership seeks to do more than merely appease anger and pander to the desire for simple solutions. It means asking second, third, and even fourth questions, and seeing beyond the immediate outcomes. Innovative nonprofits do not train the unemployed for jobs that either do not exist or will quickly become outmoded; they do not place their clients in minimum-wage jobs with no future merely to meet the immediate performance standards of the Labor Department. They do not buy into the notion that the complex issue of violent crime can be solved through a three-strikes-you're-out mentality or by filling jails to capacity. They know enough to distrust "gut" reactions and simplistic solutions.

The innovation capacity consists of two major subcategories: creativity, which generates the ideas, the possibilities for change, and planning, which selects from the possibilities and eventually translates them into concrete change projects or initiatives. Creativity and planning are an inseparable team. Lots of creativity without a well-developed planning capacity is a recipe for unrealized potential, frustration, and little important change. And a good planning process that is run by people with little opportunity to build or express their creativity will severely limit the possibilities for innovative action.

Creativity

Think innovation, and creativity comes immediately to mind; the two concepts go hand in hand. Although they are frequently treated as one and the same thing, I believe it makes sense to view creativity as the capacity that undergirds and enriches the innovation process. Creativity is the supplier of the "newness" that the innovation process will translate into practice. An ill-defined concept having as much mystery as science about it, creativity involves seeing in one's mind patterns that have not been seen before. It means going beyond the tried-and-true and transcending the conventional wisdom when responding to environmental challenges.

Developing the creative capacity that is at the heart of a non-profit's capability to innovate is more than anything else a matter of developing the creative capacity of the individual people within it. People are more or less creative, not the systems that support decision making, and no planning process, no matter how sophisticated its design, can fully compensate for inadequate individual capability.

Planning

Planning, especially of the strategic variety, can be the innovation machine that transforms creative ideas into practical innovations; therefore, it can be a preeminent driver of nonprofit change. Unfortunately, strategic planning has over the past quarter of a century earned a reputation for generating more paperwork than action, deforesting much of America in the process. This is by no means a bum rap. In actual practice, if not in theory, strategic (or long-range) planning has tended to be control—rather than innovation—focused, basically taking what an organization is already doing and projecting it forward three years, five years, or more. Of course, since the world refuses to oblige us by remaining static or by changing in a nice, neat fashion, such mammoth globs of paper have quickly become outdated and have routinely ended up on dusty shelves, rarely if ever consulted.

My guess is that professional planners—most likely working in the Soviet ministries of the past—with their penchant for order created the three-year, five-year, and—God forbid—ten-year planning cycles. They correspond to no natural cycle in human affairs and have never delivered the future they promised. If the benefits of formal planning have been scant, the costs have been high. For one thing, the illusion of control that bloated documents can create has lulled many nonprofits into a false sense of security. Believing they are in control of their destiny they actually become more vulnerable than if they had never done formal planning. For another, the time spent writing, editing, printing, and binding such plans might better have been spent gathering intelligence on environmental trends and conditions and focusing on specific change targets. In addition, going through the planning motions for no useful purpose has bred cynicism among managers, making it all the more difficult to build support for serious planning.

Yet, just because strategic planning has been misused does not mean that it cannot produce powerful results. In reaction to the traditional wheel-spinning in pursuit of the illusion of control, serious planning reforms have revitalized the process over the past decade or so. A significant new variation on the strategic planning theme, typically known as strategic management, has been successfully tested in hundreds of organizations, including several nonprofits.

In a nutshell, a serious strategic management process results in the identification of "change challenges," strategic issues in the form of opportunities to move closer to an organization's vision or barriers blocking progress toward that vision. It selects the challenges or issues to be addressed immediately and develops change initiatives to address the selected issues. Taken together, the change initiatives form a kind of organizational change portfolio or agenda that must be managed separately from day-to-day operations if it is not to be overwhelmed.

As I will discuss in greater detail in Chapters Six and Seven, a nonprofit's annual operational planning and budget preparation process can also be a source of systematic organizational innovation, although on a smaller scale than strategic management. Because operational planning is by its very nature control focused and is a kind of cockroach of management tools—a long-surviving, hearty breed with little glamor—its innovative potential has received less attention than it actually deserves.

Capacity Three: To Implement

The gap between intent and practice, between plan and action, is frequently not successfully bridged. The following case is all too familiar.

> The two days could not have gone better for the board and staff of the Center for Family Services. Millhaven was a superb facility, offering spacious, well-equipped conference rooms, a sylvan setting, and numerous recreational opportunities. The facilitator did a great job of steering the group through a complex process of visioning, assessing external conditions and trends, and identifying several issues that appeared to deserve closer attention. The group even had time to narrow the issues down to four that everyone agreed should be explored in greater detail in the coming weeks: an expected cut of 30 percent in next year's United Way subsidy; a proposed merger with the Children's Services

Agency; the need for an aggressive financial development program; and eroding board enthusiasm, as evidenced by several resignations and the cancellation of two board meetings for failure to attract a quorum. Loud applause greeted the chair's closing comments, the meeting ended on a high note, and everyone drove home keenly anticipating some positive changes on the horizon.

But days, weeks, then months went by. Copiers and faxes spewed out paper, the staff were up to their eyeballs just getting through each day without a major mishap. One or another board member would occasionally ask about following up on the retreat, which was well on its way to becoming a hazy memory. Things went along pretty much as usual. Fortunately, some last-minute lobbying resulted in a smaller than expected cut in the United Way allocation, and only a couple of positions had to be eliminated. Filling three board vacancies made achieving quorums easier, but lack of enthusiasm was still very noticeable.

This downbeat scenario probably sounds depressingly familiar. Examples of the breakdown between verbal intentions and actual practice are everywhere around us. The fact is, planned change is frequently not implemented for three major reasons: *unrealistic implementation planning, inadequate implementation structure and process,* and *a milieu that is unfriendly to change.*

Through detailed implementation planning, an organization determines for particular change initiatives or projects: precisely what steps must be taken or jobs done to carry out the initiative; the people who are accountable for seeing that each step is taken; the timetable that will be followed; and the resources required to implement the plan. A realistic plan will pay close attention to the required resources, looking not just at the obvious cost—dollars—but also at staff skills that may have to be upgraded to ensure full implementation. There may be no point in moving forward with an image-building strategy, for example, if a part-time person is not hired to handle media relations.

Change initiatives or projects can easily be overwhelmed by the press of day-to-day events, oozing away like a crustacean whose shell has been removed. A change structure and implementation process that are kept separate from the day-to-day management process can provide the protection, nurturing, and oversight required to keep change initiatives alive and well. Many organizations have created special change programs, with a steering committee composed of management team members who meet regularly for the sole purpose of overseeing the implementation of change initiatives or projects, a team member who serves as the coordinator of change projects and as the quality control officer, and staff task forces accountable for the many details involved in implementing the projects. Everyone involved wears only his or her "change hat" when participating in the program, which is kept well away from normal operations. Thus, change matters never become the ninth item on crowded Monday morning staff meeting agendas.

A nonprofit's internal milieu is another factor with substantial influence on the implementation of change. An organization's milieu is in large measure its culture. Schein (1985) defined culture as a "pattern of basic assumptions—invented, discovered, or developed by a given group as it learns to cope with its problems of external adaptation and internal integration—that has worked well enough to be considered valid and, therefore, to be taught to new members as the correct way to perceive, think, and feel in relation to those problems" (p. 9).

The organizational milieu also consists of the current climate, including the feelings and attitudes of the staff. Obviously, an organization lurching from one crisis to another over a period of weeks or months, with a fatigued or nervous staff, will have a harder time concentrating on the implementation of change than one with a more secure and peaceful climate. Furthermore, a staff that has been burned on a number of occasions by abrupt, seemingly irrational changes of course is likely to hold both commitment and energy back when asked to participate in a new change process.

Changing to Get Ready for Change

In this chapter, I have briefly described the three key organizational capacities that a nonprofit organization must develop if it is to lead and manage change successfully: the capacity to lead; the capacity to innovate; and the capacity to implement. Developing these essential capacities and thereby building a foundation for continuous self-generated and guided change will itself involve organizational change. Therefore, nonprofits would be well-advised to tackle capacity building early on, even while they are responding to change signals from the external world by fashioning new strategic directions, programs, and services. This will require virtuoso juggling, as a nonprofit at the same time works on capacity building to enhance its capability to respond to the changing world while also having to respond to specific external opportunities or threats when the stakes are high enough.

To take a practical example, let's say that a nonprofit nursing home without a contemporary strategic management process has, in a recent management team meeting, taken note of the growing consumer demand for "one-stop" retirement living that offers a full range of accommodations and services for residents. As they live longer and healthier lives, seniors want to be able to begin their stay in a retirement community with truly independent living in detached cottages, then move through a range of living styles until the day comes when they may need skilled nursing care in a traditional nursing home setting. The strong market demand dictates that the organization begin to explore strategies for expansion from its current traditional nursing home. At the same time, the team has decided that it must take a more systematic approach to identifying and acting on strategic issues in the future, so it has also decided to create a task force to design a new strategic management process for this purpose.

It would not be feasible to ignore the changing world outside the nonprofit for very long, while focusing exclusively on building the internal change leadership and management infrastructure. The key is to create an overall change agenda or portfolio that balances the need to respond to external events with the internal capacity-building need, making sure that first things are put first. For example, strengthening the leadership of a board that is not fully involved in setting strategic directions but that is not malfunctioning in any important way should take second place to dealing with the imminent loss of a grant that supplies one-third of the budget. In contrast, a board that is up in arms about its role and angry enough to consider firing the chief executive would merit concerted attention before consideration is given to diversification options for a long-term growth strategy.

A nonprofit's board, chief executive, and management team must work closely together to keep the change agenda balanced from year to year, ensuring that it responds effectively to external challenges and opportunities while continuously strengthening the essential capabilities on which effective change leadership and management depend. Their choice of change initiatives should be based on a realistic assessment of what is at stake for their organization. Their responsibility is to create a mix of initiatives that promises the greatest benefit, including loss reduction, at an affordable cost.

In Summary

This chapter identified several major characteristics of successful efforts to lead and manage change, including a clear strategic framework, rational priorities, humaneness, comprehensiveness, balance, creativity and innovation, realism, and self-maintenance. It also outlined the 3CAP approach to change, which involves the development of three key organizational capacities: to lead, to innovate, and to implement. Leadership involves applying new approaches to chief executive and board leadership. Innovation comprises two subcapacities: creativity and planning, particularly a variation on the broad strategic planning theme known as strategic management. Implementation is the capacity to translate plans into action, which involves management structure and process as well as a nonprofit's internal culture. Finally, the chapter explained that nonprofits must face the inevitable dilemma of building their internal capacity to lead and manage change while at the same time responding to external demands for change.

Chapter Three

Strengthening Chief Executive Leadership

Coming Attractions

In Chapter Three, the reader will find:

- A description of the traditional view of the chief executive as the top administrative manager and leader
- A fleshing out of the chief executive role based on accountability to produce five organizational outcomes that are critical to effective change leadership
- A discussion of three character attributes that are at the heart of effective chief executive leadership

The Preeminent Partnership

A nonprofit organization's chief executive officer and governing board together constitute the preeminent partnership for leading change. Unless the two partners work in harmony, significant, planned, and well-managed change is unlikely to occur. This discussion of nonprofit leadership capacity appropriately begins with the chief executive because much of the responsibility for building the partnership and for assisting the board in strengthening its own governance role rests on the chief executive's shoulders.

My aim is not to examine the subject of chief executiveship comprehensively here. Rather, I will focus on the chief executive's role in leading change, the principal outcomes of chief executive effort that appear critical to effective change leadership, and three fundamental chief executive attributes that are of essence in producing these outcomes. An inevitable spinoff of meeting this objective is the expansion of the nonprofit chief executive model beyond the two legs that have traditionally supported it: administrative management and overall organizational leadership.

As I know from firsthand experience, many nonprofit chief executives are doing a good job of leading change, and much of the practical wisdom in this chapter draws on their successes. Many others seem to feel that change is in the driver's seat and are finding day-to-day organizational life an ever more frenetic race to catch up with events. This chapter is intended to be an important step in the empowerment of these executives as change leaders. Growing in the capacity to lead change is a never-ending journey that will continue as long as there is change itself. No quick fixes will substitute for sustained time and attention or avert the pain that accompanies growth. But if chief executives are willing to pay the price in time and energy and to face squarely the anxiety that change induces, they can follow the guidelines in this chapter to make their journeys more positive and productive.

Let's begin with a look at the archetypical nonprofit chief executive in the throes of coming to grips with a challenging world. A composite of many real-life examples, she will surely strike a chord with most readers.

This Is the Top?

Sitting in her study early one Saturday morning, barely noticing the autumnal gift of brilliant oranges, reds, and yellows outside her window, Barbara Carlson, RN, MBA, felt exhausted and more than a little discouraged. Although not usually given to self-pity, she felt like putting her head on the desk and having a good cry. After years of hard work and obstacle after obstacle overcome during an arduous journey to the top—the executive directorship at Rest Haven Home—the top now felt like the bottom!

Reflecting on the climb, Barbara couldn't fault herself for lack of passion, discipline, or tenacity. She also knew she was in the right field. She'd known since high school, when she worked as a nurse's aid at a nursing home and discovered that she really cared about the elderly residents she met there. They mattered, their lives and dreams deserved respect, and helping to make their last years comfortable and enjoyable mattered!

It was not that Barbara's powerful professional vision had

cleared the way of obstacles. Working her way through school was
an exhausting experience. Putting her career aside to stay home
with her children Bart and Megan for ten years had been a major
detour. And there was the pain and financial stress that divorce and
single motherhood had brought. But she had never caved in. She
had managed to complete her master's degree on weekends with
financial support from a local foundation. She had then worked
her way steadily up the professional ladder at Rest Haven Home,
a nonprofit elder care facility with 145 beds and a $20 million
budget. Her appointment as executive director four years ago
had been a vision realized and a dream fulfilled.

So why does it feel as if things are going to hell in a hand-
basket? she wondered as the fall colors grew more brilliant with
the rising sun outside her window and her coffee cooled. Well,
maybe that was too dark an assessment, but things did seem over-
whelming these days, and working harder and spending more
hours on the job didn't seem to help much. It was bad enough,
she mused, that health care had become so topsy-turvy, with
merger after merger, accelerating institutional mortality, and the
federal government chipping—no, chopping—away at Medicaid.
It was tough enough coming up with an annual operational plan
and budget that made sense, much less some kind of long-range
plan. In fact, Barbara remembered, it was time to produce another
update of the five-year plan. Where was it, anyway? She couldn't
recall having seen it for months, perhaps a year or two. What was
the point of updating a plan that was never used? Still, she knew
several of the veteran board members would expect a new version
to appear on schedule.

And then there was the board itself. Something was going on
there, but she couldn't put her finger on it. They were clearly no
longer happy campers, but she did not know what they wanted.
Board mailings were finally getting out on time, the finished
packets very carefully prepared. Despite being well nourished with
paper and consequently well informed, they seemed to be getting
pickier and pickier, going through even routine action items with
a fine-tooth comb. The efficient two-hour monthly meeting had
become a fond memory, replaced by marathon sessions that left
everyone drained. What was wrong with the ingrates? She couldn't
work harder to send them a top-notch packet, and on time, too!

Added to all of this misery was Barbara's suspicion that it was
not possible to stay on top of the advancing field of management,
which seemed to be passing her by. Was this what obsolescence felt

like? Three board members in the past two weeks had called to ask her what she was doing about total quality management (she wasn't exactly sure what that was, anyway, and certainly didn't know when she would ever have time to learn). There was that damn strategic plan to be updated, but surely a five-year plan didn't make any sense given the state of the world. Was there any alternative to going through the wasted motion just to please some board members?

There were other problems, too. Her chief of nursing had sent another memorandum on staff empowerment, which seemed to have to do with task forces—or was that quality management? And she still hadn't gotten an e-mail address, despite her best intentions to do so. Oh, and the already high turnover among less skilled staff was growing even worse. Without a personnel director, who had time to dig into the problem?

The Chief Executive Role

Chief executives reading this book will have no trouble relating to the fictional Barbara Carlson. She is a familiar figure in my consulting work with nonprofit organizations. There is no doubt about it, it is tough being a nonprofit chief executive these days, and there is no relief in sight. The only hope is to develop a definition of the role—a model, if you will—that fits these challenging times. Unless they learn to lead and manage change in their nonprofit organizations, many smart, hardworking chief executives will fail to meet the challenge and suffer needlessly, and their organizations will consequently pay a high price.

Any book dealing with the leadership and management of change must pay considerable attention to the chief executive because that individual is in the best position to influence and guide organizational change. In theory, a nonprofit board has more influence and formal authority than the chief executive, but only in theory. In practice, board members devote most of their attention to affairs outside the board; indeed, their typically busy and high-achieving lives, often involving service on other boards, keep their board service at the backs of their minds most of the time. By contrast, the chief executive, who is usually a full-time employee, has ample opportunity to influence how and when organizational change occurs.

Let's start with a simple definition of the position. The chief executive officer is the highest-ranking paid staff person in a nonprofit organization. This individual reports only to the board of directors or trustees and is accountable to the board for all internal organizational operations. In the nonprofit sector, the chief executive is most often given the title executive director or director, but president is becoming more popular.

Most readers will find nothing objectionable about this simple definition, but they will rightly insist that it be fleshed out. In attempting to satisfy this appetite for detail, I inevitably run into a fundamental problem: for all of the thinking and writing about chief executiveship, there is no clear, detailed description of the role that fits the times. What we basically have at a detailed level is two very different slants on the job that are essentially distinct and unintegrated, and could not, even if woven together, serve as a reliable model. In my experience with some three hundred nonprofits, chief executives tend to go back and forth from one stream to another in their careers. The more agile have a better chance of surviving than their slower-moving peers.

Administrative Management

One perspective on the chief executive's position is that of administrative management. In this view, the chief executive oversees and provides direction to a number of technical administrative functions or systems, such as planning, production or service delivery, marketing, information management, and financial, personnel, and facility management. The extent of an organization's investment in systems and the depth of the chief executive's involvement depend on the organization's resources and its needs. In a two-person community development corporation, for example, the chief executive is likely to be the only marketing person and will directly deliver many of the services; also, a sophisticated financial management system will be neither necessary nor affordable.

Closely allied with the administrative management view is what I call the command-and-control style of leadership, typified by such macho-sounding rhetoric as "The buck stops here" or "It happened on my watch." Although the administrative management perspective has proved far too narrow in practice to support successful chief executive performance, it continues to be popular, perhaps in part because it is easily teachable and remains a common route to the chief executive office.

Chief Executive as Leader

The other view of the chief executive is as the organizational leader. This concept is much more nebulous than that of administrative management. It rises above the technical administrative management functions and focuses on the human relationship between leader and followers, drawing on such fields as psychology, organizational behavior, philosophy, and political science. No one would confine leadership to the chief executive; anyone can be a leader, whatever his or her position in an organization.

I have not come across a precise definition of leadership that is universally accepted. Although it would be pointless to spend much time surveying the voluminous leadership literature, a brief excursion down that path to highlight major viewpoints will be helpful here. A good starting point is John Gardner, whose highly regarded book *On Leadership* (1990) proposes a simple definition that is probably still the popular view: "Leadership is the process of persuasion or example by which an individual (or leadership team) induces a group to pursue objectives held by the leader or shared by the leader and his or her followers" (p. 1). In other words, the chief executive gets people to board the change train.

Experience has taught that the chief executive who is an effective leader may not be very interested in or very good at directing the administrative functions, and vice versa. In fact, leadership students are fond of pointing to former president Jimmy Carter as a prime example of the consummate administrative manager who couldn't lead and, as a result, lost popular support. Others have fleshed out the definition, probably no one more prominently and eloquently than Warren Bennis, who has for years carefully studied real-life leaders in search of common themes. Bennis (1989) has identified and described four core leadership competencies: management of people's attention through clear vision; management of meaning through communication of that vision; management of trust through reliability and constancy; and management of self through positive self-regard and goals.

Kouzes and Posner (1996) suggest that effective leaders have learned and put to good use seven basic principles: the importance of taking immediate action; the importance of having personal credibility—that is, character; the importance of having a visionary and a practical side; the importance of fostering shared values; the power of leading by example, not just words; and, finally, a concept of leadership as something that can be accomplished by anyone, not just the higher-ups.

In *Leading Change* (1995), James O'Toole makes a compelling case for the suggestion that a preeminent characteristic of highly successful leaders is their focus on fundamental values rather than ephemeral details, and he offers a number of public and corporate "Rushmoreans" (such as Abraham Lincoln) as examples. Max De Pree (1989), a highly successful chief executive himself, points out that the only convincing proof of leadership is its results. He notes that leadership can't properly be measured by the "quality of the head, but the tone of the body. The signs of outstanding leadership appear primarily among the followers. Are the followers reaching their potential? Are they learning? Serving? Do they achieve the required results? Do they change with grace? Manage conflict?" (p. 12).

Richard Beckhard (1996) sees the leader as the "center of a number of forces, each with its own agenda" (p. 126). These forces, or domains, which are outside and inside the organization as well as inside the leader, demand responses. The leader must "decide how to respond to both individual demands and the interactions between various demands" (p. 126).

Howard Gardner, a leading cognitive psychologist who has studied the creative process, presents an interesting variation on the leadership theme: the leader as storyteller (Gardner and Laskin, 1995). Defining leaders as people who "significantly influence the thoughts, behaviors, and/or feelings of others" (p. 6), Gardner observes that the "ultimate impact of the leader depends most significantly on the particular story that he or she relates or embodies, and the receptions to that story" (p. 14).

Stories can be communicated in words or by example. Their intent is to convince followers of a particular vision or view. They communicate not only to the intellect but also to the emotions of the listener, and "stories of identity—narratives that help individuals think about and feel who they are, where they come from, and where they are headed" exert the greatest influence (Gardner and Laskin, 1995, pp. 42–43). That Ronald Reagan was such an influential president almost certainly had more to do with his superb ability to tell stories that recalled America's pioneer spirit and made people feel optimistic and proud of their heritage than with any programmatic direction he took.

The Bottom Line of Chief Executiveship

The nonprofit manager aspiring to become a chief executive can surely find gold in these two lodes. Leadership helps people influence those whose support they require to get things accomplished, while the technical, administrative functions are essential for a smoothly running organization. But even if serious attempts are made to integrate these two very different perspectives on the chief executive role, they will never add up to a whole picture of what a nonprofit chief executive must be in these challenging times. A more powerful chief executive model is needed, one that is multifaceted enough for these challenging times. The best place to begin is at the beginning: determining the intended outcomes— the bottom line of chief executiveship.

If we think in practical terms about the nonprofit chief executive's role in leading and managing change, one powerful bottom-line result stands out. *As a result of the chief executive's efforts, a nonprofit organization realizes its promise—as contained in its vision and mission—as fully as possible by maintaining the most favorable balance between organizational resources and external conditions.*

Two key concepts are at the heart of this result: a promise is made through vision and mission statements and a promise is kept by conscious investment in organizational resources to capitalize on external environmental conditions, taking advantage of opportunities and coping with barriers and threat. Five very important outcomes of chief executive leadership that together contribute to this preeminent outcome and, hence, to the effective leadership and management of change are:

1. A nonprofit organization that is united around a common vision and mission

2. A nonprofit organization whose organizational parts are defined and aligned so as to function with maximum effectiveness
3. A nonprofit organization that is stable and secure
4. A nonprofit organization that is a source of major, systematic innovation
5. A nonprofit organization that consists of empowered people

By no means should the chief executive be seen as being able alone to achieve such powerful outcomes. Rather, the chief executive is principally accountable for seeing that they are achieved. In doing so, today's chief executives cannot rely on a simplistic model that has them merely dipping into the leadership and administrative management streams. Rather, they need to supplement leadership and administrative management by becoming an organizational designer; a facilitator of organizational activity who helps the board and staff to carry out their roles effectively; and even a therapist of sorts, who is committed to helping board and staff members to grow individually and to exercise greater creativity.

A final observation about the five key outcomes: far from being neatly differentiated and mutually exclusive, they overlap and reinforce each other. Thus, nonprofit chief executives must be sure to ask the right questions about the work they are doing and produce as much positive impact on their organizations—and their clients and customers—as they can.

Unity Through Vision and Mission

Widely shared organizational values, a vision, and a mission are critical to, if not the preeminent producer of, a nonprofit organization's unity. *Values* are the fundamental truths that form an overarching ethical framework for all organizational planning and operations; they are the bedrock principles that compel an organization to move in certain directions and deter it from engaging in certain activities. A *vision* sets forth a multifaceted picture of the desired future, a picture that can be painted in terms of the organization's desired impact on its environment, of the organization's desired role in that environment, and of the organization's desired image in the eyes of others in that environment. The *mission* is a description of the nonprofit's basic business now, in terms of its customers and clients, its products and services, and its major roles and functions.

These three elements form the nonprofit's strategic framework. They differ in purpose as well as content. Values give organizations guidance in determining courses of action and in setting limits to organizational behavior. For example, if one of an art museum's overall values is wide community use, then it will over the long run be encouraged to invest in outreach and discouraged from raising admission prices, assuming that the value is explicitly stated and taken seriously. In contrast, a vision is intended to inspire and to motivate; visions are goads to growth and innovation drivers. For example, if a nonprofit employment and training organization envisions as one of its long-term impacts significant growth in high-tech, high-wage employment in its metropolitan area, then it will be encouraged to invest over the long run in customized training programs for relocating high-tech firms.

If the vision is by its very nature expansive and growth-oriented, the mission serves a more disciplinary purpose, clarifying to the wider world exactly what the organization is and what it isn't. The mission keeps a nonprofit from embarking willy-nilly on growth and diversification, from expanding its boundaries without a second thought. Chapter Seven delves much further into the three elements of the strategic framework; for now, I will look at the chief executive's responsibility for upholding the framework and ensuring that it plays an active role in organizational life.

The leadership literature sees values and vision as the most precious currency of strong leaders. Through the clear articulation and effective communication of values and vision that they take seriously and apply in their own behavior, strong leaders inspire commitment, loyalty, and confidence in their followers (Bennis, 1989; Bennis and Nanus, 1985; O'Toole, 1995). On the grander political stage, even if many voters don't agree with all the values or the vision a leader communicates, they still tend to feel more trust and confidence in a leader with firm beliefs than in one who waffles, as David McCullough's magnificent biography *Truman* (1992) demonstrates so well. A leader's passionately held, effectively communicated values and vision are capable of building support even among people who have strong programmatic disagreements with the leader, as Bennis and Nanus (1985) observed of President Ronald Reagan.

On the smaller stage where nonprofit dramas unfold, the chief executive who merely thinks through, articulates, and communicates his or her own values, vision, and mission to others in the organization is more likely to produce resistance than commitment. Board members and staff these days expect to play an active role in fashioning their organization's strategic framework, so the challenge for the chief executive is to design a participatory process for generating values, vision, and mission statements and to facilitate their participation, ensuring that the strategic products are generated fully and on time.

Thus, the chief executive must make sure that everyone involved knows exactly what they will be producing and how they will participate in producing it. For example, the superintendent of a school district I worked with several years ago decided to form a task force to prepare for a two-day board-management retreat. Consisting of selected board and staff members along with the superintendent, the task force fashioned the values and vision statements to be presented, discussed, and revised in a plenary session that was the first event in the retreat. His design also included an outside consultant's facilitating both the task force deliberations and the retreat.

To give the values, vision, and mission statements meaning, the nonprofit chief executive must ensure that they are widely communicated, that they are seriously used as planning and decision-making tools, and that the chief executive never violates them in any major way. Otherwise, they will quickly lose their power to inspire, motivate, and shape behavior. The chief executive of a nonprofit national association with which I am familiar accomplishes this by ensuring that his board's planning committee—in an annual daylong work session with management team members—reviews departmental annual operational plans while keeping the vision in mind, explicitly asking how each plan contributes to accomplishing key vision elements and making sure that no planned initiatives contradict the vision in any major way. If there is a conflict, the staff go back to the drawing board.

A chief executive's ability to build organizational unity and cohesion by ensuring that values and vision statements are developed and communicated depends not just on planning and communication skills but also on adherence to the values in his or her behavior day after day. People have learned to discount words, hedging their bets until actual behavior over a period of time confirms the validity of particular values.

I recall vividly a young, ambitious, fast-track college chief executive with whom I worked several years ago. He was an avid consumer of the latest management thinking and could go on at length about one innovative technique or another. A favorite hobbyhorse at one point was participatory management and team building. Indeed, waxing eloquent on the subject of teamwork as a key to organizational innovation, his eyes would even tear up on occasion, he was that sincere! His "espoused theory," as Chris Argyris (1993) would put it, was that teamwork was a highly prized value, good for the spirit and essential to the college's success and should, therefore, be actively promoted. But his "theory in practice" was something else. The Wednesday cabinet meeting at which he presided over the assembled vice presidents and directors could have been designed by the Marquis de Sade or Josef Stalin. Heads bowed, participants fervently hoped that if they kept quiet the president would not direct his scathing wit or humiliating critiques at them. His monologues, often punctuated with screams of rage, were the rule. The common theme was the tremendous burden that an incompetent management team had put upon him, the heroic, overworked, and possibly soon-to-be-martyred chief executive. It is not difficult to guess how enthusiastically the cabinet members promoted participation throughout the institution.

Seeing That the Pieces Fit

Organizations are complex and dynamic puzzles consisting of ever-shifting pieces. There are the people organized into entities, such as the board, the management team, departments, divisions, programs, projects, and other units. There are the systems and processes that support the people: strategic and operational planning; budget preparation and management; financial management; information management; and many others. And there are the developing technologies and methodologies that can be applied in systems and processes, for example, total quality management techniques in operational planning and computer hardware and software advances in information management.

One of the most challenging roles of the modern nonprofit chief executive is to ensure that a comprehensive organizational design is developed and maintained so that the pieces of this complex puzzle fit and work together well, as a principal means of ensuring full achievement of organizational vision and mission. Let's take the board, for example. Herman and Heimovics (1991) have observed that the "primary behaviors that characterize effective chief executives are those associated with board-centered leadership, and we believe that the most effective chief executives engage their boards in special ways to see that they are ready and able to deal effectively with externally induced challenges" (p. 90).

Every nonprofit organization has a board. There are some critical questions that must be asked and answered if the board is to carry its share of the organizational load. Is the board's role clear? Does it reflect advances in the field of nonprofit governance? Does the board have the membership, structure, and governance processes that will generate the outcomes the organization needs? If not, what enhancements are needed and how can they be achieved? (See Chapter Four for a detailed discussion of nonprofit governance and board development.)

Certainly, a nonprofit chief executive should not try to answer all of these questions alone or attempt to identify and implement the enhancements alone. But it is without question the chief executive's job to see that they get asked and answered effectively—sometimes by taking the lead, at others by leading from behind. In other words, the nonprofit chief executive must pay close attention to the board's performance and the culture of the board, their attitudes and feelings, looking for signs of malfunctioning and dissatisfaction. The chief executive must also keep abreast of the nonprofit governance field, keeping up to date on the governance experiences of other nonprofits and understanding advances in the field.

Boards do not and cannot alone develop their governance capability; they must rely on the chief executive as both partner and supporter in the process. Board members often do not even see the need to improve performance; they can become comfortable with familiar routines even if the routines prevent them from doing their job fully. I have worked with many chief executives over the past twenty-five years who knew without doubt that their boards would benefit from a daylong examination of their governance roles and responsibilities in a retreat setting. But they also knew not to ask directly, "Would you like to spend a day together thinking about governance?" Nor were they foolhardy enough to add, "You need it, and I'm recommending you do it!" The inevitable answer would have been, "No, thanks." Instead, they employed less direct, more sophisticated strategies to help their boards discover the need themselves. Some shared pertinent articles on governance with their boards; others sent certain board members to governance workshops and conferences as appetite-whetters. No matter how direct or convoluted the strategy, the chief executive took accountability for moving board governance forward, for making sure that this piece of the organizational puzzle took appropriate shape.

The chief executive should also determine if the strategic planning or management process already in place involves board and staff members creatively and reliably produces practical innovations that respond to change in the wider world. Perhaps the nonprofit is saddled instead with an outmoded five-year long-range planning process that mostly just chews up trees while generating pounds of paper that merely describe what already exists and offers only an illusion of safety and control. It is the chief executive's job to ensure that the pertinent questions get asked and answered, not only about planning but all systems and processes.

The savvy chief executive will want to involve his or her management team and other staff in asking and answering such important questions about organizational processes and systems. For example, a local nonprofit housing development corporation that I worked with a few years ago used an annual management team retreat to audit all major operating systems and processes. The team's first task was to determine what it expected of such key systems as strategic planning and budget preparation. It then roughly audited each system to determine gaps between expectations and actual performance. For example, the team members determined that the annual budget process should produce not only numbers but also measurable performance targets and extensive internal communication. But their audit indicated that objectives in the past had been too general to use as yardsticks. This led to a third step: determining annual system enhancements and fashioning strategies to produce them, such as adding a better description of performance targets to the budget preparation guidelines.

One of the chief executive's most important roles as chief designer and "celestial mechanic" of the organization is to protect both the board and the staff from premature commitment to or overinvestment in management innovations that are likely to disappoint expectations or produce an unfavorable cost-benefit ratio. Today, with tantalizing technological advances and constant encouragement to seek the quick fix, the danger of getting caught with an expensive "improvement" that yields little while causing undue pain and suffering is clear. Remember the example of the staff task force in Chapter One that used the graveyard illustration to demonstrate the many improvements that had come to untimely ends after being launched with promise and enthusiasm.

Perhaps the most oversold quick fix these days is the philosophy and operational guidelines that make up what is called total quality management. Total quality management offers important and useful concepts and tools—focusing on the customer and continuously involving teams in fashioning operational improvements, for example. But it has all too often been applied as a kind of low-cost "miracle drug" and has, therefore, already earned a dubious reputation among many disappointed nonprofit managers. Inadequately understood and haphazardly implemented, without sufficient training or a willingness to pay the other costs, total quality management has generally failed to fulfill its promise.

A few years ago, I knew a school superintendent who abruptly shifted course in the midst of implementing a highly participatory strategic management process to charge full-speed ahead into a total quality project in response to a state government initiative that involved substantial grants of financial aid to local institutions. The result, while sad, was predictable: lots of confusion, an overextended staff, the eventual loss of any benefits already realized from the strategic management process, and considerable disillusionment among board and staff members. By contrast, the director of a YMCA in a large city led his management team through a careful design process that resulted in the application of total quality management techniques within the broader framework of a strategic management process that supplied vision and strategic direction and within which total quality techniques could be applied as an operational process improvement tool. This director took the chief executive design role seriously, and his YMCA is continuing to reap the benefits.

Ensuring Stability and Security

Nonprofit chief executives can contribute to their organization's stability and security in a number of ways. Perhaps the most powerful is by taking accountability for the health of the organization's relationship with the world around it. The most effective tool for accomplishing this undoubtedly is designing and implementing a planning process that keeps the nonprofit in a dynamic balance with its environment, so that its scarce resources are invested to capitalize on opportunities for growth and to counter threats.

As long as it is not old-time mechanistic projections of the present into the future, planning can protect organizations by enabling them to anticipate opportunities and challenges and fashion responses before crises disrupt organizational peace. The more turbulent the world outside a nonprofit is, the more emphasis its chief executive should place on the planning function. Health care today is a prime example of an unruly environment that demands attention to planning from the agencies and institutions that wish to survive.

Another tool for chief executives to bring greater security and stability to their nonprofits is to regulate the pace of change so that people are not so overextended that they become anxious, insecure, and unstable. A couple of years ago I was asked to counsel a nonprofit—a department within a larger organization in the financial services field—that had launched a far-reaching reorganization without thinking through the consequences. Basically, the two top executives, in keeping with a sincere commitment to team management, chose to replace the traditional operating divisions of the department with functional teams headed by team leaders who were given somewhat vague authority and told to lead through a kind of consensus management rather than by traditional direction setting. A complex change both culturally and administratively, this reform was launched with the expectation that it could be carried out in a year's time.

But anxiety was soon rampant. The growing organizational instability forced the two top executives to bring the whole department together for a retreat. Over the course of one and a half days together, what the two hoped to achieve from the reorganization was clarified. A new implementation strategy was formulated, setting a far more realistic pace and taking much of the pressure off a dangerously overextended and frustrated group of people.

A simple tool for building internal calm and stability is to make sure that information is widely shared, and that, within reasonable bounds, staff know what important initiatives are under way at any time and understand each other's plans and activities. I long ago came to the conclusion that the old need-to-know rule for sharing information is 100 percent wrong. The more *everyone* knows the better—not only because they can use the information in their work but also, and perhaps more important, because it makes them feel better about the organization. And feelings have a lot to do with positive energy and commitment.

It is easy to share information but it is more difficult to ensure that communication actually occurs. Regular team meetings are a simple and effective tool for bringing everyone up to date on activities and thinking. But I have encountered many nonprofit chief executives who are "just too busy" to chair meetings or who think that talking is a waste of time. Over the past year, I have met two nonprofit chief executives, both heads of economic development corporations, who almost never hold staff meetings and depend on one-to-one meetings with management team members instead. Both chief executives are smart, dedicated and hardworking, humane, and likable. But both organizations underachieve because of the anxiety that inadequate communication breeds among the staff.

A feeling of trust in the chief executive also contributes to internal security and stability. Trust is primarily a function of the chief executive's behavior—rather than mere words—and behavior is basically determined by what we call character. Although personality can be manipulated to an extent, character, as Stephen Covey (1989) has observed, draws on a person's fundamental psychological makeup, core values, and principles. Over time, character is demonstrated through behavior and cannot successfully be hidden from everyone all the time. There is wide agreement that chief executives and other leaders of character know themselves intimately and that they focus on their own development before turning to those around them. Covey calls this the "inside-out" approach, putting "private victories" before public ones. He says that "it is futile to put personality ahead of character, to try to improve relationships with others before improving ourselves" (1989, p. 43).

A nonprofit chief executive aspiring to what Peter Senge terms "personal mastery" must embark on a personal growth journey that leads inside, far enough into the subconscious mind to uncover and deal with assumptions and beliefs about both himself and herself and the wider world (Senge, 1990). These beliefs and assumptions can distort self-understanding and perceptions of reality, and play a powerful role in shaping character and hence chief executive leadership. In the process of developing a speaking career over the past decade, I have come to understand the power of the subconscious to influence conscious perceptions of reality by filtering and interpreting experience. Like many new speakers, I found that a subconscious fear of being judged harshly turned every audience I faced during my early years into a group of unforgiving critics whose mission was to wound my ego. Speaking engagements felt like battles; every success was a fatiguing experience. Only by taking an inner journey and confronting my subconscious negativity was I able to alter reality. I now feel only admiration and respect for those chief executives committed to such reality.

Most people have probably witnessed chief executives who contribute to a sense of anxiety in their organizations because of dysfunctional aspects in their own characters that they seem not to recognize. A good example is the college president described earlier with the espoused commitment to participatory management who treated management team members abusively. Chief executives who do not "walk the talk" risk not being heard since actions speak louder than words. When the gap between what is said and what is practiced relates to core values rather than to tactical matters, then the disparity is sure to erode chief executive credibility, and employee trust and commitment.

Making the Organization Innovation-Friendly

In a rapidly changing world that constantly hurls challenges at non-profit organizations, building an organizational capability to innovate regularly and systematically is a matter of survival. Innovation basically means behaving in significantly new ways or producing significantly new services, programs, and processes. Chief executives can do a number of things to make their nonprofits more innovation-friendly, starting with a sincere desire and commitment to make innovation happen. The depth of this commitment has a lot to do with the strength of character already discussed. A chief executive who unconsciously feels threatened by change can become the worst enemy of innovation without even knowing it. In the name of caution and prudent management, but in reality because of personal insecurity, new ideas will be forced to run a gauntlet that few will survive.

Innovation involves a marriage between creativity—the invention process that generates new possibilities for innovation—and planning, which is the process of translating possibilities into implementation strategies. (Chapter Two discusses creativity and planning in greater depth.) Chief executives who are committed to innovation will ensure that their nonprofit's creative capacity is developed and that the planning process makes it possible to employ creativity in producing innovation.

Nonprofit chief executives can take some relatively simple steps to encourage creativity in a nonprofit. One is to provide formal developmental opportunities outside the organization. For example, the management team could go through a program aimed at training people to think more creatively. The Center for Creative Leadership in Greensboro, North Carolina, is an important resource in this regard; so is the Gestalt Institute in Cleveland. There is growing evidence that creativity can be strengthened through formal education and training in the creative process, as Chapter Five will discuss in detail.

Creative expression can be limited by unconscious motivations, including fear of failure or need to control. Chief executives can help staff understand and cope with their internal resistance. One way is to teach by example, being brave enough to think aloud about their own feelings of resistance and sharing with others the ways in which such feelings have limited their own expressions of creativity in the past. Such public disclosures of human frailty can foster trust and encourage staff to tackle their own barriers.

Smart, aggressive chief executives with a powerful drive to succeed and win in all places and times can, through their competitiveness, retard creative growth in those around them. I have met many chief executives who could hardly sit still during a discussion that was being facilitated by someone else, so great was their need to jump up and take control. One particularly amusing instance occurred while I was leading a brainstorming session involving the chief executive and several board and staff members of a national association. The goal was to consider creative ways to carry out a number of change initiatives that had been identified at a retreat several weeks earlier. A chalkboard stood behind me, and after an hour or so of general discussion, the chief executive directed one of his staff to get a piece of chalk and stand behind me to write down his solutions, which he dictated aloud. As a relatively cohesive and collegial group of strong-willed colleagues, we were unintimidated and able to continue brainstorming. In a different setting, however, such aggressive, controlling behavior can squelch creative growth.

One of the simplest steps a chief executive can take to encourage creative activity is to design opportunities for free brainstorming into organizational processes and to play the facilitator role when the occasion demands it. Every day brings many opportunities to encourage freer thinking if the chief executive is alert to them. The most obvious opportunity is the weekly staff meeting, which is frequently a forum for considering operational issues. Nothing prevents a committed chief executive from structuring opportunities for wide-open discussion of issues that come up, encouraging everyone to chime in without fear of rejection, reprisal, or humiliation. Such an undramatic practice, while in the short run likely to have little impact, will over the longer term lead to better decisions and more creative thinking among the staff.

Empowering Others

A number of readers may feel instant revulsion at coming across the term *empowerment* because it has become one of those too-common buzzwords that carry a lot of negative connotations. I do not doubt that damage has been done in the name of empowering people, but, in fact, the concept has a precious core that deserves the respect and serious attention of nonprofit chief executives. Max De Pree (1989) captures the essence of empowerment in answering the question, What is it most of us really want from work? "We would like to find the most effective, most productive, most rewarding way of working together. We would like to know that our work process uses all of the appropriate and pertinent resources: human, physical, financial. We would like a work process and relationships that meet our personal needs for belonging, for contributing, for meaningful work, for the opportunity to make a commitment, for the opportunity to grow and be at least reasonably in control of our own destinies" (p. 23).

Drawing on De Pree, I see four concrete ways in which nonprofit chief executives can strive to empower others by ensuring that

- People have substantial influence on the nonprofit's direction and, hence, on their own destinies.
- They make significant contributions to the organization's success by using fully their skills, talents, abilities, experience, intelligence, and other resources.
- They grow more capable psychologically, managerially, technically, and politically.
- Their personal needs are met as far as possible.

Nonprofit chief executives can empower the people in their organizations along the above four lines in myriad ways. Planning process design is one of the most powerful because it involves people in setting strategic directions and determining courses of action that affect all of their destinies. For example, by inviting all staff members to participate in its annual board-staff strategic work session, during which the values, vision, and mission statements were clarified and strategic issues identified, one national association I worked with took a major step in the direction of empowerment. The same association involved all the staff in task forces that followed up on the work session by fashioning detailed action strategies, and this further empowered the staff.

If a chief executive seriously attempts to build empowerment into a nonprofit's organizational culture, then management team members and supervisors too will be on the lookout for opportunities to involve people actively in decision making and will take individuals' capabilities and desires into account when filling positions and assigning tasks.

A chief executive who is serious about empowerment will avoid gimmicky approaches. Gimmicks are form without substance, and they can be terribly damaging to morale. I once worked with a group of people who had spent one day several months earlier with a so-called empowerment consultant. This facilitator had instilled principles, whetted appetites, and raised expectations, but stopped short of designing any practical follow-through. The group had talked a lot about the kind of organizational culture they wanted to build, gained a good sense of the internal problems that needed to be addressed, and even acquired some important skills for strengthening communication. But at the end of a day they did not have a detailed game plan for implementing concrete improvements. In consequence, nothing important occurred after the retreat. I found a frustrated, disillusioned group on the verge of real cynicism and anger. The accumulated negative emotion was a real barrier to moving forward with serious empowerment after that. Training someone in the skills is always just a first step; without process design to ensure actual results, this kind of training can cause more harm than good.

One sure-fire empowerment approach that I have seen work time and again is building opportunities for growth into formal planning. Several years ago I worked as a coach with various management teams that were preparing for half-day operational planning and budget briefings for a board. These were pilot tests of a significantly redesigned planning process that would be expanded to all departments in subsequent years. One of the department teams included forensic pathologists, who were among the best-educated (all were medical doctors) and highest-paid employees in the organization. I wondered at the onset whether such a brilliant, strong-willed crew had much to learn, but I need not have worried. As they struggled over the course of three lengthy brainstorming sessions to figure out how to communicate their very complex work—in both human and technical terms—to board members who lacked technical knowledge in pathology, I saw tremendous learning occur as well as real empowerment. It was inspiring to see these highly accomplished professionals learn to communicate such exotic technologies as DNA testing to a lay audience. Furthermore, learning to deal with the board as a preeminent client brought greater power to their labors in forensic pathology. For my part, I found the dark humor that helped carry them through their day-to-day activities a joy to behold.

Fundamental Attributes of the Chief Executive

For a chief executive to achieve the desired results, what attributes are most critical and how can he or she develop them? I distinguish between skills and fundamental attributes. The skills that help chief executives lead change in their nonprofits are basically technical, and hence can be learned in a relatively straightforward fashion as long as there are motivation and commitment. At the technical end of the spectrum, there are planning, financial management, time management, budgeting, information management, and many other skills. At the human end are such skills as listening, communicating, and facilitating.

These skills certainly are important, and they are not easily learned. Experience has taught me that I, along with most nonprofit chief executives I have met, need a lot of work on skills such as listening and communicating. I constantly return to Covey's powerful time management matrix in *The Seven Habits of Highly Effective People* (1989) for a booster shot when urgent, unimportant activities once again begin to overwhelm more fundamental uses of my time. But acquiring such skills has already been thoroughly discussed in numerous books and articles.

In contrast, fundamental attributes have to do with the character and psychological makeup of a chief executive, and this brings us face to face with the spiritual dimension of human development and inexorably leads us into the shadowy realm of the subconscious. Fundamental attributes are much more difficult to understand than skills, and more difficult to develop and to change. In fact, many people believe that they are hopelessly fuzzy and subjective and thus not a valid subject of attention. Others question whether one's character can be developed or significantly changed later in life. And we have all often heard the sobering conclusion, "People just don't change."

Based on my professional and personal experience, I disagree with both viewpoints. Indeed, I believe that serious attention to the fundamental attributes is the only sensible course for chief executives of nonprofits to take in these challenging times. Managers aspiring to be chief executives must work hard to develop these fundamental attributes if they intend to lead change successfully.

Scott Peck (1978) calls the journey of spiritual development "the road less traveled" because the inevitable fear and pain involved deter many people from even embarking on it while others look for easier detours before many miles have passed. Acquisition of fundamental attributes does not lend itself to the formal classroom. Indeed, much of the development in this realm is necessarily individual and deeply personal, and more is likely to happen during a retreat or on a long walk in the woods or during a session with an analyst than while taking notes in a classroom. Because fundamental development is so alien to the good old no-nonsense school of management we have grown accustomed to, it is even more mysterious and threatening. My counsel to aspiring nonprofit chief executives is to anticipate the pain and the human resistance to developing these fundamental attributes and to accept the price as well worth it. And in the process, they should resist the notion that quick, feel-good fixes offer any real help.

Because the barriers to fundamental development are normally so high, our best friend is often a traumatic event; ironically, the worst things can turn out to be the best in the long run. In my professional development, one of the most positive events was being fired almost thirty years ago from a position that provided a good salary and enough prestige to feed my ego. In addition to the shock I felt at suddenly being unemployed, an added trauma was that I was given the news somewhat brutally on the eve of my marriage, no less. Of course, this event did not immediately lead to a period of introspection with resultant insights and revelations. On the contrary, I soon found another job that provided no more passion than the first. No sea changes were made. For another five years or so I could not even think about the event without feeling tremendous anger over my mistreatment and humiliation. But the door had opened, if only a crack, and another road could be glimpsed, if only hazily. I now count this horrible memory as a blessing long disguised.

What are the fundamental attributes that appear most critical for a chief executive who wishes to lead change? Three loom largest as I reflect on my work over the past quarter-century: *true humility, realistic self-knowledge,* and *courage.* They are certainly intertwined and may even be essentially just different facets of the same thing, but the variations seem important enough to merit individual discussion.

True Humility

It seems contradictory to speak of true humility and strength in the same sentence, but I have learned that the two go hand in glove. If a chief executive's strength is measured by positive accomplishment and the ability to motivate and help others to contribute in more powerful ways to the achievement of a nonprofit's vision and mission, then the strongest chief executives I have encountered in my work are the humblest, and at the same time the most fundamentally self-confident. Often, those who appear the strongest on the surface—those who are loud, combative, self-assertive—turn out to be the weakest when it comes to actual results. Truly humble chief executives do not fit the stereotype of the macho leader astride a white horse issuing commands and leading charges, never shedding a tear or admitting to any of the frailties that bedevil lesser mortals. Truly humble chief executives are keenly aware of their mortality and their human frailties, and they are the stronger for this essential humility.

True humility is the cornerstone of successful change leadership: it inspires trust, it steers a firm course that builds confidence and commitment among colleagues and followers, it allows for the listening and learning that are critical to creativity and growth. Truly humble people see themselves not at the center of the universe but as one part of a grander scheme, a transcendent force for good. They never compromise in the hurly burly of day-to-day affairs. There is nothing of the namby-pamby about the truly humble; their steadfastness in the face of adversity, a natural consequence of belief in more than just themselves, inspires others to persevere in troubled times.

Not being the end-all, be-all of existence, the truly humble chief executive does not need to expect or demand perfection in himself or herself, or in other people, and thus has no need to preserve face at all costs. Being able to admit shortcomings and mistakes before peers and subordinates and to forgive them in others, the truly humble person helps others to be open and to engage in the occasionally risky behavior that fosters learning and creativity. And because the truly humble chief executive believes that all people have a purpose, a place in the grand scheme of things, and that everyone has an important contribution to make, he or she encourages and actively supports colleagues in expressing that unique contribution.

Some years ago, I facilitated a management team meeting in an organization that was experiencing great tension over a reorganization that had been pushed through unrealistically fast. The woman at the helm and her top lieutenant were widely viewed as responsible for much of the trauma, and rightly so since they had conceived and pushed the reorganization plan forward. In one of the preparatory meetings at which a retreat design emerged, we came up with the idea of having the chief executive and her sidekick spend an hour sitting on stools at the front of the room in a completely unstructured dialogue with the group, without an agenda or any preconceived notion of outcomes.

Worried that the situation could easily lead to an exceedingly unpleasant confrontation, we were relieved when the group responded positively. The willingness of the top executives to share not only their rationales for the steps that had been taken but also their misgivings about the pace of the reorganization and their expression of a desire for advice and help from the team turned what might have been a debacle into a learning event. It was a highly successful morale booster, and it also ultimately led to a better planned transition from the old to new structure.

People tend to feel safe and secure around truly humble chief executives, mainly because they observe day after day that their values are never compromised, although tactics may shift and even take on a Byzantine quality at times. They also know that the truly humble chief executive will not lash out at the least provocation because of the self-hate that often results from the perfectionistic tendencies of arrogance and false humility. (Can anyone question that self-flagellation easily leads to a sadistic tendency to inflict damage on others?) Truly humble, undefended chief executives make better decisions because they are able to listen and learn, freed from the imperative to be right on every issue.

After years of work with chief executives, I believe that I have learned to spot truly humble ones pretty fast. One of the surest signs that I am in their presence is the quiet they keep as they listen carefully and patiently and resist the temptation to jump in, take control, and demonstrate their expertise. One of most effective change leaders I have ever observed was superintendent of a school district with more than its share of problems, a district that benefitted greatly from his wise leadership. I will never forget how impressed I was when we met. After the usual break-the-ice chit chat, he simply said, "Tell what you know about strategic planning" and proceeded to listen for the next two hours, interjecting occasional pertinent questions but basically just listening, with nary a phone call or other interruption. He did the same the second time we met. I knew that his essential humility boded well for leading change, and it did.

Donald's Pulitzer Prize–winning *Lincoln* (1995) paints a picture of a truly humble leader whose essential humility contributed to his becoming a historical figure of mythic proportions. According to Donald, Lincoln was keenly aware of his place in the universe. From early in life he "had a sense that his destiny was controlled by some larger force, some Higher Power" (p. 15). His essential humility made him an avid on-the-job learner. He was able to tolerate huge egos and outrageous behavior around him in the interest of the greater good. For all his competitiveness in law and politics, Lincoln never had to be "right," and this quality has endeared him to succeeding generations. I think we appreciate his true humility all the more when we see him as a whole man rather than a saint—an ambitious, sometimes devious attorney, a brawling, down-and-dirty politician who relished the rough and tumble, a man who made plenty of bad decisions as president and admitted it.

Truly humble chief executives tend to attract and retain strong, creative people with ideas to share and contributions to make, and they are willing to overlook stylistic differences in the interest of learning. There is probably no better example of this than Harry Truman's strong relationship with Dean Acheson, as recounted in *Truman* (McCullough, 1992). Was there ever an odder couple than the former Missouri farmer and failed haberdasher who earned his spurs in the Kansas City political machine and that reserved, elegant, Ivy-League educated Eastern establishment figure, Dean Acheson? It is a testimony to Harry Truman's true humility that the relationship developed and deepened quickly. American foreign policy benefited mightily from this unlikely partnership.

Realistic Self-Knowledge

I have worked with chief executives who could not capitalize on the talents and commitment of strong women on their teams because they found such strengths threatening. I have worked with chief executives who were unsuccessful in building critical partnerships and joint ventures with other organizations because they saw the world as a dark and dangerous place filled with competitors waiting to do them in. I have worked with chief executives whose need for security and control made them intolerant of the give-and-take of wide-open discussion and led them to impose on their organizations mechanistic long-range planning processes that substituted neatness and order for creative questioning and exploration.

In these and other cases, what has struck me is the absence of conscious awareness on the chief executives' part that they were filtering reality through an internal lens that distorted reality, ensuring that what the chief executives "knew" fit largely subconscious preconceptions and expectations. The cost of such distorting of reality can be quite high in untapped human potential, lost opportunities for creative partnership, and wasted motion.

Chief executives committed to seeing the world around them realistically and to being open to its manifold possibilities have no choice but to embark on an inward, psychological journey, in search of those aspects of self that have disappeared from their consciousness but exert power over their perceptions. Only by visiting these facets of the self that have been stripped away and relegated to the subconscious realm—by making them conscious— can their influence to shape perceptions be recognized and controlled. Only by rediscovering what Jung (1990; Au and Cannon, 1995) called the shadow side of the self and bringing light to bear on it can chief executives avoid projecting their perceptions onto others. This process is vividly described by Conger in *Spirit at Work* (Conger and Associates, 1994, p. 28): "Why must we go in and down? Because as we do so, we will meet the violence and terror that we carry within ourselves. If we do not confront these things inwardly, we will project them outward onto other people. When we have not understood that the enemy is within ourselves, we will find a thousand ways of making someone 'out there' into the enemy."

A chief executive I knew found it extremely difficult to work effectively with a bright, highly capable, but very assertive woman on his staff. He could not understand the feelings of coldness and anger he felt whenever she challenged one of his ideas. His feeling of being harshly criticized and humiliated was so obviously out of proportion to what actually was said that he eventually consulted a psychologist to help him deal with the situation, which was quickly becoming unworkable for both parties. It did not take long to discover that an overbearing mother's scathing criticism of his least offence had left a festering wound whose power to color his perceptions had grown stronger over the years. This chief executive did not, so far as I know, do enough inner work to stop completely the projection of a harsh mother onto this and other innocent assertive women whose paths he crossed, but he did learn to distrust his negative feelings and not act on them.

Unfortunately, such an inner journey is probably a rarity among chief executives coming of age in a society that so prizes extroverted behavior and extols the virtues of positive thinking. Success itself can make a chief executive immune to the danger signals, especially when operating outside of the usual milieu. The classic case, which I have witnessed countless times, is the successful business chief executive serving on a nonprofit board who passionately resists any attempt to reform board process in the interest of more effective governance. More often than not, so far as I have been able to tell, the passionate opposition to reform results from a deep-seated fear of being displaced or of not measuring up to the new task rather than from serious governance concerns. I have never heard anyone disclose such a motivation, but in the absence of any other compelling rationale for the passionate opposition, this is the only conclusion I can draw.

Courage

Leading from a values base takes courage because our values do not always lead us where we would like to go. It is far easier if less noble to hold up a wet finger and let the breeze determine our course. A chief executive can lead from a base of self-understanding only after taking the inner journey, confronting the demons, and freeing perception from their distorting grip. Joseph Campbell (1968) vividly describes the terrors ahead on this hero's journey: "The unconscious sends all sorts of vapors, odd beings, terrors, and deluding images up into the mind—whether in dream, broad daylight, or insanity; for the human kingdom, beneath the floor of the comparatively neat little dwelling that we call our consciousness, goes down into unsuspected Aladdin caves. There not only jewels but also dangerous jinn abide: the inconvenient or resisted psychological powers that we have not thought or dared to integrate into our lives" (p. 8).

The courage that enables chief executives to withstand pressures to compromise their values and arms them to undertake the interior journey to self-understanding, is not, in my experience, a matter merely of intellect, willpower, ambition, or discipline, although these can be useful tools. The wellspring of such courage, the vital force that infuses it with such strength, is far more mysterious: faith in a transcendent being, a divine force standing above all humankind but also residing within each person, what Thomas Merton has called "the divine image in our soul" (1961, p. 121). Closely allied with the concept of faith among the courageous chief executives I have observed is love, which is the most precious and freely given gift of the Supreme Being, who frees each of us to love himself and herself. What faith and love appear to produce is a fundamental self-confidence and the true humility that I discussed earlier. Thomas Merton says that the "root of Christian love is not the will to love, but *the faith that one is loved. The faith that one is loved by* God" (1961, p. 75). Or as Wilkie Au (1989, p. 28) put it, "Only by embracing the totality of who we are as people uniquely fashioned by the Lord can we progress spiritually."

Whether such faith is developed and nurtured in a formal religious setting or not, a strong spiritual life appears to be the bedrock foundation for enduring courage. By spiritual life, I mean nurturing faith by preserving and protecting the interior life, regularly taking time away from the madding crowd to be alone, to turn inward, to commune with the Supreme Being, to seek direction in the silence, to accept the free gift of love, and then return to the world armed with healthy self-regard and renewed courage. A strong spiritual life can be a vital partner with rational thought, deliberate will, and discipline in the essential task of translating values and vision into actual practice.

Things to Do

What are some practical steps that nonprofit chief executives can take to develop true humility, grow in self-understanding, and build courage through faith? Such concerns are obviously outside the realm of textbooks and formal course work, yet the increasing number of chief executives I have met over the years who are committed to growth have used certain developmental tools successfully. Formal religious observance is one way to approach life's spiritual dimension. Thomas Moore (1992) comments that religions "demonstrate that spiritual life requires constant attention and a subtle, often beautiful technology by which spiritual principles and understandings are kept alive" (p. 204). Even if estranged for years from the religion of one's childhood, renewed participation in familiar rituals can awake long-buried feelings. Standing in a Methodist church for the first time in over thirty years, motivated more by the pain of divorce than by something more affirmative, a person I know was jolted by emotion and taken aback by the tears coursing down his cheeks barely a stanza into an old familiar hymn.

Reading religious texts, such as the Hebrew Bible, the Koran, or the New Testament can put one in touch with the spiritual dimension of life. Tales of divinely inspired courage abound, as do parables that demonstrate the transformational power of love and the necessity of death (in the sense of freeing oneself from a preoccupation with the demands of the day-to-day world) for rebirth—and transformation—to take place. Reading the spiritual and psychological literature, works such as Wilkie Au's *By Way of the Heart* (1989), Scott Peck's *The Road Less Traveled* (1978), and Thomas Moore's *Care of the Soul* (1992) or the more technical writings of such psychologists and psychiatrists as Carl Jung (1990) and James Masterson (1988), can also help pave the way to the inner journey. It should be noted, however, that reading and thinking alone can effect little beyond intellectual growth.

Time alone for meditation and renewing the connection with the unconscious mind can be very helpful. In this regard, retreat centers can provide a suitable setting and spiritual directors can offer valuable advice and counsel in making the spiritual journey.

Chief executives are increasingly feeling free to discuss their beliefs and feelings about spirituality with their colleagues, and even seeking out the company of other chief executives who are open to this dimension of life. Sharing personal experiences is becoming more common and can help build confidence in spiritual exploration. I can attest to the powerful impact I felt when a highly successful chief executive told me over lunch one day about a dream he had had one night that guided him in making a critical professional move. His openness encouraged me to share an experience that had deeply influenced my own development, but which I would normally have kept to myself.

I also urge chief executives to consider experimenting with psychotherapy as a potentially powerful tool for making the inner journey, for surfacing deep-seated feelings that have blocked self-understanding, and realizing greater creativity as a result. In this regard, I wholeheartedly recommend an elegant, deeply moving little book by Alan Wheelis, *How People Change* (1973), which tells his personal story of one traumatic boyhood summer that impeded his professional and personal development and of the steps he later took to free himself.

In Summary

A nonprofit's chief executive officer is its preeminent change champion, the person who is in the best position to influence and guide change in the organization. This chapter went beyond the traditional views of the chief executive as a leader and top administrator to provide a more comprehensive view of the chief executive as the primary producer of five organizational outcomes that are critical to successful change leadership: unity through vision and mission; a coherent organizational design; stability and security; an innovation-friendly organization; and the empowerment of people. The chapter concluded with a discussion of the three fundamental attributes that enable chief executives to produce these outcomes: the true humility that enables learning from others and inspires confidence and trust; the self-knowledge that leads to realistic understanding of the wider world; and the courage to travel the road of spiritual and psychological growth.

Building Boards That Lead

Coming Attractions

Chapter Four will look at the following subjects:

- Nonprofit boards as a rich resource for their organizations
- The ineffective passive-reactive approach to governance
- The reasons for the prevalence of the passive-reactive approach
- A more effective approach driven by a board's development of its own leadership design
- The elements of board leadership that are critical to its role in leading change: board membership and self-management; the board-chief executive partnership; the board role in planning; and the use of board-staff retreats as a leadership tool

The Board-Chief Executive Partnership

Although the chief executive is the primary change champion in a nonprofit, the board is an indispensable partner in the change process, providing authority, legitimacy, technical advice, and financial support. An aggressive chief executive can achieve some change without board support, but not to any significant degree, and strong board opposition will kill any large change initiative. In light of the stakes involved, one would expect that capitalizing on the board as a resource and maintaining a strong board-chief executive partnership would be a top concern for every nonprofit chief executive and a premier issue in the field of nonprofit management. Yet this has not been the case, and the process of change has had a rockier road to travel as a result.

A Rich Resource

To judge from the lamentations that I hear on my travels, one would think that governing boards of directors or trustees were the invention of a sadistic creator intent on turning chief executives' skies cloudy, their hair grey, and their tenure brutal and brief. I hear again and again such comments as, "They just beat me to death on whether to paint or wallpaper the new conference room but spent all of ten minutes reviewing my $20 million operating budget!" "They're always asking where we're headed, but I can't get a quorum for a half-day Saturday strategy session, no matter how hard I beg." "They seem really interested in telling me how to do my job but don't have a clue what they're supposed to be doing." Overhearing a typical executive gripe session, you might get the picture of a group that at best produces a modest product while doing no real harm and at worst really makes life miserable.

Yet when I consider the people who make up the thousands of nonprofit boards in this country, I have to wonder why, blessed with such a superb key ingredient, the governance recipe so often fails to produce a gourmet's delight. Having worked with thousands of nonprofit board members over the years, I have concluded that they are a rich resource for those nonprofit organizations whose chief executives and management teams are willing and able to capitalize on them. They are often highly motivated to do good and sincerely want to make a difference, consciously using their board service to pay back society for the blessings in their lives. I can count on one hand the board members I've met who have brought any real malevolence to the governance job.

In my experience, board members are usually well educated, intellectually nimble, and capable of giving complex questions the sophisticated attention they deserve. They like to think, and they have typically sharpened their analytical skills over the years in dealing with challenging issues. The average board member is a high achiever who has accumulated impressive knowledge and expertise in the business or volunteer worlds. Board members tend to know a lot about leading and running organizations and about what is going on in the world around them generally.

Many are or have been chief executives, vice presidents, chief financial officers, and senior managers in an amazing array of businesses. They can knowledgeably discuss strategic planning, financial management, marketing, performance management, computer technology, and other complex subjects. They are often successful attorneys, physicians, and other professionals; sometimes they head their own nonprofit organizations. Through service on other boards, many have learned a lot about the process of governing.

Many nonprofit board members are able to write a substantial check to a nonprofit's treasury, but even those without deep pockets often can help put a nonprofit in touch with funding sources. Typical board members have over the years built a network of associations, and these connections can often be put to good use by a nonprofit.

A Largely Unmined Resource

Good intentions, intelligence, knowledge, expertise, leadership skills, money, and connections: there is no question that boards are a rich lode to be mined by savvy chief executives. Yet nonprofit boards are often underexploited as a resource or become dysfunctional governance families, doing more harm than good (Carver, 1990; Eadie, 1994; Herman and Heimovics, 1991; Houle, 1989). The following tale of Kevin James, a new board member, is a fictional account that draws on hundreds of real-life cases to paint a familiar picture of initial high hopes and ultimate disappointment.

> Kevin James was really pleased about the invitation to join the Downtown Development Corporation Board of Directors. He was looking forward to working with the board's planning committee in shaping the Vision 2020 plan that was to be adopted in the next two months. After fifteen years of working his way up the ladder at Mystic Sports Stores, he felt ready to contribute more to the community. A former varsity basketball star for Johnson State, Kevin had started out on the sales floor at Mystic's downtown store, at the time the lowest producer of the chain's four stores, and within a year was leading its dramatic turnaround as Mystic's youngest store manager. A keen mind, a great way with people, and an apparently bottomless reservoir of energy combined with

a passion for sales and marketing fueled Kevin's steady ascent to a well-earned position of vice president of marketing at Mystic, which had expanded to fifteen stores throughout northern Ohio. Kevin knew marketing inside out. He couldn't wait to get started in his new volunteer role, helping to fashion a strategy that would revive the very neighborhood where he had got his start at Mystic fifteen years earlier.

Nine months and three board meetings later, Kevin still felt at sea about his role as a board member. He remained unclear as to exactly what he and his colleagues were expected to achieve for the Development Corporation. The governance job seemed basically to consist of reading thick packets of material that arrived like clockwork one week before each board meeting. The executive committee was apparently where most of the detailed policy work was done, whereas full board meetings consisted largely of a review of informational reports, with occasional action items such as approving consultant contracts.

If the overall experience was less than scintillating, the planning committee's work on Vision 2020 was downright disappointing. It had consisted of one half-day session at which the consultants who had been retained to write the plan reviewed a vision statement for the downtown neighborhood, a set of long-range goals, and five broad action strategies. The consultants' work was solid, as far as Kevin could tell, and there were few questions during the presentation. Some suggestions for improvement came out of the meeting, but it was clear that there was no intention of throwing the thing open to detailed discussion—after all, the corporation had paid handsomely to have top professionals do what they did best. As he left that meeting, Kevin wondered again exactly what he was expected to contribute, beyond being a kind of sounding board. Maybe that was the extent of it; he hoped not.

The Passive-Reactive Approach to Governance

Kevin's experience is par for the course in the field of nonprofit governance. It demonstrates the widely practiced passive-reactive approach. This approach basically puts the board at the apex of the organizational pyramid, receiving and acting on a regular stream of written and oral communication from below, as depicted in Figure 4.1. The term *policy* is commonly used to describe the parameters of appropriate board actions in this approach, and one of the cardinal rules is to keep the board focused on policy concerns and out of the hair of the chief executive and staff, whose mission is to carry out policies—to administer. Thus, the twain are never to meet.

Another phenomenon associated with this governance approach is that the documentation going to the board should basically be finished so that policy decisions are made "rationally and efficiently." Leaving too much latitude for discussion—monkeying around—is a cardinal sin.

The passive-reactive approach remains popular among executives and managers if not board members, and the result is that thousands of boards do not make a strong contribution to organizational directions, priorities, or operations. Board work is often neither fun, challenging, nor a growth experience. Board members all too often wade through masses of paper that is for informational purposes only, and sit through oral presentations without using the information to decide anything important. Being well informed is clearly not the same as being influential (Carver, 1990; Eadie, 1994; Herman and Heimovics, 1991).

When documents arrive already finished at the board, the decisions have, in effect, already been made. So the typical board merely validates and blesses, perhaps making some minor changes.

Figure 4.1. Passive-Reactive Board Governance.

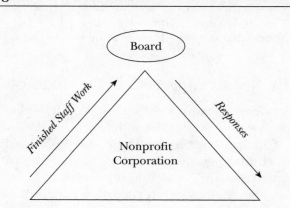

To ask many critical questions about a finished staff document, especially something as important as an annual budget, and much less to challenge it, might impugn the credibility of the chief executive and cause organizational trauma.

The passive-reactive governance approach has caused tremendous frustration among nonprofit board members, and this frustration has frayed many board-chief executive relationships to the extent that chief executive tenure has suffered. But many nonprofit board members have resigned themselves to a passive role, diligently thumbing through finished documents without exerting particular influence. Consequently, many pay the closest attention to, and appear to exert the greatest influence on, relatively minor details, because such fiddling can do no harm and it feels better than doing nothing at all. So, in lieu of a serious role in setting strategic directions, a nonprofit board might look at the travel line item in the proposed budget, asking if four staff people really have to attend the conference in Phoenix, or if a few dollars could be saved by sending only two. Policy making might take the form of reviewing the new personnel procedures manual and dealing with such earth-shaking questions as the sick pay accrual procedure and vacation carryover from one fiscal year to another.

In the passive-reactive approach, the nonprofit board committee structure frequently reflects what I call the tip-of-the-administrative-iceberg principle. This practice ensures low governance productivity by keeping the board's sights on administrative details. For example, finance and personnel committees ensure board members' involvement in the tip of what are basically administrative functions, relegating them to setting administrative policy. Deeper involvement would not be allowed because it would constitute meddling in administrative matters. Yet, such a structure actually invites meddling!

Another example of the tip-of-the-iceberg practice is committees that focus on particular program operations, such as the downtown development or world trade committees of a chamber of commerce board (Beals and Eadie, 1994). Once again, little in-depth board involvement is possible without bumping up against administrative prerogatives. After all, it is *our*—the staff's—job to run programs, so if *you* dig too deeply you are doing our job.

Why the Passive-Reactive Approach?

Why did such an unproductive, frustrating approach ever become so widespread in the first place? One foundation stone of the passive-reactive approach is the adversarial tradition of American government. Legislative bodies (the forbears of today's nonprofit boards), whether city councils or state and federal legislative bodies, are basically guided by a checks and balances philosophy that has legislators watching the administrative critters to make sure they do what they promise and in the process do not steal the store. This basically adversarial approach appears to have greatly influenced the development of nonprofit boards, and it certainly militates against creative board-executive collaboration. Of course, every board has a valid watchdog role, making sure that the organization is carrying out its mission effectively and efficiently. There is a serious problem only when this becomes the board's *predominant* role, at the expense of more serious participation in setting organizational direction.

Because of the adversarial tradition, on the administrative side nonprofit managers aspiring to be chief executives have been taught that their preeminent role is to keep their boards under control, vigilantly protecting staff from board incursions into administrative and program operations. In addition to this inherently negative role, managers have learned that, as staff, they are not responsible for, nor should they even get involved in, developing their board's leadership. Board is board, staff is staff; their paths should never cross except under very controlled situations.

In addition, the traditional view is that boards are essentially policy-setting bodies and that there is a clear boundary between policy setting and administration. This view too has helped perpetuate the passive-reactive board leadership approach. In fact, policies in the popular mind are essentially rules that set boundaries and limits on organizational behavior. Most rules relate to administrative matters: the work week is 37.5 hours, tuition for 1997 will be $185 per credit hour, employees must be evaluated annually as the basis for salary determinations, and so on. The most effective way to get the rules enacted is to have the staff draft documents for the boards to review and adopt. This static view, which downplays the board's involvement in the creative process, has also impeded the development of a fuller board leadership role that would capitalize on it as a rich resource.

Carver (1990) has taken a more sophisticated approach to policy, proposing that boards focus on ends-related policies while leaving means-related (administrative) policies to the chief executive. But as Herman and Heimovics (1991) point out (and as I have found in my own experience), "The problems, opportunities, and changing conditions that any nonprofit organization faces do not come labeled as 'major policy' or 'administrative means.' Not only must a board and an executive sort out what are their major policies and ends, they must also be prepared to adjust them as conditions change. The rapidity and ambiguity of change make simple policy-administration and ends-means standards impossible to consistently implement" (p. 44).

Those familiar with the literature of nonprofit management know that until relatively recently, board leadership was not the subject of serious research. While Carver (1990), Eadie (1994), Herman and Heimovics (1991), Houle (1989), and the National Center for Nonprofit Boards have advanced the field considerably over the past decade, this work is just beginning to have widespread impact. A great number of unfortunate little golden rules still influence behavior; for example, "Small boards are always better" and "Boards should always receive finished staff work."

Why Keep a Bad Thing Going?

If the passive-reactive model cannot involve nonprofit boards creatively in producing important results or provide board members with a satisfying experience, why has it managed to endure for so long? Well, for one thing, expectations have always been pretty low, so despite growing frustration among nonprofit board members, many envision no other role for themselves. Rule making and acting as watchdog have been around for a long time, and while they may not be exciting activities, they are familiar and concrete—compared, say, with updating a nonprofit's vision.

The power of the vested interests of long-tenured board members should also not be discounted. They often have stuck around for years, slowly learning the ropes and becoming effective at rule making and acting as watchdogs. They are good at their role on the board, and it provides substantial ego fulfillment. They will not lightly tolerate changing the traditional rules of the governance game if they perceive their status is threatened. Furthermore, the few new board members trickling in are unlikely to challenge the entrenched practices of their elders, in keeping with the widespread belief that newcomers should keep quiet until they have learned the ropes.

The frequent practice of appointing as members people who have earned the award of board membership through their program volunteering can also hinder board development because it helps perpetuate the narrow governance perspective. As a matter of fact, volunteering in program operations has nothing in common with governance; expertise and dedication in one area does not qualify a person for the other.

Is There More to Life on a Board?

Nonprofit board members are not condemned to a purgatory of low expectations, unimportant and unsatisfying work, and constant frustration. An alternative to the traditional passive-reactive model is for the board and the chief executive officer to work closely together in fashioning their own *board leadership design*. In designing their own governance method, boards and chief executives can draw on principles that are aimed at empowering the board and form a more contemporary board leadership model:

- Rather than being merely the apex of the organizational pyramid that reacts to a flow of paper, the nonprofit board should be seen as a business within the wider organization, explicitly accountable for producing its own bottom line, for adding value.
- The board should be held accountable for its own governance performance. Therefore, it should set clear performance standards for itself and monitor and enforce them.
- The board should ensure in its governance design that the experience, skills, connections, and other resources that its members bring are fully utilized.

- The board and chief executive officer should function as a partnership, with the chief executive assisting the board in developing its leadership capability.

The Design Process

Briefly, designing a board leadership role involves matching desired impacts and outcomes for the board with the structure, process, and resources required to produce them, as illustrated in Figure 4.2. The design is best created during a retreat, when there is enough time to put the major pieces in place. Furthermore, the design process must involve the board intensively if true understanding and commitment are expected to develop. Merely presenting a board with a leadership design that was produced by the staff or consultants will virtually guarantee that it ends up on the proverbial shelf.

A good place to start the design is by identifying the major areas within which a board produces outcomes. In my experience these are the board's operations, planning, organizational performance, external relations, and financial resource development. Second, the most important outcomes desired within each of the areas should be identified. For example, in the area of board operations, impacts might include a board that stays focused on

Figure 4.2. Board Leadership Design.

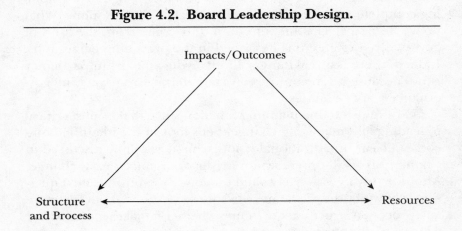

Impacts/Outcomes

Structure
and Process

Resources

strategic and high-level policy matters, a board whose members are well oriented on their governance role, and a board with a diverse membership. In the area of planning, a board's impacts might include: a clear organizational vision and mission, long-term direction, growth targets, measurable annual operational objectives, and a balanced budget. In the area of external relations, impacts might include: positive working partnerships with key stakeholders, greater public knowledge and understanding of the nonprofit's vision and mission, stronger public support for the nonprofit's mission, and a more diverse revenue base.

Every board is not so unique that its design process will uncover dramatically different outcomes of board leadership. Most are likely to find their way to vision and mission as truly high-level outcomes of a board's participation in the planning function. But by going through the outcomes identification process, a board can approach the design of its own governance structure and methods from a base of better understanding of the nature of the ongoing governance process.

Let's think about how this contrasts with a board that focuses on a particular high-level issue. I recently worked with a nonprofit nursing home that, against the odds, managed to build a beautiful new state-of-the-art facility to replace a dreary old building. The details of fund raising, design, and construction consumed a tremendous amount of board and staff time; in fact, it was all-consuming. At the end of the process, with their magnificent building completed, the board sat back and asked the question, "What do we do now?" The answer could only come from the kind of governance design effort described in the preceding paragraphs. Indeed, there is a real danger in involving a board in particular issues because it can confuse roles and detract from ongoing governance responsibilities.

Let's return to the planning function since that is most critical to leading and managing change. Let's look at the identified outcome, a clear organizational vision, which, as will be discussed in Chapter Six, is the preeminent driver of organizational change. After identifying vision as a valid outcome, the obvious next question is how to produce it, and this raises questions about structure and process. A structural question is whether it makes sense to have a board planning committee take responsibility for its role in producing such planning outcomes as vision. On the process side, what steps need to be taken, by whom and when, to produce a vision statement? Many nonprofit boards with which I have worked have chosen to fashion an updated organizational vision statement at an annual two-day strategic planning retreat involving both the board and management team members. That unvarnished statement then might be refined by the planning committee for ultimate adoption by the full board.

A word about staff involvement is in order here. Whenever a board undertakes a governance design effort, it should be in partnership with staff, not only because they have useful knowledge and experience to offer but also because they must be accountable for carrying out and supporting any design process. For example, deciding that a retreat is the best way to involve the board in fashioning an organizational vision does not, in and of itself, produce a retreat. Myriad details have to be taken care of before such a complex event as a board-staff retreat can take place, and most of this preparatory work is a staff responsibility.

Getting the Design Done

Getting a nonprofit board to participate in setting its own governance course through a systematic design effort is primarily the responsibility of the chief executive officer, who is the one person most likely to see the need for it and to be able to push the process along. The first steps for the chief executive are to get the board chair committed to the design process and then recruit a small group of board members who are willing to serve as the design champions. In this capacity, they take responsibility for convincing their peers to participate. The executive can then circulate monographs and articles on governance to whet appetites; two good sources are the National Center for Nonprofit Boards and the Society for Nonprofit Organizations, which publishes *Nonprofit World*. Selected board members might also participate in governance workshops—at the annual national conference in the nonprofit's field, for example.

Of course, resistance is natural. It should be expected. Most people have grown accustomed to inheriting past practices and do not question them, much less wish to get involved in designing something new. Again, many board members—through longevity and hard work, combined with a high frustration threshold—have over the years found a comfortable niche on the board that they will not lightly jeopardize for something unknown. Furthermore, the word *design* has a cold, unfamiliar ring about it and many find it abstract and intimidating. Many board members will automatically ask, "Have I bitten off more than I can chew? Do I have the time and energy to become more heavily involved than I already am?"

Two years ago, I witnessed firsthand the power of resistance when a poorly prepared design process collapsed. A relatively new community development corporation whose basic mission was to organize and support neighborhood planning councils decided to hold a board-staff retreat for the twin purposes of setting long-term directions and developing the board's leadership capability. One of the more influential board members, the chief executive of a highly successful national development firm, had been unable to attend any of the meetings at which the retreat was planned. Still, the retreat was held. At the end of a productive and enjoyable morning of brainstorming at the retreat, the facilitator asked the group to begin to consider the role of the board in governing the new nonprofit. But before anyone had a chance to respond, this board member stood up to announce that there was nothing to discuss.

"It's simple," he said. "Board members should spend lots of time in the neighborhoods so they get to understand what it's really like out there. Then, when neighborhood councils come up with ideas for projects, we, as the board, help as much as we can to get them funded and carried out. That's the whole story. I don't intend to get caught up in a lot of fancy bureaucratic stuff, and that's that!"

Because no one in the group thought that board leadership was an important enough issue to take on such a powerful person in public, the effort to tackle governance design ground to a halt. In subsequent discussions, it became clear that this well-intentioned board member was motivated by a simple mission: to assist neighborhoods and to make sure no "poverty bureaucrats" slowed things down. This was a personal mission that had virtually nothing to do with governance, which was a concept that he did not understand.

And because he had not been involved in preparing for the governance design session, he had no background on which to draw. As a result, the sorely needed board development at a very important nonprofit organization was, at least for the time being, derailed.

The People on the Board

Like all organizations, boards are essentially people. While a well-designed structure and a fine-tuned process are important to governing, the people themselves determine the quality of a nonprofit's governance. The people serving on a board bring experiences, talents, skills, connections, and pocketbooks to the table. They also bring reputations that can polish the image of a nonprofit, serve as a magnet to attract other strong leaders to the board, and make it easier to implement change.

Thus, the quality of a board's participation in leading and managing change is obviously directly related to the people on it: how carefully they are selected, how methodically they are oriented and trained in playing the governance role, and how well planned their involvement in leading change is. Getting the right people is obviously the first and most important step.

Many nonprofit boards have found that it makes sense to have the executive committee, or sometimes the nominating committee, take responsibility for systematic membership renewal that starts with a detailed profile of the kind of members desired for the board. The profile might include somewhat generic characteristics, such as commitment to the mission of the organization, prior experience on other nonprofit boards, and willingness to commit the time required. More specific characteristics that relate closely to a nonprofit's current and anticipated situation might also be developed in recruiting and screening new board members. For example, one nonprofit nursing home board that was dealing with a rapidly changing health care environment that places a premium on partnerships and alliances wisely chose to increase the number of board members who represented other health care providers—such as hospital chief executives—and of persons who were knowledgeable about acquisitions and mergers.

However, viewing the board as a collection of experts can erode its overall governance mission. In *Boards That Work* (Eadie, 1994),

I discuss what I call the expertise trap: "To the extent that board members are encouraged to play the role of resident experts, the primary governance mission of a board will suffer. Additionally, resident experts on boards may diminish the sense of collective accountability of the board in key areas. The board as a whole should be accountable for, and knowledgeable about, the financial status of the association, whether or not a standing committee is employed to enhance the board's involvement in finance. Such accountability should never be informally handed to a corporate chief executive officer who happens to serve on the board" (p. 54).

Another danger of a board of experts is that they may have more interest in their field of expertise than in the welfare of the organization. I encountered this phenomenon a couple of years ago when I was working with the board of a national mental health association whose mission was to promote more effective treatment and ultimately reduce the incidence of a group of related mental disorders. In the early days, this group of disorders was not universally recognized in the mental health field, so the original board largely consisted of mental health professionals—psychiatrists and psychologists for the most part—and former sufferers of the disorders. It focused almost all of its energy on defining the new field and achieving recognition and legitimacy in the wider mental health profession. But as the association grew and began to grapple with broader corporate issues, such as membership recruitment and retention, diversification of products and services, and revenue growth, the narrow professional perspective of the board became a hindrance. Indeed, several board members had no real interest in growing the association; their allegiance was to the mental health profession, not to the health and growth of the nonprofit corporation itself.

I do not recommend that as a general rule nonprofits divert lots of time and energy to finding superstar board members, and certainly not if they are to serve on the masthead by name only. But there are times when finding just the right person for the board can make very good sense. Such plums are notoriously tough to pick; they are always busy and they are always desired by many other nonprofits, so a special recruitment strategy is frequently a prerequisite for a successful hunt. Many years ago, I observed a nonprofit social service agency that was successful in finding that kind of special person for its board.

This agency was just starting to recuperate from a period during which its very existence had been threatened. A management study had identified the need to establish a board management committee to oversee a major overhaul of the financial and personnel management systems and to upgrade staff. Some old-timers were sure to lose jobs and outsiders to arrive on the scene; paranoia could be smelled in the air. The young executive director and new chief operating officer knew that the management committee would lead the charge into the future, and so they needed a person so capable, so strong, and so respected that he or she would be above the fray and impervious to the inevitable political machinations as the old guard fought for the agency of the past. They found that person in the chief executive of one of the community's most successful firms, a real estate developer known for his commitment to community welfare, his no-nonsense approach to management, and his rigorous, plainspoken honesty.

The executive director and his chief operating officer put together a recruitment package that articulated the new vision, summarized the consultant's report that the management committee would take the lead in implementing, reviewed the committee's charge and the role of the chair, and explicitly pledged their support to make the committee work. It took three long meetings in the man's office, but he finally agreed to take the role. He was a superb leader as the recommended administrative reforms were successfully implemented. Ultimately he served for a critical decade and saw the agency quadruple its programs and revenues. This man was truly the one right person for the job, and the agency was justified in going after him.

However, talented, experienced, and dedicated people, even when supported by a strong process, do not automatically appear or grow on the job, and so another very important task of the executive committee is to fashion and implement a strategy for continuous board member capability building. I have worked with many boards that put new members through a detailed orientation process that not only introduces them to a nonprofit's mission, programs, and funding situation but also clearly outlines the board's role, structure, and processes. An executive committee might also keep track of opportunities for governance education, such as the circulation of articles and monographs and attendance at workshops. One of the most productive approaches I have seen is a formal mentoring program that assigns every new member to a mentor who is responsible for helping the new member learn the ropes during the first year.

Self-Management

Just getting the right people to serve on a nonprofit board does not ensure their success in the governance business. Clearly defined roles and responsibilities, detailed performance expectations, thorough orientation, and regular self-monitoring are essential to ensure members' effectiveness. Major board roles and responsibilities should be a product of the governance design process, but more detailed performance expectations and indicators are essential for effective self-management. Such indicators, which are often developed by a board's executive committee, can relate both to required activities and to limitations on behavior.

For example, many boards have required their members to participate actively in the committee structure, not to exceed a certain number of unexcused absences, to come to board meetings well prepared, not to interact with staff members without the knowledge of the chief executives, and regularly to attend fundraisers and other special events. Board members have also been required to speak regularly on behalf of their nonprofits in appropriate forums, including testimony before congressional committees, to assist in raising money, and to contribute financially.

No chief executive with a well-honed survival instinct would attempt to become involved in monitoring board performance. So if specific performance requirements are to have teeth, the board itself must be accountable for managing its performance. The willingness to take action in the case of poor performance is necessary for the process to have any credibility, even if that action is merely a formal warning or an offer of assistance. Otherwise, the message being sent loudly and clearly is that underperforming board members are just as acceptable as their more industrious counterparts. Thus, it is a mistake to have board members whose names add luster to the roster but whose faces are never seen in the board room, demonstrating by their absence a two-caste system—board members who must work to keep their positions and board members who are too important to work.

I have worked with several boards over the past several years that have reinvented their executive committees to play a much more positive role than the traditional one as elite, petite boards making decisions between full board meetings. This new role essentially uses an executive committee as the standing committee on board operations. In this capacity, the executive committee is responsible for regularly renewing board membership, which includes: developing a profile of qualifications and attributes and recruiting new members, developing board performance indicators and monitoring board performance, and coordinating the work of the board's standing committees. This practice has proved to be a powerful tool for upgrading board performance that, in the process, helps the chief executive resist foolish excursions into dangerous territory.

Boards and Their Chief Executives

Early in my career in management, I absorbed the conventional wisdom about the board-chief executive partnership. It goes something like this: The board is essentially responsible for setting strategic directions and establishing policies. The chief executive is the top staff person, the only one reporting directly to the board, and he or she is responsible for administering the organization in accordance with the board's long-range directions and established policies. The board's business is the board's business; the staff's business is the staff's business. Neither partner, if truly committed to the health of the organization, meddles in the affairs of the other.

It did not take me long out in the real world to recognize that in well-managed organizations, the board and chief executive work closely together in shaping directions and policies and the content of plans is enhanced by close collaboration. No board alone could set sensible directions. So the basic point of the old-time leadership model seemed to be one of formal authority: no matter how a policy is made, only the board can enact it. True, one is tempted to say, but so what? A far more dynamic partnership is required for successful change leadership today. At its heart is the assumption that a complex, rapidly changing environment demands flexibility in the definition of the board and chief executive roles and responsibilities and in the division of labor (Eadie, 1994; Herman and Heimovics, 1991). Another key assumption is that the primary responsibility for making this close-knit, dynamic partnership work is the chief executive's. Of the two partners, only the chief executive can find the time to devote to building and nurturing the partnership. As Herman and Heimovics note, "We believe that the most effective chief executives engage their boards in special ways to see that they are ready and able to deal effectively with externally induced challenges" (p. 90).

Regarding division of labor, I can think of hundreds of examples of nonprofit boards that have become involved in operations with the blessing and active support of their chief executives where it has done no damage to the organization nor caused any confusion about the basic board-staff division of labor. Every instance involved a clearheaded decision to violate the conventional wisdom in order to get an important goal accomplished in the absence of enough staff time or expertise to do the job. For example, the state-of-the-art nursing home discussed earlier would never have been built if board members had not become actively engaged in the myriad details of building design and contracting. Similarly, committee members of a community development corporation with which I worked rolled up their sleeves and went through detailed loan applications in the absence of staff expertise, keeping a very important program moving in a community that badly needed rehabilitation money.

In my experience, those chief executives who think of themselves as peers of the board tend to do a better job of building and sustaining the board-staff partnership than those holding the more traditional view of the chief executive as merely the chief staff person. Chief executives with the more contemporary view tend to spend more time thinking about and planning for the partnership and to be less defensive and more creative in their thinking about roles and responsibilities. The chief executives I have worked with who saw themselves primarily as top staff tended to fall captive to the we-they adversarial mentality far more often than those with a view of the position as a kind of hybrid, neither completely staff nor board.

Does this mean that chief executives should actually fill a seat on the board, making themselves formal peers? I do not have the information on which to base a definititive answer to that question. I do know that the creative chief executives I have worked with who were committed to a strong board-staff partnership did not need to be board members in order to think and act as their peers. The ability seems to have more to do with psychological orientation than formal organizational structure.

It is commonly argued that a chief executive should never sit on a board because doing so would conflict with the board's responsibility to provide direction to and to evaluate the performance of the chief executive. This viewpoint makes sense in theory, but I am not aware of strong evidence either way. It sounds suspiciously like a variation on the old-time "watch the critters" approach to board leadership. I have worked with several chief executives over the years with seats on their boards whose boards who had no apparent problem giving them direction or evaluating their performance. The fact is, when the board retains authority to hire and fire the chief executive, his or her membership on the board can probably do little harm—it might even strengthen board-chief executive teamwork.

In terms of the board's responsibility for leading change in partnership with the chief executive, two of the most important contributions the board can make are choosing the right chief executive and regularly evaluating his or her performance. I want to comment on each of these responsibilities briefly since I have so often seen them poorly done, and in the case of evaluation, not done at all.

First, I believe that selecting the right chief executive has more to do with systematically thinking through current and anticipated organizational circumstances and needs than with any other factor. In addition to the obvious generic chief executive qualifications that would appear on any job description—education and training, written and oral communication skills, experience in financial management, and so on—a board search committee will want to identify special requirements. For example, a local nonprofit hospital in a market experiencing rapid consolidation might want to find a person with extensive merger experience and demonstrated diplomatic skills. A national association with a serious image problem that is hindering membership growth may need a new chief executive with a strong public relations background. Similarly, a board interested in having a chief executive with strong change leadership skills might request evidence of such skills in the form of specific change targets that have been accomplished.

Second, regular, in-depth board evaluation of the chief executive is a rarity in my experience. Frequently, it is done informally, if at all, and when it is done, evaluation lite seems to be the rule. In other words, boards rely on a generic checklist of functions that are relatively open ended, such as "represents the organization well externally," "provides capable supervision to staff," "manages the financial resources well," and the like. A far more substantive and useful evaluation is based on bottom-line performance promises that are explicitly negotiated at the beginning of every fiscal year. Every chief executive will obviously be judged on planned organizational performance as set forth in the annual operating plan, but above-the-line promises unique to the chief executive should also be made and measured. These performance promises will relate to the chief executive's direct use of his or her own time.

A bottom-line promise, for example, might be "To diversify revenues by obtaining at least two grants from nongovernmental sources amounting to at least $500,000," or "To have a new strategic planning process fully operational by July 1," or "To increase membership by 15 percent." In negotiating the bottom-line targets, the board might also set some parameters, such as to maintain internal peace when implementing a new system or not to spend more than a certain amount in a membership campaign. The board's contribution to achievement of the goals should also be spelled out when its contribution is critical—for example, its willingness to commit the time and money for a retreat that will kick off the new strategic planning process.

The benefits of regular board evaluation of a chief executive's performance against bottom-line expectations are so obvious that one may well wonder why such evaluation is not more common. There are two important barriers. One is the natural reluctance of peers to evaluate one another. For example, I was once approached by the chief executive officer of a large foundation, who asked me for advice on evaluation. He knew that it was important, but he was having a hard time getting his board to agree to judge his performance. They were worried about offending him. A second barrier is reluctance to commit the time to do a really substantive evaluation. A functional checklist is appealing because it takes little thought, effort, or time. However, in the interests of both the chief executive and the organization, a savvy chief executive will find a way to convince the board to carry out its evaluation responsibility fully.

The Board Chair and the Chief Executive

I have observed close, positive board chair and chief executive partnerships characterized by a clear division of labor and substantial mutual respect that have facilitated large-scale organizational change. I have also seen dysfunctional relationships that impeded or even derailed change. The board chair-chief executive partnerships that work best, in my experience, are grounded in a fundamental division of labor: the board chair is the chief executive of the board itself, not of the whole organization; the chief executive is accountable for the whole organization. The board chair directs the board's operations and is responsible for the board as an effective governance body; the chief executive makes sure that the whole organization works well.

This division of labor is clearly different from the conventional views of the board chair as a kind of head of state and the chief executive as prime minister. Unfortunately, the conventional view has caused much damage in the past, as the two parties have tussled for the overall organizational leadership role, at one pole, or at the other, the chief executive has all of the fun while the board chair is a figurehead with nothing important to do. Employing the board chair in a clear role as head of the nonprofit's most important organizational unit, its governing board, is a far better arrangement.

This does not mean that the two partners do not have to work out their roles and responsibilities on an ongoing basis. Both, for example, will be seen in the wider world as spokespeople for the nonprofit, so they need to decide who will perform which public duties, such as testifying before a congressional committee or addressing the United Way allocations committee. These ad hoc divisions of labor can be smoothly accomplished if the basic division is firmly established.

By the way, when a board chair is the elected president of a membership association, the situation can be confusing because the board chair will look suspiciously like a chief executive. Indeed, I am aware of at least one case, a women's club, where the elected president, a full-time practicing attorney, publicly declared herself the chief executive and the club's executive director its chief administrative officer. This caused real confusion, in both the club and the wider community, and impeded development of a full-fledged chief executive function. In membership organizations, the ceremonial role of the board president is likely to be more substantial, including chairing the annual conference, for example, but there is still no reason why a basic role distinction cannot be maintained.

It should be remembered that, no matter how close the relationship between board chair and chief executive, no board chair should ever give direction to the chief executive on behalf of the board or evaluate his or her performance on behalf of the board. That the chief executive report to the board as a whole is essential for both progress and internal peace. I have seen real problems develop in national associations when board chairs with one-year terms tug and pull on the chief executive to go in one direction or another, while the board sits in the corner confused and frustrated. In this situation, the chief executive has no choice but to refuse to be pushed and to insist on accountability to the board as a whole; the only alternative is to look scatterbrained and unresponsive.

The Board's Role in Planning

A board that passively receives a finished strategic plan for review and approval is not likely to feel any ownership of the content or to be inclined to support its implementation. But ownership question aside, change initiatives and plans produced without intensive board involvement cannot take full advantage of the experience, expertise, knowledge, and perspectives of the board members. Opportunities will be missed. Innovative implementation strategies will not be explored. Icebergs that might sink the change ship will not be spotted. A critical funding source will be overlooked.

The nonprofit chief executive is the guarantor of productive board involvement in planning for change. In this capacity, he or she needs to design a planning process that will engage the board fully, capitalizing on the board as a rich resource, help the board understand the process, secure its commitment to participate, and facilitate such participation. These are likely to be challenging tasks for several reasons.

The field of strategic planning is going through a radical rethinking (see Chapter Six for more on this). The term *strategic plan* today may conjure up a picture of an ineffective, bloated Soviet five-year agricultural plan, a bureaucratic production incapable of feeding anyone, or of a more svelte innovation-focused document aimed at producing action now. In either case, although reviewing finished planning documents may not be exciting, it requires less thought and time than actually helping to produce the plans, so many board members are reluctant to become involved in a more substantive and demanding role. But the chief executive cannot afford to let them off the hook, in the interest not only of better planning but also of ultimate plan implementation. Furthermore, the chief cannot just ask simplemindedly, "Do you want to play a larger role in planning?" since the likely answer will be, "No thanks, we're really pleased with the way things are going and don't want to get in your way." A more sophisticated strategy is to collaborate with the board's planning committee in coming up with a design that allows for fuller board participation without requiring a mind-boggling time commitment. One proven way is to involve the board in front-end brainstorming on high-level questions, such as values, vision, mission, and strategic issues, but not in the more arduous task of fashioning the action plans. Since a retreat is an efficient way to accomplish intensive board involvement, I will now talk about designing effective retreats.

The Retreat as Vehicle for Board Involvement

There is probably no better way to involve a board substantively early in the planning process than to stage a well-designed, carefully facilitated retreat, preferably at least a day long and away from the press of day-to-day affairs. But I could fill the second half of this book with nothing but the horror stories about the "retreats from hell" that hundreds of board members have recounted over the years. I doubt there is a board member living who has not had at least one terrible retreat experience that left a sour taste and made him or her forever leery of going away for a day again. Life is just too short to repeat such an experience, so retreats are really a tough sell.

Shuddering at the memory, they tell about a whole morning devoted to discussing in excruciating detail every last word in a one-paragraph mission statement that, so far as anyone can tell, inspired no one to do anything really new. Or they tell about the long lists of tantalizing possibilities filling a hundred worksheets and the green, yellow, red, and blue sticky dots used to "vote" on their relative importance—all then forgotten, having made no discernable difference in their organization's affairs. I hear about the elaborate team-building exercises that for a brief shining moment opened people up to each other, revealing minds and souls never before seen so honestly, and leaving tremendous disillusionment in its wake when Monday morning brought back business as usual with a vengeance.

I believe the horror stories; after all, I have endured retreats myself that have been exercises in futility. Failure appears to be the result of three key flaws: there is no clear idea of what is to be accomplished or how; there is inadequate board leadership and ownership; and there is an absence of follow-through. But experience has taught that there are also practical ways to ensure that retreats are highly productive tools for planning change, as well as enjoyable experiences. Among the most important, board members should be involved in fashioning a detailed retreat design and should be put in strong leadership roles in the retreat. Premature decision making during the retreat should be avoided, and staff and key stakeholders should be invited. Finally, a comfortable location off-site should be chosen for the retreat, adequate time allocated, and a professional facilitator employed.

A common practice is to use an ad hoc retreat design committee involving the board chair, chief executive, and three to five board members to design the retreat. Often led through the design process by the professional facilitator who will ultimately facilitate the retreat itself, the committee creates a comprehensive design for the retreat, specifying the objectives to be achieved, the structure, the participants, the agenda, and such details as timing and location.

The retreat objectives should be specific and outcomes-oriented. For example, a nonprofit nursing home I worked with recently identified five desired outcomes for a one-and-a-half-day retreat: to update values, vision, and strategic directions; to understand the implications of conditions and trends in the health care field generally and in the immediate market area; to identify critical issues facing the organization; to identify targets of opportunity to be acted on in the coming year; and to identify practical ways to clarify and strengthen board leadership.

The key structural questions are how the outcomes will be produced, who will participate in producing them, and how the meeting will be led. A popular and productive approach is to break into groups to focus on specific outcomes. For example, a women's civic association used nine different groups in three different rounds, in each of which three groups met concurrently: values, vision, and mission in the first round; conditions and trends, internal resource assessment, and performance assessment in the second round; and program and revenue diversification and growth targets, image and stakeholder relations targets, and capability-building targets in round three. These "break-out" groups are a powerful retreat tool because they produce substantial content in a short time, are highly participatory—hence making the retreat more interesting—and provide board members with a significant leadership opportunity.

A well-planned retreat can be fun. I recall many instances when break-out groups have, through their creative reporting in plenary session, added pizzazz to retreats. For example, one group, during a retreat of a children's services agency, used group members as sandwich boards, taping the flip-chart sheets on the front and back of each member. Another presented their report in the style of TV's "McLaughlin Group." And one group, concluding that a tremendous barrier to the agency's success was its outmoded policy, marched into the plenary session humming Chopin's Funeral March and carrying a makeshift coffin with the name of the policy printed on the side.

By involving board members in the design of the retreat and using them as the leaders of break-out groups, board ownership of the retreat is created, thereby increasing the odds of having a productive retreat and successful implementation of follow-up activities. Because board members are typically high achievers who dislike the idea of public failure, their involvement as retreat leaders virtually guarantees that break-out groups will work well. In many years of retreat facilitation I have never seen an exception to this rule, provided that the board members who are leading groups were prepared to do so. This may mean an orientation session focusing on guidelines for facilitating groups and on the specific content that each group is intended to produce. It is not uncommon to find a person sitting in the chief executive's seat who has never facilitated a retreat group, so some orientation and training are almost always a sensible course.

The use of break-out groups can produce an amazing amount of information, especially if the groups employee a free-flowing, brainstorming approach without right or wrong answers. Faced with the prospect of generating, say, a hundred flip-chart sheets over the course of a day or two, the board and chief executive may be tempted to use some kind of formal decision-making process for voting or at least rank-ordering ideas. The thought of leaving loose ends dangling can seem a violation of the puritan ethic, but in fact premature consensus can limit creativity, actually do damage to strategy, and kill a retreat's credibility.

My work in innovation and strategy formulation has taught me that a problem early on in the innovation process is more likely to be too much rather than too little discipline. Instead, it is necessary to generate as much good thinking about complex matters as possible in a short time and to leave time after the retreat for second, third, and fourth thoughts. (Chapter Eight offers a detailed discussion of this phenomenon.) A sensible objective for a retreat is to surface possibilities and to raise questions, not in such a short time to provide answers. Time and again I have heard nonprofit board members complain that the list of possible growth targets that was winnowed down from twenty-three to nine last Saturday looked much less impressive the following week. In fact, on reflection, three or four items that were eliminated in the rushed voting process that day now look like they should have made the list.

There are simple ways to avoid mechanistic consensus tools and the illusion of precision they produce while also eventually getting the loose ends tied up. One is to have the facilitator of the retreat prepare a detailed report that analyzes the information produced and recommends action and present that report in a follow-up session with the retreat participants. Another is to have the retreat break-out groups meet two to three times after the retreat to refine their work down to the highest priority items that they are willing to recommend to the assembled retreat participants. A board committee might take the work of a retreat break-out group and do the winnowing job. Of course, combinations of these approaches might work well, too. For example, a national association had the retreat facilitator present his report and followed that by establishing task forces to analyze the report recommendations under the overall direction of the board's planning committee, which ultimately recommended action to the full board. This approach produced values, vision, and mission statements that were adopted by the full board several months after their original versions had been developed in brainstorming sessions at the retreat.

It makes sense to invite as many staff members to the retreat as can be included without making the board feel overwhelmed. Staff not only bring important information; they are the ones who will follow through on what is produced during the implementation process. Furthermore, the bonding that can occur in a well-designed and facilitated retreat can strengthen the board-staff partnership, especially important during times of rapid change and stress. Stakeholder organizations—the outsiders with which the organization has an important relationship—can also be valuable participants. They bring information from the outside world while they learn more about the organization, and their knowledge can make building partnerships in the future much easier.

As already noted, at least a full day is required for a serious retreat; many organizations devote one and a half to two days. A shorter period is likely to cause more harm than good, generating half-baked ideas that leave everyone with a feeling that they have enjoyed some delicious appetizers but no main course. Meeting in a comfortable, off-site location is a good way to "suspend the rules," stimulating new thinking free of the business-as-usual feel of headquarters. Also, using a third-party professional facilitator skilled in group process normally makes it easier to generate considerable content without becoming bogged down in repetitious discussion or drawn off track by emotional debate.

In Summary

This chapter opened with a discussion of the passive-reactive governance approach that has resulted in the underutilization of nonprofit boards as a rich resource to their organizations, while also causing disappointment, frustration, and even anger among board members. A more contemporary model that can be employed in developing a nonprofit board's leadership design was described in terms of four key principles: the board as a business within a wider business with its own bottom line; board accountability for its own performance; full utilization of board members' capabilities; and a cohesive board-chief executive partnership.

The governance design process matches desired outcomes and impacts of the board with the structure, process, and resources required to produce them. Key outcomes for boards are found in the areas of board operations, planning, operational oversight, external relations, and financial resource development. The chief executive officer is primarily responsible for ensuring that a board actively participates in designing its own structure and process, and a certain amount of resistance to doing so should be expected.

This chapter also discussed how a board can develop its membership, manage its performance, and build an effective board-chief executive partnership that necessarily changes over time as organizational needs and circumstances evolve. The chapter closed with tips on how to use board-staff retreats as a powerful vehicle for the board's involvement in change leadership.

Nurturing Creative Capacity in Nonprofits

Coming Attractions

Chapter Five will examine the following issues:

- The link between creativity and innovation
- The dimensions of creativity
- The ways in which a nonprofit's chief executive, serving as its chief creativity officer, can foster and promote creative capacity

Creativity's Contribution to Innovation

Although the terms *innovation* and *creativity* are often used interchangeably, I find it useful to distinguish between the two. Innovation is basically the process of bringing something new into being—a product, service, program, or management system, for example. Innovation involves the exercise of three key capacities: creativity, planning, and implementation. The essential role of creativity in the innovation process is to supply the possibilities—ideas for new programs, services, customers, clients, systems, revenues—beyond what a nonprofit organization is already doing. In other words, creativity supplies the newness in the innovation process. The greater the creativity involved in innovation, the greater the departure from current practice is likely to be. The essential job of planning is to translate creative possibilities into strategies (action plans) that must then be implemented if change is to amount to more than rhetoric.

The creative process obviously does not have to be linked to formal planning to produce important results. For example, creativity can help solve day-to-day operational problems, improve service delivery and refine products, and strengthen working relationships. But the explicit linkage of creative capacity with planning, and specifically with the strategic management process, is the surest way to produce large-scale organizational innovation.

An organization's creative capacity enriches the content of action strategies, serving as the "fuel" that makes planning a more powerful innovation engine, since it expands the opportunities for innovation that can be considered in fashioning change initiatives during the planning process. Without the expansive power of creativity, the strategies that a nonprofit ultimately fashions are likely to be mere incremental variations on current themes—the strategies already in place that define the present organization. Creative capacity fights the natural tendency to limit one's possibilities to the familiar; it goads an organization into questioning the conventional wisdom and raising uncomfortable questions about what it is and what it does. The more creativity that is brought to bear in responding to environmental challenges, the more likely that significant new responses will be fashioned.

The Challenge to Be Creative

Let's look at two nonprofit organizations, a civic club and an employment and training agency. The situations of both call for the exercise of creativity.

The Women's Civic Club of Greater Amity

The nominating committee of the Women's Civic Club of Greater Amity is in a quandary. One of the five volunteer vice presidencies (for community programming) remains unfilled after a seven-month search—a first for this prestigious, volunteer-driven association—and a second vice president (for administrative operations) has tendered her resignation. Something is going on that sets off alarm bells in the minds of concerned board members. Certainly, a second look is needed.

For over fifty years, the club has served well both its community and the women who are its membership, providing them with an opportunity to participate in well-conceived and capably administered community service programs, such as the hugely popular civic issues forum last year, as well as frequent social occasions, such as the monthly teas at the University Club. Furthermore, members have always been proud that so much is routinely accomplished with only two paid staff members. The volunteer vice presidencies, although very demanding of time, were traditionally coveted positions, the objects of aggressive if civil campaigns by ambitious members eager to ascend the volunteer career ladder. But in recent years, it has not been easy to fill these positions. Turnover has become a serious problem. "What is happening and what can we do about it?" is the frequent refrain at board meetings.

Mallard County Private Industry Council

Mallard County Private Industry Council (PIC) staff members are perplexed and anxious. PIC trustees have begun recently to call for a strategic planning session to take stock, figure out what is happening in the employment and training arena, and set some new directions. A new ball game with new rules has left the PIC in an ambiguous position.

Funded principally by grants under the federal Job Training Partnership Act (JTPA), the Mallard County PIC has plodded along for years, doing a solid if unspectacular job of training eligible "disadvantaged" participants and getting them placed in jobs. Federally determined performance standards are regularly exceeded. Most staff members are good at, and dedicated to, what they do.

By conventional standards, the PIC is a model agency. But in a time when job training is sorely needed at the local level in order to meet the needs of a rapidly changing economy, Congress is cutting JTPA funding while seriously considering the creation of a more comprehensive national employment and training system. Where PICs will be in the new system once the dust settles is currently unclear but, in the meantime, does it make sense to continue delivering the same programs in the same way? If not, what should be changed, and how can an anxious and defensive staff be encouraged to participate fully in determining a new direction?

The Women's Civic Club and the Mallard County Private Industry Council are not nonprofit organizations in the throes of crisis, but their futures look bleak if they do not begin to respond—now, not in five years—to ominous signals from the environment. If they wait too long to take action, the cost may be prohibitive or their very existence may be threatened. Their situations are typical of many nonprofits in today's challenging world, in which business-as-usual approaches appear to be a potentially perilous course. Although relatively minor environmental change may call for only incremental adjustments—tinkering a bit with program content, for example—increasingly the challenges demand a more dramatic break with current practice. In other words, significant innovation is needed, and this in turn depends on the nonprofit's creative capacity.

For the Women's Civic Club it would be all too easy to stick to a tried-and-true solution: scour the countryside for more of that vanishing breed, the full-time volunteer woman, in order to fill club vacancies. Second and third thoughts might surface other possibilities, such as untangling board and administrative volunteering so that administrative vice presidents do not serve on the board, thereby reducing the time that each volunteer position demands. Or the organization might consider increasing paid staff and reducing or eliminating volunteer administrators. Variations on these themes would surface in a creative brainstorming of possibilities, greatly increasing the likelihood of producing an innovative solution to the challenge.

As for the Mallard County Private Industry Council, in an antigovernment, probusiness environment, it might want to consider reinventing itself as an economic development organization that employs job training as a tool rather than continuing to see and describe itself primarily as a training agency. It might also want to consider learning to sell services to business customers in order to generate revenue, rather than relying on governmental support, or to pursue innovative partnerships with organizations once seen as competitors.

It is creative capacity that generates these possibilities for innovation, from which the planning process will select, and flesh out, the change initiatives, which will produce the organizational innovation.

The Planning Connection

Creative capacity alone, however, cannot lead to innovation. Creativity achieves its impact through a planning process that, as I will discuss in detail in Chapters Six and Seven, is designed to welcome, and to make full use of, the creative capacity of the people doing the planning. Long-range strategic planning does not have a proud history in this regard; think of the many weighty tomes projecting business-as-usual into the future that line organizational shelves. I will never forget the sense of waste and futility that my colleagues and I felt some twenty years ago as we participated in an elaborate five-year planning process that involved endless lists of goals and the projection of current programs into an unpredictable future. None of us took the process seriously; its basic purpose seemed to be to convince the public at large that we were serious. Nothing innovative came out of the process, as far as anyone could tell.

Indeed, more harm than good is likely to come from building the creative capacity of a nonprofit's staff without explicitly connecting it to the planning process. I have seen dozens of examples of off-site creativity training followed by highly conventional, control-oriented planning that stymied the exercise of creative capacity and produced frustration, anger, reduced commitment, and low morale rather than innovation. When I have encountered such abominable yet avoidable situations, I have wondered why anyone would want to develop a refined palate and a taste for gourmet foods if he or she will only sit down to a meal of a Big Mac and fries?

The Chief Creativity Officer

Creative capacity basically resides in the minds of the individuals working in an organization. Nonprofit boards and chief executives who are committed to developing the creative capacity of the individuals in their organizations will venture into complex and incompletely mapped territory that is marked with constantly shifting guideposts. In light of the stakes involved for every nonprofit organization in these turbulent times, I can say without reservation that every nonprofit chief executive must make a serious attempt to understand the creative process and to promote the development of creative capacity in his or her organization as a powerful route to innovation.

The contemporary nonprofit chief executive who seriously intends to lead his or her organization in producing innovation must, in effect, serve as the organization's "chief creativity officer" rather than merely delegating the role to a consultant or the training department. It is the chief creativity officer who ensures that employees grow in individual creative capacity and sees to it that the planning process makes full use of this creativity. Detailed knowledge of every feature of the creativity terrain is obviously not required to promote creative capacity building, but a chief executive must understand the major landmarks to be an effective creativity officer for his or her organization. I have no question that it is just as important these days for a nonprofit chief executive to master creativity development as it is to master financial planning or performance management or any other more traditional function.

Defining Creativity

There is no universally accepted definition of creativity, creative capacity, or the creative process. Through much of human history, the term *creativity* was commonly used to describe a largely romantic and mysterious capacity and process by which giants in various fields of endeavor arrived at their brilliant creations, discoveries, or inventions. Creativity was more the province of philosophy and religion than of science. The demystification of creativity began in the early years of the twentieth century, when Freud and his successors in the field of psychotherapy claimed a place for creative capacity in the subconscious mind.

Although not denying the subconscious an important place in their study of creativity, cognitive psychologists have researched creativity as a conscious mental process that can be observed and taught, thereby making creativity training programs—such as those offered at the Center for Creative Leadership in Greensboro, North Carolina—a realistic path to organizational creativity (Boden, 1991; Csikszentmihalyi, 1996; Gardner, 1993). Students of leadership and organizational development such as Peter Senge (1990) and Warren Bennis (1989) have taken a balanced approach. They draw on both the philosophical/spiritual/psychoanalytical and the cognitive streams. They have also taken advantage of a rapidly accumulating body of real-life case experience in recommending practical ways to build creative capacity (Gryskiewicz, 1993; Gryskiewicz and Hills, 1992).

The creative process has been most clearly mapped out as a methodology for problem solving and issue resolution that can be taught and learned. For example, Russell and Evans (1992) have identified five key steps in the creative process: *preparation,* including information collection and problem analysis; *frustration,* when no solution comes immediately to mind; *incubation,* during which conscious work on the problem is suspended and unconscious processes seem to continue the creative task; *insight,* which supplies one or more solutions, sometimes as an "aha!" event; and *working out,* which involves fleshing out the insights and turning them into full-blown solutions.

My experience with nonprofits confirms that these problem-solving steps work and do produce innovative solutions to identified issues and problems. However, a full understanding of creative capacity must go beyond a narrow problem-solving framework. Chief executives who intend to take the lead in building creative capacity must draw wisdom from both the study of conscious cognition and the exploration of the more hidden and mysterious processes of the subconscious mind.

In the realm of cognitive psychology, perhaps the research that is most pertinent to the subject of nonprofit leadership is that being done by Csikszentmihalyi (1996) and Gardner (1993) on the lives of highly creative people. Csikszentmihalyi's research indicates that "an idea or product that deserves the label 'creative' arises from the synergy of many sources and not only from the mind of a single person. It is easier to enhance creativity by changing conditions in the environment than by trying to make people think more creatively. And a genuinely creative accomplishment is almost never the result of a sudden insight, a light bulb flashing on in the dark, but comes after years of hard work" (1996, p. 1).

Csikszentmihalyi and Gardner have both identified three key components of a creative system: the person; the domain (the subject matter, such as mathematics or management); and the field (the people with enough influence to decide what constitutes the domain). Csikszentmihalyi's definition of creativity, then, is that it occurs "when a person, using the symbols of a given domain such as music, engineering, business, or mathematics, has a new idea or sees a new pattern, and when this novelty is selected by the appropriate field for inclusion into the relevant domain" (1996, p. 28).

Delving deeply into the various research going on in cognitive psychology is beyond the scope of this work, but readers should be aware that useful work is being done in the area of artificial intelligence. Basically, it involves using computer modeling to demonstrate how the human brain generates creative ideas. Very influential in this regard is Margaret Boden (1991), whose basic thesis is that a truly creative idea is one that could not have been produced by applying existing "generative principles" (the rules that lead to ideas), that computational concepts assist in specifying the generative principles, and that computer modeling helps us to determine what sets of generative principles can or cannot do.

The Subconscious and Spiritual Dimensions

Despite serious research aimed at clarifying key aspects of the creative process, the concepts of creativity and the creative process are far from well-defined. Debates over their meaning and how best to go about developing creative capability abound; one does not have to venture far before leaving the realm of hard science. I am convinced, based on extensive personal experience and in-depth work with hundreds of nonprofits, that serious attention must be paid to the mysterious workings of the subconscious minds of the individuals in a nonprofit if greater creative capacity is the goal.

Building creativity was, and in many circles still is, seen primarily as a matter of realizing creative potential by freeing oneself of subconscious limitations or barriers through the process of psychoanalysis. The courage to take the inner journey into the subconscious mind is often seen as coming from faith, and so the creative process is widely seen as having a spiritual dimension. Closely related capacities—such as being insightful and intuitive—are today commonly described as creatures of the subconscious realm, doing their important work in a mysterious fashion not yet fully understood. Even cognitive psychologists involved in the more scientific study of creativity do not deny its subconscious dimension (Boden, 1991; Csikszentmihalyi, 1996; Gardner, 1993).

This means that in leading the creativity charge, a nonprofit chief executive must move beyond straightforward problem-solving techniques that can be fairly easily taught and learned into a more shadowy realm that is not well understood and is also controversial. However, I believe there is no other choice: the powerful role of the subconscious in the creative process has been demonstrated so many times that it cannot be ignored without compromising any serious attempt to develop creativity capacity.

We may think of the subconscious mind not only as a reservoir of ideas that seem to appear from nowhere, sometimes in dreams, sometimes popping into consciousness after a period of rest (the "aha!" phenomenon), but also as a complex of deep-seated emotional barriers to creativity whose removal is essential for realizing a person's creative capacity. Anyone who has been involved in significant organizational change has confronted many instances where reality seems to be perceived in a distorted way and resistance to change appears irrational. Such resistance is difficult to deal with because of its largely hidden motivations. An impressive body of evidence supports the notion that creativity is closely linked to bringing such subconscious forces into consciousness so they can be examined and dealt with.

Jung (1969) expressed the limitations of conscious cognition and the importance of balance between the two minds: "The unconscious as we know can never be 'done with' once and for all. It is, in fact, one of the most important tasks of psychic hygiene to pay continual attention to the symptomatology of unconscious contents and processes, for the good reason that the conscious mind is always in danger of becoming one-sided, of keeping to well-worn paths and getting stuck in blind alleys. The complementary and compensating function of the unconscious ensures that these dangers . . . can in some measure be avoided" (p. 20).

The psychologist Rollo May (1975) links the unconscious mind directly to creativity, seeing this shadowy realm as a rich resource to be employed in the creative process, with "potentialities for awareness or action which the individual cannot or will not actualize." In his *Search for the Real Self* (1988), the eminent psychiatrist James Masterson identifies creativity as one of the ten "key capacities of the real self," defining creativity as "the ability to replace old, familiar patterns of living and problem solving with new and equally or more successful ones" (p. 44). Masterson goes on to note that creativity is not only the "ability to find solutions for life's problems in the world around us, it is also the ability to rearrange intrapsychic [subconscious] patterns that threaten to block self-expression without which there can be no creativity" (p. 45).

A common example of the failure to eliminate the intrapsychic patterns blocking self-expression—which I encounter over and over in my work with nonprofits—is the person who will not, in the company of peers, go out on the proverbial limb to share a creative idea for fear of criticism from others. Although time and time again fears of criticism—and, worse, rejection—turn out to be unfounded, to the fearful person it feels quite real and truly fearsome, thank you.

There is ample evidence that such self-consciousness and fear of rejection are often the reaction of the child inside the adult who is responding not to the actual world today but to harsh criticism and judgment in a past long gone. The fear is thus real, if not realistic, and it does block creativity. Such blockages bring a high price when repeated countless times in millions of organizations. No management system or training program, no matter how state-of-the-art, is likely to overcome this kind of strong and secret barrier to creative thinking, which call for an inward journey beyond conscious cognition.

A Word About Mindsets

Every human being who comes to the creative process brings a largely hidden mindset or filter that has a powerful impact on what his or her mind perceives. A mindset may be thought of as a mental filter that powerfully affects how a person perceives and interprets external events; this filter is modified by experience and training. Sir Geoffrey Vickers (1965) has described this mental filter as a person's "appreciative system," which is " a set of readinesses to distinguish some aspects of the situation rather than others and to classify and value these in this way rather than in that" (p. 67). Over a lifetime, we run into lots of people who have what is popularly known as the half-empty-glass view of the world, while others' views are more optimistic. Although it may on the surface sound trivial, an organization cursed with too many half-empty views is likely to see far fewer opportunities in the external world than one with a more positive mindset, and therefore, to generate fewer of the possibilities that are the preeminent product of the creative process.

Mindsets certainly simplify getting through the day-to-day, but they can, as we all know, militate against getting beneath the surface of complex issues. They lend themselves to snap judgments that can prevent the understanding on which creative change depends. In a world of grey, mindsets can easily produce black-and-white gaps that cannot be bridged. National debate these days over such complex issues as public welfare and criminal justice dramatically illustrates how phenomena are amenable to startlingly different interpretations depending on the perceptions of the party in question. A nonprofit organization needs to understand its own collective and individual appreciative systems—its mindsets—as well as those of key actors in its environment. Otherwise, it may overlook or misinterpret critical information, or misread the reactions and motives of important external actors.

At a recent meeting, senior managers of a nonprofit organization involved in preserving the natural environment were discussing environmental developments over the prior few months. When they began to mull over the meaning of the new Republican majority in Congress, and especially the phenomenon of the aggressive, often brash speaker of the house, Newt Gingrich, the sound of the collective mental gates crashing down was almost audible. I could imagine the wagons being drawn into a tight circle in response to an apparently clear and present—and unambiguous—threat. Therefore, the initial responses were largely defensive and overly adversarial. It took some time to open the discussion to a more searching examination of the phenomena, one that allowed a deeper look at root causes—such as skepticism of governmental motives and practices—and to distinguish between rhetoric and action. Only by opening the mental filters more widely could we truly know the phenomena we were examining. The result was the identification of creative strategies to build common ground with the "foe."

A few years ago, I directly experienced the power of mindsets in dealing with so-called objective facts. I was facilitating the board-staff retreat for a nonprofit corporation whose mission was to promote wider home ownership and the upgrading of housing stock in the community through the use of a large revolving loan fund.

One of the several brainstorming groups that we used to generate information was assessing the corporation's performance over the past year. All the group's members were looking at the same performance data, whose accuracy was not questioned. The group consisted of three bankers and two community organizers. The bankers' assessment was strongly negative, based on a history of tardy loan repayment. The organizers' assessment was glowing, based on the corporation's success in loaning so much money to so many deserving people so quickly. Same data, same table— completely different perceptions.

A year or so later, I facilitated the board-staff retreat of a non-profit corporation engaged in efforts to reduce the incidence of domestic violence. Mention of the term *feminism* late that first afternoon ignited an emotional debate that almost derailed the meeting. To one group, largely board members, the term conjured up the kind of radical image that impeded fund-raising efforts. The other saw a powerful force for good that had led to the creation of the agency.

About that time, I also facilitated a board-staff retreat for a non-profit economic development agency with an African American board. When we assessed the agency's strengths and weaknesses, the older members of the board saw no problem with the lack of racial diversity, based on their negative experience with white-dominated institutions over the years. But some younger, newer board members lamented the absence of diversity as a sign of provincialism that would impede growth.

In this section, I have drawn on some fairly obvious examples of differing views on the same set of facts to illustrate the power of mindsets in interpreting so-called objective events and conditions. The reader should keep in mind that often mindsets are so narrow that important signals from the external world are not picked up at all, much less analyzed.

Anxiety: Friend and Potential Enemy

Anxiety, that usually unwelcome sense of foreboding and dread, can in fact play a positive and important role in the creative process. However, anxiety never feels good, and if it is not controlled it can bring a halt to creative thinking.

Anxiety contributes positively to the creative process by making a person uncomfortable enough to want to take the journey into the subconscious mind and, hence, to grapple with the barriers standing in the way of creative expression. I like to tell my clients that one way they will know that they are taking a creative journey in their work is the presence of anxiety as a traveling companion.

Danish philosopher Soren Kierkegaard, whose work brilliantly captured the essence of what psychoanalysis later revealed more explicitly, described the role of anxiety: "Whoever is educated by anxiety is educated by possibility, and only he who is educated by possibility is educated according to his infinitude" (1980, p. 156). This passage refers to the creative tension that promotes dissatisfaction with an existing situation and goads a person to go beyond it. Anxiety here is clearly a friend, no matter how painful it may feel. As Kierkegaard observed, if a person boasts of being always anxiety-free, "I will gladly provide him with my explanation: that it is because he is very spiritless" (p. 157). Yet the anxiety that can goad one to greater creativity can also, if not checked, stymie creative expression. Great courage may be required to go very far into the creative realm and to grapple with what Rollo May (1975) calls the "creative confrontation."

In sum, it would be a mistake to think of creativity as a straightforward process that merely requires cognitive skills and freedom from external constraints on thinking along with a large dollop of self-reflection. As Kierkegaard and other students of the creative process have noted, faith in a power greater than oneself appears to be the most effective guardian against anxiety's becoming debilitating. We must, therefore, bring the spiritual dimension into play in any serious attempt to build a nonprofit's creative capacity, and in this regard, mythology can serve as a source of inspiration and understanding.

Mythology as a Source

Mythology is a rich lode to mine in understanding the creative capacity and its link to the subconscious mind. Joseph Campbell's groundbreaking work, which was introduced to a wider public by the popular Bill Moyers series on public televison, explained that universal myths of rebirth and creative growth that transcend cultures and eras are closely linked to the concept of the subconscious. Campbell describes the subconscious as containing "all the life-potentialities that we never managed to bring to adult realization, those other portions of ourself. . . . If only a portion of that lost totality could be dredged up into the light of day, we should experience a marvelous expansion of our powers, a vivid renewal of life" (1968, p. 17).

Campbell saw the mythological journey of the universal hero as basically an inward passage, "where obscure resistances are overcome, and long lost, forgotten powers are revivified, to be made available for the transfiguration of the world" (p. 29). When Campbell advised "follow your bliss," he was not speaking as a self-indulgent aging hippie; instead, he was asking us to take the journey inward, embrace creativity, and realize our true possibilities in this world.

Creativity in the Management Realm

The important role of the subconscious in the creative process has begun to penetrate the consciousness of management educators. For example, as he brilliantly weaves together the five disciplines essential to the learning organization, Peter Senge (1990) notes that what "distinguishes people with high levels of personal mastery is they have developed a higher level of rapport between their normal awareness and their subconscious. What most of us take for granted and exploit haphazardly, they approach as a discipline" (p. 162). Stephen Covey (1989), while cautioning that we must not be held captive by what he calls "psychic determinism" (that is, our parents did it to us so there's no way to change our suspicious view of the world), notes that self-awareness is a key element in building a creative life.

For several years in my workshops with nonprofit boards and executives, I have routinely asked what works people are reading or have recently read that have had a positive impact on their leadership and management skills. In the past three or four years an increasing number of people, often the majority of a group, mention Scott Peck's *The Road Less Traveled* (1978) and Thomas Moore's *Care of the Soul* (1992) among the works that were influential in their professional lives. When I ask how many find the spiritual dimension of their work very important, most hands in the room usually go up.

The Chief Executive's Challenge

As we have seen, the capacity to innovate is critical to leading and managing change effectively in these challenging times, and significant innovation is fueled by the creative process. Thus, nonprofit chief executives who are committed to effective change leadership have no choice but to take the lead in developing and fostering their organization's creative capacity.

Of course, this is easier said than done. As we have seen, creativity is not even a well-defined concept, much less a system that can be tailored to fit a nonprofit's unique situation and then installed in turnkey fashion. Assuming various shapes and drawing on dramatically different wellsprings, creativity defies easy understanding. Chief executives contemplating what to do and where to move on the creativity front may be tempted to throw up their hands and retire from the fray. But abdicating the role of "chief creativity officer" would come at too high a price in these perilous times, when innovation is often the price of survival, much less growth.

Fortunately, there are some practical steps that committed chief executives can take to develop creative capacity. Taken together, they will not add up to anything remotely resembling a system, but this may actually prove more of a strength than a weakness in light of the rapid evolution of creativity as a field. The last thing we need is a neatly packaged "creativity system" that will become another quick-fix gimmick that inevitably disappoints while slimming the nonprofit pocketbook.

By taking five important steps, a chief executive can strengthen creative capacity:

- Make understanding and practicing creativity a high personal priority.
- Establish creativity as a major organizational value.
- Lead by example and sharing, providing a living model of creative growth.

- Provide opportunities for education and training in creativity.
- Guarantee that creative capacity actually fuels serious organizational innovation.

Making Creativity a High Personal Priority

If creativity is not high on the list of personal priorities of the chief executive, he or she is much less likely to be successful in building an organization's creative capacity. Making something a high priority means devoting significant time and attention to it, keeping it at the top of the list of to-do's, and not letting the press of day-to-day business drive it out of sight and mind. A chief executive truly committed to building creative capacity must first learn about the subject. While attempting to become an expert on every facet of creativity would be unrealistic, at least becoming familiar with the major facets of creativity will be indispensable to understanding and promoting it in the wider organization.

A firm grasp of the creative process will require going beyond the field of management into philosophy, psychology, spiritualism, and even mythology. As Joseph Campbell (1968) has noted, familiarity with the universal myths that describe the hero's journey within can inspire one with the courage to make the personal journey: "Furthermore, we have not even to risk the adventure alone; for the heroes of all time have gone before us; the labyrinth is thoroughly known; we have only to follow the thread of the hero-path. And where we had thought to find an abomination, we shall find a god; where we had thought to slay another, we shall slay ourselves; where we had thought to travel outward, we shall come to the center of our own existence; where we had thought to be alone, we shall be with all the world" (p. 25).

Doing rather than merely reading about something is a powerful path to understanding, and in this regard, a chief executive seriously interested in creativity will constantly be on the lookout for opportunities to practice creative skills, alone and in group settings. One way is to follow a formal creative logic in tackling complex issues and problems, such as the one Russell and Evans describe in *The Creative Manager* (1992). This will require resisting snap judgments, living with inevitable frustration for a time because immediate solutions are not generated, and allowing time away from the problem so that the necessary incubation occurs. In the process of formally employing a creative process, a chief executive can also be alert for the mindsets that simplify, but also sometimes distort, seeing and understanding.

An equally important but far more difficult approach to understanding is to seek a closer connection between conscious cognition and the subconscious mind so that the power of the subconscious can be put to better use in the creative process. Work with a psychotherapist would probably be the most direct way to pursue self-understanding, but simpler approaches such as setting aside significant time for quiet and meditation and paying attention to dreams as messengers from the subconscious realm are also useful paths to travel in the quest for self-knowledge.

Over the past two years I have found spending at least one day a month at a Jesuit retreat center, all alone except for an hour or so with a spiritual director, such a powerful way to stimulate creative thinking in my work that I now firmly believe I cannot afford not to spend this time there. Far from being merely an escape from the madding crowd, it is a way of becoming engaged fully in the process of living and working creatively. The decision to write this book, for example, despite deeply ingrained barriers—"Do I have anything worth saying?"—that stood in the way, was made during one of my daylong retreats. They might better be called *advances,* by the way.

Personal experience has also taught me that the regular examination of dreams is another powerful way to recognize and understand deep-seated emotions that can profoundly affect our conscious behavior. As Jung (1990) observed, "Dreams are the commonest and universally accessible source for the investigation of man's symbolizing faculty" and "indeed the chief source of all our knowledge about symbolism" (p. 70). I now regularly employ dream examination as an important means for strengthening my own creative capacity through self-understanding. My wife and I routinely describe our dreams to each other and discuss the meaning of the symbols through which dreams speak. We have been frequently amazed at the practical wisdom that is offered.

Here is another story told me by a chief executive with whom I worked four years ago. The winter before had been one of the most difficult he had ever experienced. He was in the midst of spearheading the development of a new nonprofit subsidiary that promised significant client and revenue growth, and at the same time he was chairing one of the most important committees of his state association. Neither the organizational development initiative nor the leadership role in the state association was going as planned. His tried-and-true response to adversity thus clicked in: push hard and then when fatigue sets in, push even harder. If eleven hours a day don't get the job done, put in twelve or thirteen.

One night in the middle of what was becoming a very depressing period, he had a dream. In his dream, he saw a child being beaten, apparently to death, by a shadowy figure. Apparently a powerless observer, he sadly left the room with the child's body lying on the bed. But returning later in his dream, he found the child, who looked very much like his own son as a baby, undressed him, and gently lay him in a warm bath, where the child awakened and greeted the dreaming chief executive with a warm smile.

"Doug," he said, "when I awoke that morning, it was with a clear understanding of the harsh self-judgment that had been at work and a strong sense that I needed to be more of a nurturing father to myself, to be more forgiving, to adopt a more reasonable schedule, and to trust that all would be well." And so he eventually did.

To judge from the dream experiences that an increasing number of chief executives have shared with me in recent years, I am not alone in seeing dreams as a powerful path to self-understanding. By the way, I have on a number of occasions shared my own dreams with chief executives, whose response has been uniformly positive.

Taking the time to learn about the creative process will be challenge enough to overburdened chief executives, much less setting significant time aside for reflection, meditation, and interior journeying. The press of daily events will militate against spending time this way, and the interior journey will initially feel uncomfortable and even threatening to many chief executives, who have been well trained to focus on concrete bottom-line results and to maintain a rat-a-tat-tat pace. I can only say that the price of this discomfort is modest compared with the potential gain in individual and organizational creativity.

Making Creativity an Organizational Value

Explicit values statements that are developed collaboratively, formally adopted by a board, and widely publicized within an organization can confer legitimacy on desired behaviors and encourage their practice. They comprise the most important part of what we might call the official ideology of the organization. The chief executive's job in this regard involves both design and facilitation: designing a planning process that includes values formulation as a key component and ensuring through facilitation that creativity is seen as an explicit value.

Of course, values statements have been known to end up on shelves, little noticed or consulted. A nonprofit chief executive can reinforce the importance of creativity by serving as its verbal champion, publicly extolling it as a virtue on every possible occasion and educating board and staff members about it, explaining why it made the values list in the first place and what it means in both theory and practice. To be sure, neither written statements nor verbal exhortations can alone strengthen and sustain creative behavior, but they can lay a foundation on which other efforts can build.

Inspiring by Example and by Sharing

Max De Pree (1989) has observed that the "best way to communicate the basis of a corporation's or institution's common bonds and values is through behavior" (p. 101). Experience has demonstrated for most of us the truth of that old saw, "Actions speak louder than words." Nobody's actions are watched more closely than the chief executive's in determining acceptable behavior.

The people I have worked with in nonprofit organizations are all smart enough to be able to spot espoused theories that are contradicted in practice and to choose practice rather than theory as their guide. They are not about to jump on the creativity bandwagon in response to their chief executive's exhortation; they know enough to board it only after the chief executive has taken the driver's seat and started the engine.

Of course, the truest test of a chief executive's commitment to creative capacity building is a personal willingness to participate in process along with staff, rather than disappearing after the exhortatory speech has been given or engaging in contradictory behavior. If the team is going off to an intensive weekend with a facilitator, the chief executive must be there as one of the team. Furthermore, the chief executive must practice resisting the desire to control—keeping quiet and listening in meetings rather than jumping in immediately with the right answer—and leaving room for creative ideas to emerge. Chief executives should also resist the temptation to criticize the creative ideas that emerge in meetings, suspending judgment until choices must be made. Another valuable trait is to forgive mistakes that are the natural result of experiments in creative thinking and that are not the result of disobeying explicit directions or violating fundamental organizational principles.

Five years ago, I learned a valuable lesson about leaving room for creativity from my twelve-year-old son. The lesson had a definite impact on my work as a facilitator of strategic planning sessions. In fact, I remember the day every time I am tempted to exert control rather than leave space for others to be creative. That day, having dropped his sister at summer camp in Michigan, William and I decided to spend a couple of days at Deerfield Village near Detroit, a beautifully restored nineteenth-century community that includes Thomas Edison's laboratory and the Wright brothers' workshop. The first morning at breakfast, in the grip of a planner's need to structure the day ahead, I pulled out a village map and began a monologue on our options for the day.

A couple of minutes into this one-sided planning session, I noticed that William was silently doodling on his napkin, not at all captivated by the choices I was outlining. As a good father my immediate inclination was to call him to attention, but before speaking I made an uncharacteristic decision to turn the day's plans over to him, to surrender control over both the process and the outcomes. I just handed William the map and said, "Please plan the day. You lead the way, I'll follow."

With a huge smile, William grabbed the map and began to outline a route with gusto. Neither his enthusiasm nor energy waned throughout the day and William demonstrated great creativity in leading us through a wonderful tour.

One way a chief executive can lead by example in the creative realm is to share deeply personal experiences with staff members, not only to demonstrate the courage that is at the heart of creativity but also to build intimacy and trust. One chief executive's recounting of a dramatic dream that had helped him make a critical decision encouraged his management team members to be open to dreams as a source of creative insights and to be brave enough to share their own dreams with each other. Because this chief executive was secure in his position and a physically imposing person, it heightened the impact when he was willing to share something that could easily have been seen as weak or even "flaky."

More dramatically, another chief executive I know was courageous enough to share with his management team an intensely personal experience that vividly demonstrates the close connection between unconscious cognition and creativity. He had a couple of years earlier joined fifty other people in a southwestern city for five consecutive twelve-hour days together in an intensive, professionally facilitated personal development program. The third night, at about eleven o'clock, the facilitator had announced that the next day each of them would have five minutes to present, before the assembled group, an expression of their individual creativity. It might be through song, dance, rhetoric, pantomime, or some other mode. The "show" was to begin at ten the next morning. The participants were told to select their mode of expression before leaving that night and to inform one of the staff assistants. The facilitator offered only the simplest counsel: "Be yourself, be creative."

The chief executive's immediate internal response was probably shared by most of his fellow participants: he felt tightly enclosed in the "bands of steel" that Alan Wheelis so movingly describes in his eloquent little book, *How People Change* (1973). To perform alone in front of fifty people did not feel at all like an opportunity to create but rather like a punishment to survive! But being a frugal man, and having paid his money, he was in for the duration. So, after a few moments of thought, he announced his choice would be an interpretive dance and left for his hotel. "What an idiot you are," he recalled thinking as he entered the hotel room. "You don't dance at all, even with someone else in relative anonymity, much less solo before an audience, and you are now going to play the fool."

What he experienced that night as he created his dance and what he saw the next day brought home to him vividly the creativity that can be unleashed by lowering the barriers between conscious control and the shadowy world of the subconscious mind. His performance was a dance symbolizing the death and rebirth of the spirit into a world of hope and expanded opportunity. It came into being only after he had given up the planning that was getting him nowhere that night, relaxed control, and slipped into a kind of meditative state. When the ideas and the related choreography emerged, from God only knows where, they had the feel of rightness and truth. He also witnessed that day wonderful demonstrations from others of the courage to be creative in action, and he learned from everyone he talked with that their ideas had come only after they had quit trying to control the process of creation. Finally, he experienced the joy of sharing creativity in a safe setting, without fear of criticism or judgment.

Of course, this courageous chief executive knew that, as we say in the retreat business, "Monday always comes; welcome back to the real world." Readers will recognize the script. It's one thing to cavort on stage in some faraway city with people you won't, if you're lucky, ever run into again in this lifetime. It's another out there in the real world, where trust and playing the fool come at a stiff price. But even after two years, this chief executive has preserved the memory as a treasured example of creativity in action, and as a challenge to learn how to expand the practice of creativity in more businesslike settings. And most important, he was brave enough to share this experience with his management team. They were thus inspired and emboldened to undertake their own interior journeys into the realm of creativity.

Providing Opportunities for Education and Training

If you mention education and training in any field, from creativity to financial management, most nonprofit chief executives will think of looking for something "out there": sending staff members away for a day or a week to a training facility or bringing in a consultant to present a workshop. But in the area of creativity, the pickings are slim although the choices are growing as creativity is increasingly being recognized as a powerful force for innovation. The Center for Creative Leadership, located in Greensboro, North Carolina, is probably the leading research center and training facility in the business of explicitly developing creativity skills. More common are business or management school programs that focus on teamwork and, although they may also dabble in creativity, have a more get-the-job-done focus.

Explicitly developing creative process skills is not the only avenue available to a chief executive committed to strengthening the creative capacity of the staff. It also makes sense to consider opportunities for individual emotional and psychological growth through participation in a facilitated group process such as the interpretative dance described earlier. The range of choices is wide, from the "finding the child within" type of experience that is based on a fuller integration of the conscious and subconscious minds, to the highly regarded work of the Covey Leadership Institute, which is more oriented to conscious principles-driven behavior than exploration of subconscious forces.

Whatever the methodology chosen, sending the people away for a day or a week to develop their creative capacity can be an expensive course of action. It can also be risky. First, quality control is a real issue; the chief executive who has not actually gone through a program personally should let *caveat emptor*—let the buyer beware—be the rule. Second, there is always the danger that the external experience will be out of sync in some important way with the organization. Although perhaps a valid way to effect organizational change, this is one of the more disruptive approaches.

A chief executive will not want to neglect the many important opportunities for self-education and training. An option for larger nonprofit organizations is to appoint a training director, or even to create a full-fledged training department. In my experience, however, the training field generally does better in providing mid-level technical skills training (such as time management, budgeting, reading financial reports) than guidance in the vague and more demanding creativity arena. Indeed, I question whether it is possible for an organization to produce a creativity skills training program of much value by itself.

One low-cost approach that many nonprofits have successfully used is to build a top-notch leadership and management resource library. Books and journals are relatively inexpensive resources that can be used again and again, and a library can be especially valuable when combined with facilitated discussion groups. One chief executive I know has set aside a half-day every two weeks for a discussion session with her management team, each one focusing on a particular book or article. Management team members lead the sessions, and everyone is expected to be prepared. Thus, a book like Russell and Evans's *The Creative Manager* (1992) can be the subject of one or more such sessions in an inexpensive way to build a fuller understanding of creativity.

Being the Guarantor of Eventual Innovation

The only purpose of developing a nonprofit's creative capacity is to produce concrete change—to innovate. Therefore, one of the most important jobs of the chief executive is to ensure that creative capacity actually fuels innovation. If the connection is not made, creativity inevitably becomes unrealized potential, and this is one of the surest routes to frustration, disillusionment, and cynicism. Furthermore, without significant innovation, the nonprofit remains at risk in this rapidly changing, always challenging, and frequently threatening environment.

The essential connection is between creative capacity and that innovation engine, the planning process, and the design of this connection is the responsibility of the chief executive. Chapters Six and Seven examine this issue in detail.

In Summary

Creativity is the fuel that drives the innovation engine. It produces the possibilities that the planning process will translate into practical innovations. This chapter examined ways to understand and learn about the creative process. We can gain insights into the mysterious workings of the subconscious mind with the help of psychoanalysis and through harder scientific approaches, such as those taken by Csikszentmihalyi and Gardner.

This chapter also looked at the mindsets that can block creativity and examined anxiety as both a goad to creativity and a possible barrier to it. Mythology and spirituality were also discussed; they are closely tied to creative capacity.

Finally, several practical ways that chief executives can serve their organizations as "chief creativity officer" were described, including making understanding and practicing creativity high personal priorities; establishing creativity as an organizational value; leading by example and by sharing; providing opportunities for creativity education and training; and ensuring that creative capacity is used in a serious innovation process.

Strategic Management as an Engine for Innovation

Coming Attractions

Chapter Six discusses the following:

- The inadequacies of traditional long-range planning as an innovation tool
- Strategic management, an important variation on the broad strategic planning theme
- How to develop a strategic management process design
- How to realize more fully the innovation potential of annual operational planning and budget preparation

Realizing the Potential of Planning

This chapter and the next are about tapping the tremendous potential of planning as a practical—indeed, the preeminent—innovation tool that is available to nonprofit organizations. Through the planning process, the possibilities—the innovative ideas—generated by an organization's creative capacity are eventually translated into schedules of planned activities that can be budgeted and implemented. Happily, these two chapters are able to draw on the rapidly accumulating experience of the nonprofits that are blazing new trails in realizing the innovative potential of the planning function in practice (Bryson, 1995; Eadie, 1991, 1995).

This chapter provides an overview of the strategic management process, a variation of strategic planning that has proved particularly powerful as an engine for innovation (Eadie, 1994, 1993).

Free of the grandiosity of traditional strategic planning, realistically avoiding long-term projections of activity into the unknown future, selective in its focus on particular change challenges, and emphasizing immediate action, strategic management is well suited to an unruly increasingly unpredictable world and has already demonstrated its utility in the innovation process.

Although the strategic management process may be considered the thoroughbred of nonprofit innovation deserving the lion's share of attention, it would do a disservice to the reader to ignore completely the innovation potential of a lowlier beast—the annual operational planning and budget preparation process. Strategic planning has always had the edge in the glamor department (who, given a choice, would want to be known as a sound operational type rather than a strategic type?). However, when it comes to their applications, that's another story.

An Operations Bias

There has never been a shortage of planning in the nonprofit world. Almost every nonprofit leader and executive with whom I have worked over the past three decades has been an active, enthusiastic planner. But, for the most part, the planning had a short-term, control focus. For example, every chief executive of my acquaintance has been addicted to that popular planning tool, the daily and weekly to-do list. The to-do list is unquestionably a planning device because it schedules and allocates the time and energy needed for various activities. Such lists can be a great help in accomplishing high-priority items. In addition, their very concreteness is a source of satisfaction as each item is checked off with the passage of hours, days, and weeks. However, anyone who finds himself or herself revising a list at the end of the day to match what actually transpired may want to take a relaxing holiday!

Moving beyond individual planning, we come to that Mississippi River of organizational processes: the annual operational planning and budget preparation process. Fundamentally about productivity, efficiency, and control, it is an effective vehicle for making incremental adjustments in financial allocations, fine-tuning ongoing programs, identifying operational improvements, and generating performance indicators to be used in measuring operational effectiveness. No more reliable control device has ever been invented than the monthly report of actual versus budgeted dollars by department, cost category, and program.

Although organizational flirtations with strategic planning have tended to be sporadic, brief, and painful, often leaving disappointment and cynicism in their wake, annual operational planning and budget preparation, like the cockroach, is a survivor. It plods along, exciting little passion but doing its job nonetheless. We might not want to caress an annual plan, but we could not do without it in running an organization. Without erasing the distinction between strategic and operational planning, this chapter looks briefly at a practical way to make operational planning an important source of organizational innovation.

The Failure of Traditional Long-Range Planning

Controlling existing programs and dollars and enhancing the productivity of current operations are important goals. Most of the nonprofit leaders and managers I know feel comfortable with, if not passionate about, short-term operational planning because it reliably achieves these goals. But historically, when an unruly environment presented an organization with challenges that called for significant innovation, the traditional planning solution—comprehensive long-range or strategic planning—proved woefully inadequate, leaving dashed expectations and an anti-long-range-planning bias in its wake. Indeed, this kind of bad feeling constitutes one of the tallest barriers I have encountered to the successful application of the strategic management process in nonprofits. Although the occasional professional planner might surreptitiously fondle a weighty long-range planning tome in a closet (probably violating a state law in the process), most such documents end up on the shelf, seldom remembered or consulted.

Mintzberg (1994) issued a strong indictment of traditional strategic planning: "Strategy making needs to function beyond the boxes, to encourage the informal learning that produces new perspectives and new combinations. As the saying goes, life is larger than our categories. Planning's failure to transcend the categories explains why it has discouraged serious organizational change. This failure is why formal planning has promoted strategies that are extrapolated from the past or copied from others. Strategic planning has not only never amounted to strategic thinking but has, in fact, often impeded it" (p. 109).

Generally, I assign the blame for the inadequacies of traditional long-range planning to the professional planning field, with its fondness for theory over practice and its penchant for rationality, order, and neatness, even at the expense of realism. Specifically, three basic design flaws are at the heart of long-range planning's failure to deliver impressive results. First, the common requirement that detailed long-range plans be prepared for a three- or five-year cycle has forced managers to take a mechanistic approach to their projections, increasing activities by five percent a year, for example, because it is impossible to predict the environment accurately much beyond one year hence. Second, the bottom-up, accumulative approach—compiling departmental or programmatic long-range plans into a big blob of a plan—has ensured that the plans flow along established channels, basically continuing the present into the future. Third, the departmental planning approach has meant that what I term *change challenges,* that is, strategic issues that transcend departments and programs, tend to fall through the organizational cracks.

Here is a case in point. Some fifteen years ago, I did a study of the strategic planning process at a large postsecondary institution with over thirty thousand students, three new campuses, and a budget of approximately $100 million. Adorned with a number of bells and whistles, the process required all budget units to fashion five-year goals and objectives. These were then compiled into divisional plans, which eventually grew into three-pound campus plans, which were ultimately turned into a hefty nine-pound, beautifully bound institutional plan.

I studied every major investment in significant innovation—whether in educational content or management systems—over the five-year period covered, including the new high-tech business training center that was being constructed at that time. In not one instance could I find an innovation that had been generated by this elaborate planning process; rather, it merely recorded any recent decisions to innovate once they had been made and codified them in the annually updated five-year plan. Nor did I find any evidence that these regularly updated tomes were ever used as yardsticks for measuring progress.

Apparently, this tremendously time-consuming effort served a political purpose (evidence of institutional seriousness that was provided to state legislators) and was viewed as a team-building exercise (process as product). In an interview, the very capable young planning director, who later went on to more meaningful work elsewhere, candidly admitted that he focused more on editing, graphic design, paper stock, and cover art than on any substantive issues once the giant blob of paper reached his desk. So much time to produce so little impact! No wonder the process had over time become the butt of jokes on all the campuses.

Underutilizing Operational Planning

Even though Sovietlike comprehensive long-range planning is an obvious target of contempt, over and over again I have witnessed hum-drum annual operational planning and budget preparation processes that only incrementally adjust existing functions, programs, and dollar allocations without exploring creative ways to strengthen program effectiveness or enhance productivity. More often than not, such ho-hum operational plans are then sent finished to the board, whose only choice is to play a passive role, thumbing through a complex tome asking relatively low-level questions. No wonder planning has so many grudging adherents and so few passionate advocates!

So Much Potential

Past sins committed in the name of planning can teach valuable lessons about what not to do, but the history of planning, no matter how sordid, should not keep nonprofit leaders and managers from tapping the tremendous potential of planning. It is a practical innovation tool, much more than a simple device for refinement and control of existing activities or the mindless codification of the conventional wisdom. Without the planning process, there is no practical, systematic way to translate creative capacity into concrete organizational change, to make possibilities reality. Fortunately, disgust with the failure of traditional planning as an innovation tool combined with an increasingly challenging environment have prompted many nonprofits to test new approaches (Bryson, 1995; Eadie, 1995).

Being Strategic: An Overview

Before taking a detailed look at the strategic management variation on the broad strategic planning theme, I want to note some of the important work going on in the broader field of strategic planning, much of it in response to the obvious deficiencies of traditional long-range planning. Perhaps the most fundamental account of the process of strategizing has been supplied by Nathan D. Grundstein in his remarkable book, *The Knowledge of Strategy* (1992). To Grundstein, "To strategize is to engage with the manifold of the world. To engage is to bring into play on the part of the strategist those of his powers by which to bring a something into existence; to introduce a particular directionality or relation into events; to utilize his powers so as to drive desired possibilities . . . about the manifold to their consummation as actualities" (p. 5). Grundstein has hit on the essence of strategy: going beyond the conventional wisdom and current practice to discover new possibilities and translate them into concrete change. His most powerful contribution to strategic thinking is, I believe, attention to the conscious cognitive processes that transcend mere planning practice and make real strategic change possible.

In a comprehensive look at public and nonprofit strategic planning, John Bryson (1995) provides a broad definition of the strategic planning process that is the foundation for this chapter's discussion of the strategic management variation of that process: "I define strategic planning as a disciplined effort to produce fundamental decisions and actions that shape and guide what an organization is, what it does, and why it does it. To deliver the best results, strategic planning requires broad yet effective information gathering, development and exploration of strategic alternatives, and an emphasis on future implications of present decisions. Strategic planning can help facilitate communication and participation, accommodate divergent interests and values, foster wise and reasonably analytic decision making, and promote successful implementation" (pp. 4–5).

Learning and Entrepreneurship

The rapidly growing literature on learning organizations is pertinent to any discussion of strategic management. Depending on the definition, it can encompass much of the innovation process. There is no question that organizations that systematically learn are far better prepared to use strategic management effectively in the innovation process than those that have not developed their learning capacity (Cranton, 1994; Garvin, 1993; Beckhard and Pritchard, 1992; Senge, 1990). To Senge (1990), it is through learning that "we re-create ourselves. Through learning we reperceive the world and our relationship to it. Through learning we extend our capacity to create, to be part of the generative process of life" (p. 14). Redding and Catalanello (1994) see organizational learning and strategic change as closely linked, observing that "fundamental organizational change most often results from journeys of learning—of setting out in a direction, of gaining new insights and making discoveries en route, of going back, adjusting old maps, developing revised plans, and taking new actions" (p. 7).

Cranton (1994) says that "transformational learning" occurs "when, through critical self-reflection, an individual revises old or develops new assumptions, beliefs, or ways of seeing the world" (p. 4). Garvin (1993) defines a learning organization as one that is "skilled at creating, acquiring, and transferring knowledge, and at modifying its behavior to reflect new knowledge and insights" (p. 80). He suggests that learning organizations possess five critical skills: solving problems systematically, experimenting with new approaches, learning from their experience and history, learning from others' experiences and practices, and transferring knowledge quickly and efficiently throughout the organization.

Developing the entrepreneurial capacity of nonprofit organizations is pertinent to the innovation process, because being entrepreneurial means, above all else, acting on opportunities to build and grow. Entrepreneurs are cutters of red tape who single-mindedly pursue their own growth targets. Dennis Young (1991) takes an expansive view of entrepreneurship as a process "of putting new ideas into practice. Entrepreneurs bring together and catalyze the ingredients—people, financial resources, organizational arrangements, and the like—that are necessary to implement a new concept" (p. 62). Young identifies eight skills that are critical to successful entrepreneurship: fashioning a mission, solving problems, applying creativity and ingenuity, identifying opportunities and the right timing, assessing risks, building consensus and teams, mobilizing resources, and being persistent.

Strategic Management in a Nutshell

Two core assumptions are at the heart of strategic management (Eadie, 1996). The first is that it is a waste of time and effort to attempt to project detailed organizational activity much beyond a year into the future, especially in today's context of rapid, unpredictable change. The second is that two basic planning streams or agendas—the strategic and the operational—flow concurrently, and although they are closely related, they must be kept parallel and separate in order to generate concrete results, as shown in Figure 6.1. In contrast, traditional planning theory saw strategic planning as an umbrella process from which flowed increasingly detailed operational plans. Of course, in practice, when the strategic plan was finished, it was put away, and operational planning proceeded largely independently, little influenced by the now-shelved strategic plan.

Strategic management also differs from traditional strategic planning in several other ways, summarized in Figure 6.2.

Strategic management pays attention to the *strategic framework*—the values, vision, and mission of an organization—as the preeminent driver of change and the only part of a plan that can be projected more than a year or so into the future.

Figure 6.1. The Strategic and Operational Streams.

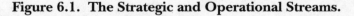
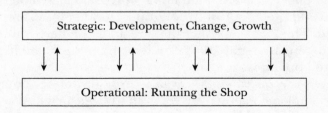

Strategic: Development, Change, Growth

Operational: Running the Shop

Figure 6.2. The Attributes of Strategic Management.

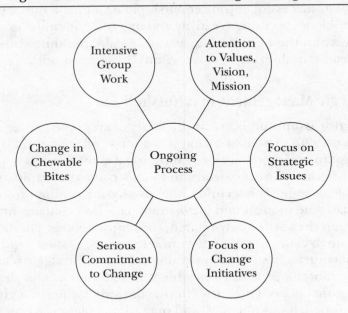

In strategic management, specific *strategic issues* or change challenges—that is, opportunities to move closer to the vision or problems and threats blocking progress toward the vision—are selected as the focus of detailed strategy formulation, in recognition of the finiteness and scarcity of time, money, and other resources. Supermarket shopping lists of tantalizing possibilities are not the stuff of strategic management, which aims serious attention at only as many issues as an organization can realistically tackle in a given year.

Change initiatives or projects to address selected issues—an initiative to pilot test a new adult literacy program, based on evidence of need and the opportunity for grant funding, for example—are selected. The strategic issues that are addressed are found in the gap between an organization's strategic framework and its current plans and operations.

There is a *commitment to change* through the development of detailed implementation plans for each strategic initiative or project.

Organizational change need not be grandiose—change can

take the form of modest, *chewable bites*. Change can mean capability-building initiatives (such as reorganizing the board to strengthen its leadership capability) or have more external manifestations (such as bringing in new clients or developing program innovations).

Recognizing the need to gain diverse perspectives and to identify issues that do not fit established departments and programs, as well as the importance of fostering a feeling of ownership when the change initiatives are eventually implemented, strategic management requires *intensive group work*. Such work, including board-staff retreats, is carried out in top-down fashion—rather than the bottom-up accumulative approach of traditional planning.

Finally, strategic management is an *ongoing process* that pays as much attention to managing the implementation of strategic change initiatives as to the annual identification of new issues and the formulation of new change initiatives.

A nonprofit organization that seriously applies this kind of strategic management process basically produces and manages what we might think of as a kind of *change portfolio*. At any given time, the portfolio consists of the strategic change initiatives—the change projects—that are being implemented. The portfolio is kept separate from day-to-day program operations being managed by established organizational units, ensuring in this way that the planned changes or initiatives are not overwhelmed by the inexorable demands of daily operations.

The concept is simple. But although it is modest, it is beautiful because it works. For example, let's look at a local library system that at its annual retreat selected three issues to tackle, above and beyond the management of ongoing operations, from a list of fifteen originally identified. The three issues are: declining usage in a neighborhood that is experiencing rapid demographic change; an outmoded card catalogue that is not linked with the countywide computer system; and a growing community demand for censorship, which violates one of the library's strongest values—open accessibility. Task forces in each of these three areas have fashioned detailed change initiatives, which have been adopted and budgeted and that are being implemented—above and beyond the mainline operational budget. The initiatives are being carried out with the guidance of the board's planning committee and the management team, who are meeting once a month as a change steering committee. Our library is actually implementing changes that are important but practical, that are tied to its long-term vision but are not wishful thinking, and that are affordable in time, money, and other resources. This is the kind of serious change that is the stuff of strategic management.

Strategic Management by Design

Chapter Seven describes in detail each of the major components of the strategic management process: fashioning and updating the strategic framework; scanning the external environment; assessing organizational resources; identifying and selecting strategic issues; and fashioning strategic change initiatives. Finally, the initiatives are implemented. Figure 6.3 summarizes these steps.

These steps are intended as part of a broader logic; they do not represent a step-by-step recipe to be followed slavishly. There is no

Figure 6.3. The Strategic Management Flow.

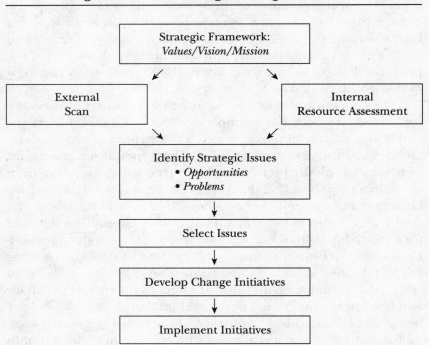

such thing as *the* strategic management process for all places and seasons; there is only the particular application that fits a particular organization. The wide variations among nonprofits in terms of circumstances and capabilities make an all-purpose application impracticable.

The most effective strategic management applications with which I am familiar have been guided by a detailed design that ties together strategic management, operational planning, and budget preparation in the framework of an annual planning cycle. The planning design ensures that a nonprofit achieves what it wants from the planning process, when it wants it, and at a cost that it can handle. It guards against the danger of carrying out mere rituals that do not produce serious outcomes and of having breakdowns midstream in the process. The key elements of the planning design are the detailed *planning of objectives or outcomes, the parameters of the process, a schedule of planning events,* and *the resources required to carry out the process.*

The process of fashioning a planning design is very important because it can build understanding, commitment, and ownership of the process among key planning participants, including the board and management team members. Therefore, a participatory approach makes good sense. For example, a nonprofit's board planning committee, the chief executive, and key staff might in a half-day session fashion the planning outcomes and parameters and a general schedule, after which the management team might flesh out the rest of the process for eventual review and approval by the committee and adoption by the full board. Because serious planning always costs something—lots of time if not money—participating in developing the design is a way to understand and agree to the costs.

Planning Outcomes

Even though some of the discoveries made during an intensive outcomes definition session may seem obvious, specifying outcomes is the most effective way I have found to build in-depth understanding of the planning process and to make sure that the eventual planning steps make sense. Outcomes can be thought of as the products, benefits, and impacts of going through the planning motions and they can be direct or indirect. A direct outcome can usually be documented—a values, vision, or mission statement, a change initiative, or a departmental object-of-expenditure budget, for example. An indirect outcome is a kind of process spinoff, such as widespread understanding of the purposes of the nonprofit among board and staff members, for example, or enhanced morale.

Direct outcomes determine the content and the format of planning documentation. Should an updated vision statement be part of the strategic management phase of the planning cycle? If so, a vision statement must be defined in terms of its content and format before the process to produce it can be designed. If the concept of a vision is left vague, how can the steps that must be taken to produce it be determined?

Process spinoffs can greatly influence how planning participants go about producing a direct outcome. For example, let's say a nonprofit wants an updated vision statement and in the process of developing it wants to build ownership of, and commitment to, that statement among board and management team members. Given this process outcome, it would be a mistake for a chief executive to draft a vision statement and send it to the board for review and adoption; rather, the nonprofit will want a planning design that involves board members actively in producing the vision statement. This may mean incorporating a retreat early in the planning process to facilitate intensive board participation in shaping key planning products, thereby enhancing ownership and commitment. The process might provide for a board committee or staff task forces to refine planning products that are generated in a front-end retreat.

Here's another example of a process outcome. A nonprofit might want the planning process to produce wider public understanding and support for its vision, mission, and programs. One design solution would be to invite key community stakeholders (organizations with a stake in the nonprofit's work) to participate in the two-day strategic work session that kicks off the annual planning cycle. Another solution might be to ensure that the planning process produces an attractive, brief executive summary document that can be mailed to community stakeholders.

A nonprofit education and training organization with which I worked determined that one of the key outcomes of its strategic management cycle would be significant curricular innovations.

After deciding that the environment had been so hostile to innovation in the past that special incentives would be required to elicit the kind of creative thinking they wanted, the design team came up with the idea of a competitive grants process to be supported by a special innovation fund of $50,000. Without sustained attention in the beginning to the meaning of innovation in curriculum, they would likely not have arrived at this dramatic process solution that was ultimately adopted.

Planning Parameters

The planning parameters provide rules and limits that must be taken into account in designing the planning process; basically, they tell participants what they cannot do. For example, an organization might establish the rule that every change initiative generated by a task force as part of the strategic management process must specify a source of funding other than the general fund and include a detailed strategy for tapping that source. In the operational planning and budget preparation phase, a rule might be that any new expenditures must be funded by reductions in existing budgeted expenditures.

Another kind of parameter is what Professor Nathan Grundstein (1992) calls a "growth rule." A growth rule establishes directions and boundaries for proposed new programs and activities and expansion of current programs. Examples of growth rules that organizations have created are: growth must be in areas where the likelihood of continued growth in both activity and revenue is very likely; growth must make our organization more competitive by strengthening our technical expertise or building our reputation and credibility in high-growth areas; growth that leads only to short-term revenue increases should be avoided; growth that will entail significant low-level administrative processing that is not clearly justified by the benefits generated should be avoided; growth that erodes our position in our basic business should be avoided. As the result of such a growth rule, one nonprofit I know refused to accept grants to do low-level skills training because doing so was seen as technically unchallenging and, hence, not a capacity builder, as a reputation degrader, and as a voracious consumer of administrative time in reporting to the funding agency.

Planning Steps and Resource Requirements

This facet of the design spells out in detail all of the work that must be done to produce the planning outcomes that have been determined, within the parameters that have been established. Does the process begin with an intensive strategic work session or a retreat in order to update values, vision, and mission and to identify strategic issues facing the nonprofit? If so, when will the retreat be held? Who will attend it? How long will it last? What will be on the agenda? How will it be facilitated? What kind of preparation will be done? Will there be a follow-up report? What will the contents and format be? Who will receive it?

This piece of the planning design should not only spell out the process in detail but also make accountability clear. For example, if a trends/conditions report is to be prepared for the retreat, who will be responsible for putting it together? The planning director? A task force of board and staff members?

The time and money needed to carry out the planning process should also be spelled out in detail in the design so that no one is caught by surprise as the process moves forward. This is also a good time to think through the skills that will be needed to participate actively in the process and, in the event of apparent deficiencies, to build in the required education and training. Let's say, for example, that the staff task forces that are expected to produce change initiatives as part of the strategic management process will be required to do some brainstorming early in their work. If many participants are not familiar with the brainstorming process, then the design must build in some orientation and training, which means that accountability for preparing and delivering training materials must be specified and perhaps even money for training consultants allocated.

The Strategic Management/Operational Planning Nexus

Operational planning/budget preparation and strategic management are now widely seen as parallel processes that serve different purposes. They must be kept separate, and strategic change is no longer seen as the long-range extension of departmental operational planning. However, the two processes are, in my experience, most effective when they intersect at the beginning and end of the planning cycle, as shown in Figure 6.4.

Every program and every major operating unit should take into account its organization's strategic framework in updating its operational plans/budget, explicitly responding to the updated organizational values, vision, and mission in its operational planning. Nothing prevents board members from asking how unit heads have addressed the evolving strategic framework during the annual operational planning retreat.

In addition, strategy formulation task forces formed to address strategic issues that are identified and selected in the annual strategic planning session can report their recommendations at the annual operational session, at which time the costs of implementing the strategies can be addressed.

Innovation Through Operational Planning

Chapter Seven describes in detail how strategic management can be a powerful source of innovation, so a word on the innovative potential of operational planning will be useful here. The annual operational plan and budget is often called a nonprofit's preeminent policy statement. Although this may overstate the case, there

Figure 6.4. Making the Strategy-Budget Connection.

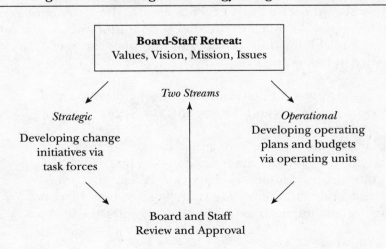

is no question that the familiar line-item, object-of-expenditure budget does its cost control job quite effectively, with little muss or fuss. Budgets, unlike strategies, are routinely produced year after year, and they are actually used to manage associations. Again, this cockroach of planning tools is the hardiest of survivors, going about its business with few admirers, generating little excitement, and being generally impervious to fancy reform efforts, from once-popular zero-based budgeting to currently ballyhooed quality management approaches.

By its very nature a conservative and control-oriented process, budget preparation typically involves making incremental adjustments in current program activities and expenditure plans to ensure that a nonprofit's revenues and expenditures remain in balance throughout the fiscal year. And the process of producing the annual budget is typically an administrative concern, involving nonprofit boards at the tail-end, when about all they can do is sift through an incredible amount of detail, asking relatively minor questions.

However, without losing the cost-control benefits that financial budgeting confers on a nonprofit, the process can be designed to serve as more of an innovation tool, if only a pale shadow of strategic management in this regard. One way that I have seen work in practice is to have an intensive one-day board-staff operational planning session that precedes the financial budget preparation and follows the strategic work session by four or five months. In preparing for such a session, department or program heads may be asked to consider serious innovations that can be accomplished within the operational plan/budget. Typical items are the following:

- An updated mission statement (regarding products and services, customers and clients, operating functions) for a unit or a program
- An organizational structure and current revenue and expenditure budget for a unit or a program
- Significant environmental changes pertinent to a unit's mission and plans, including changing needs and technologies and the implications of those changes for the unit

- Planned outcomes or accomplishments for the coming year in addition to routine functions, such as innovations in administration and service delivery that are tied explicitly to the organizations strategic framework, as updated at the annual strategic work session at the beginning of the nonprofit's planning cycle
- Any policy-level issues affecting program implementation that appear to merit board attention, including anticipated expenditures that will appear in the ultimate recommended expenditure budget if the board agrees
- An implementation plan consisting of key milestones that will serve as performance indicators for board monitoring purposes

In Summary

Starting with a description of the strong operational bias of planning as it has commonly been carried out, this chapter looked at the inadequacies of traditional strategic long-range planning as an innovation tool. Its uselessness is primarily the result of an arbitrary, unrealistic time frame; a bottom-up, cumulative approach; and organization by existing departments or programs.

A relatively recent variation on the broad strategic planning theme that has proven productive as an innovation tool—strategic management—was shown to be different from traditional planning because it pays serious attention to values, vision, and mission; selects specific strategic issues to work on; develops change initiatives to address the issues; commits to actual change that does not have to be earthshaking; employs intensive group process; and focuses on implementation.

This chapter also described how a nonprofit can go about developing its own strategic management process design and in the process build understanding, ownership, and commitment among design participants. The main job of the design process is to match the planning process with the desired direct and indirect planning outcomes. Also important is spelling out the parameters that will constrain the planning process. Finally, the chapter suggested ways to take advantage of the innovative potential of annual operational planning and budget preparation.

Applying Strategic Management to Produce Change

Coming Attractions

Chapter Seven details the steps in the strategic management process:

- Crafting a strategic framework
- Scanning the external environment and analyzing stakeholder relationships
- Assessing organizational resources
- Identifying and selecting strategic issues
- Fashioning change initiatives to address the selected issues

Building the Strategic Change Portfolio

The preeminent intended outcome that makes going through the time-consuming and sometimes painful steps required by the strategic management process is, of course, implementation of the change initiatives. The initiatives, which basically are the projects in a nonprofit's change portfolio, aim to address opportunities to move toward, or problems blocking progress toward, a nonprofit's vision.

Far-reaching change is not always necessary, of course, and frequently a nonprofit's change portfolio consists of relatively undramatic yet important and high-stakes initiatives, such as upgrading board leadership, installing a new financial management system, going after a new revenue source, or building a relationship with an important stakeholder. However, the times can call for change of greater breadth and depth; sometimes it involves the very character of the nonprofit. For example, as this is being written, a nonprofit medical insurer and HMO decided to sell the bulk of its assets to a for-profit hospital and managed care corporation, thereby forming a vertically integrated powerhouse (insurance, managed care, provision of medical services) that would be more competitive in today's complex health care market. Clearly, the board, chief executive, and management team had decided that if it made only an incremental change in the current health care environment it would miss a major opportunity and condemn the organization to decline or eventual extinction.

Before going on to discuss each step in the strategic management process, I want to note that the first four steps—from creating the strategic framework through identifying and selecting the issues—lend themselves to intensive board and staff involvement in a retreat setting. Although considerable staff follow-through planning is inevitably required subsequent to such a retreat, creative, intensive board and staff interaction in producing at least the initial cut of the strategic framework, the external scan, the resource assessment, and strategic issue identification is a powerful way to tap board and staff wisdom and to foster the understanding and feelings of ownership that are essential for eventual implementation.

Creating the Strategic Framework

A nonprofit organization's strategic framework consists of its core values, its vision for the future, and its mission. The framework is always the starting point for the strategic management process. It provides boundaries for organizational behavior, fundamental organizational aspirations and directions, and a clear definition of the nonprofit's basic business. The strategic framework also helps define the gap between aspirations and reality within which strategic issues may be found and change initiatives do their work. The strategic framework gives the strategic management process direction and purpose: if it is not taken into account, strategic management can easily become more random than rational, just as likely to cause harm as benefit.

Values

Values are the principles that guide a nonprofit's planning and operations. They finish the sentences, "We believe in . . . or "We believe that. . . ." They provide an ethical framework for the non-profit, pointing it toward certain kinds of activities and away from others. For example, a large national conservation association identified a number of core values at a board-staff retreat: pre-serving the nation's parks and cultural heritage for future genera-tions; performing work of such high quality and integrity that it elicits respect and support from the public, the National Park Ser-vice, and Congress; being nonpartisan and objective; and offering prudent stewardship of the resources entrusted to it.

A local nonprofit theater company with which I worked named the following among its core values: maintaining high artistic qual-ity; being a familial company that serves developing artists; behav-ing with professionalism; offering variety in theatrical experiences; being involved in the community; viewing the theater as an intel-lectual force that pushes the limits and develops the art form; pro-viding a platform for new voices; encouraging growing involvement of young people in theater; examining social issues; questioning the status quo.

The nonprofit foundation arm of one of the nation's largest and most successful public hospitals identified its core values as providing access to high quality health care for all local residents; acknowledging the responsibility of citizens to contribute time and money to their community; and fostering charitable instincts and feelings among the general public.

Values may seem pie-in-the-sky or so obvious that they go with-out saying. But the fact is, they never go without saying. For one thing, values inevitably evolve over time, responding to cultural and social change and to the changing cast of key characters, that is, the board and chief executive, employees, clients and customers, regulators, funders, and others. If values are not regularly rethought and restated, a nonprofit can lose touch with key con-stituencies.

Another reason for periodically restating organizational values is to surface potential conflicts that if left unstated are unlikely to be reconciled, resulting in organizational tension at best and disruption at worst. Experience has taught me that strategic issues often emerge during the values identification process and that one of the preeminent tasks of the strategic management process is to reconcile conflicting values in the interest of organizational effectiveness. I recently helped a highly regarded nonprofit nursing home make its core values explicit. The assembled board and staff members along with some key stakeholders identified sensitivity to resident needs and desires, a commitment to resident self-determination in all things related to their lives at the home, and a feeling of the fundamental sacredness of life to be among its core values. In today's world, where technology can keep people technically alive well after any possibility of enjoying life has ended and where assisted suicide is becoming more common, adherence to these values demanded creative reconciliation that could not be accomplished without making them explicit.

Similarly, the board and staff of the nonprofit theater company mentioned earlier had to figure out how to reconcile the value they put on wide community access with their commitment to innovation. In practice, they found that their avant-garde programming was hindering development of a wider audience and hence a stronger revenue base. This kind of fundamental conflict cannot be resolved scientifically; well-meaning people sitting around the same table must spend time figuring out how to strike the right balance: how to maintain an innovative focus without becoming fatally elite, how to expand the audience without stooping to another production of *Hello, Dolly*.

A nonprofit community development corporation that I worked with several years ago made good use of the values reconciliation process in a two-day board-staff strategic work session. The corporation's primary program was to make loans for housing rehabilitation from a substantial revolving loan fund. There was a pressing need for this service in a community that was experiencing rapid growth in single-parent, often single-mother, families and, as a result, was characterized by falling incomes and a deteriorating housing stock.

The break-out group focusing on values in the work session identified two of the core values: getting the money out into the community as fast as possible with as few strings as possible, and ensuring timely and full repayment of loans to maintain a healthy revolving fund. Discussion of the inherent tension between these two values led to a very practical reconciliation: a change project to expedite loan applications while also building stricter enforcement of repayment provisions.

Thus far, the examples have focused on the interface of nonprofits with their environment. However, values can also relate to an organization's internal culture. For example, a chamber of commerce board and staff envisioned the organization as one that offers to its employees and volunteer participants opportunities to use their talent, wisdom, skill, and experience; opportunities to make an impact on important community issues; a learning experience that was both rich and fun; a broad network of colleagues; and a small-town feel combined with sophisticated planning and management. A local agency dealing with the prevention of domestic violence envisioned an internal environment characterized by human development and growth; self-actualization and high self-esteem; empowerment of the individual; open, candid communication; and a consensus approach to decision making.

How can a nonprofit breathe life into its values statement, making it a practical tool for organizational renewal and change rather than a nicely framed but largely forgotten pronouncement that hangs on the wall? Nonprofits put the values component of their strategic framework to good use by taking two relatively simple steps. First, they keep the values alive by revisiting them every year during their annual strategic work sessions, forcing attention on evolving values and potential conflicts calling for creative resolution. Second, they consciously and systematically employ the values statement in assessing strategic change initiatives, making sure that the initiatives promote organizational values and in no major way contradict them. One nonprofit I know actually prints the values on a banner that hangs on the wall during all strategy review sessions, vividly reminding everyone involved that there is a higher law governing all that they do.

Vision

A nonprofit's vision is a picture of the desired future that can be painted in two basic ways: *the impact* the nonprofit ultimately wants to have on its environment (including the role that it aims to play in its environment) and *the image* that the nonprofit wants to build among its key constituencies. Before examining each of these facets of an organizational vision, I want to distinguish between two important needs that an organizational vision statement can serve: public relations and internal inspiration, on the one hand, and serious strategic management, on the other. A succinct, attractively phrased vision statement of a paragraph or two makes sense to inform the public and to build internal unity. But to be a tool for guiding strategy, a nonprofit's vision needs to be stated in a more fully developed way. In the typical board-staff strategic work session, a fully developed vision statement may run three or four pages or more.

A nonprofit organization's impact vision will describe its long-term future in terms of the major impacts it intends to produce. The statement will complete the sentence, "As a result of our efforts. . . ." For example, a religiously affiliated international relief organization with which I worked envisioned among its long-term impacts the alleviation of human suffering; the development of a model for responsible giving; personal spiritual growth; and growth in financial giving and volunteerism. A nonprofit consortium whose mission was to link high school and postsecondary institutions through technical education programs envisioned as key long-term impacts: increased placement of students in permanent jobs that fully utilize their talents and skills; increased institutional cooperation in ensuring a smooth school-to-work transition; regional economic development; and changing teaching methods and attitudes. A national association dedicated to the more effective treatment of anxiety disorders envisioned that as a result of its efforts there would be wider understanding of anxiety disorders and recognition of their seriousness; universal access to effective and affordable treatment; a dramatic increase in biological, psychological, and social research on anxiety disorders; public policy toward anxiety disorders that would promote full parity in medical insurance coverage and nondiscrimination in employment; better prevention and early intervention; an increase in the number of minority professionals in the anxiety disorders field; and reduction or elimination of misdiagnosis and mistreatment.

The organization that focused on the prevention of domestic violence envisioned as its fundamental impacts: the environment

will be significantly freer of abuse; there will be wide public understanding of the abuse issue; the public will widely support abuse
victims and the need for transitional housing; women will recognize that they can choose not to endure abuse and be able to exercise this choice; potential and actual abusers will recognize that
there are alternatives to abuse and will choose them more frequently; and school systems will increasingly offer programs dealing with abuse.

A nonprofit can also envision its impact in terms of the role it
aspires to play. For example, a local nonprofit job training and
placement board saw its role as: providing strong leadership in the
design—and the management—of the local employment and
training system; being the single most important employment and
training resource to local elected officials in planning and program development and in support of economic development
strategies; and being an organization that aggressively leads in
identifying and addressing communitywide employment and training issues. A national consortium dealing with the application of
computer technology in the insurance industry sought to play the
following roles: an objective intermediary organization that
reduces costs for companies and agencies and ultimately for the
consumer; a strong advocate for the independent agency system;
a place to go for information and assistance related to the application of new technologies; and a leader in developing innovative
technology applications.

A nonprofit can also fashion an image vision, describing how
it ultimately wants to be seen by key audiences in the world around
it. The image vision serves two primary purposes. First, it identifies
the public perceptions that appear most critical to realizing its
impact vision, and second, it serves as the primary means for directing and evaluating investments in image building and public relations strategies. By making explicit how it desires to be seen by the
wider world, a nonprofit is in a far better position to measure the
effectiveness of its image building and public relations strategies.

An image vision is based on two key assumptions. The first is
that an organization's image among key constituencies is likely to
have a strong influence on its ability to carry out its strategies. The
second is that good works seldom speak for themselves: just

because an organization is actually doing a good job does not guarantee that all, or even any, of its key audiences will be aware of its effectiveness.

It is not uncommon for nonprofits to engage unwittingly in behavior that tarnishes their image because they have not formally developed an image vision. For example, I worked with one local nonprofit planning board during a retreat to develop an image vision that included being seen by the public as warm, welcoming, and easy to work with. Later, we examined how the board's formal public meetings and hearings were conducted; it turned out that board members were seated on a platform above the public audience while people presenting testimony had to stand at a lectern. The whole group broke into laughter as they realized how actual practice contradicted the image they wished to build. At the very next meeting of the planning board, the platform was gone, and members of the public presented their testimony while seated with board members at tables arranged in a horseshoe fashion. Without thinking explicitly about the image they wished to create, it would have been much harder for this board to identify this kind of counterproductive behavior, much less to fashion image-building initiatives.

Some elements of an image vision can be pretty generic, but they still need to be included if they are meant to guide organizational planning; others will be more tailored to a particular organization's mission. For example, a women's civic association with which I worked envisioned being seen as an innovative and cutting-edge but warm and welcoming group; *the* club to join to have an impact, develop skills, find role models, have fun; movers and shakers in the community; a club for all seasons of life; a groomer of leaders; a stimulating environment; an active partner with business and government in fostering community development; a focused and purposeful group; a catalyst for creative change; and a prestigious but affordable group.

A local nonprofit health planning agency's board and staff wanted their organization to be seen as a powerful local resource in addressing community health issues; a voluntary leadership forum with substantial clout; a rich source of information on local health issues; an effective entity for containing health care costs, strengthening quality, and expanding access; a group that was sensitive and responsive to consumer needs; a think tank that was proactive, creative, and innovative.

The image vision that a local religiously affiliated women's organization developed included the following characteristics: a progressive, innovative Jewish women's organization that was committed to social action; a strong advocate for family, children, senior citizens, and people with disabilities; a sophisticated, well-managed, financially sound, and fiscally responsible nonprofit organization; an organization that put endowments, bequests, and donations to productive use in serving community needs.

As with values statements, visions can easily become mere rhetoric enshrined in rarely read planning tomes collecting dust on shelves. But many nonprofits infuse their impact and image visions with meaning by ensuring them a powerful role in the strategic management process. They identify strategic issues by examining the gap between their vision and their actual situation, asking if they should do something new to narrow the gap. The vision also comes into play when a nonprofit assesses possible strategic change initiatives, asking explicitly how each proposed initiative would contribute to the realization of a part of the vision.

Of course, no vision statement should be cast in bronze. Like values, visions evolve. Economic, political, social, demographic, technological, and cultural changes bring with them new challenges and opportunities. New client and customer needs and demands emerge; traditional markets occasionally disappear. Furthermore, circumstances can force an organization to move beyond its traditional boundaries with only scant forethought and planning, and so an expanded vision emerges after the fact. Two prime examples in American history are the Civil War, which resulted in the dramatic expansion of the vision of chief executive leadership, and the Great Depression, which resulted in a proactive vision of the federal government's intended impact that was little challenged for some fifty years.

Mission

A nonprofit's mission statement is usually a brief paragraph that describes its basic reason for being in terms of the broad purposes it serves. Basically just an elaborated slogan, such a mission statement can serve as a rallying point for board and staff and as a public relations device, but not as a serious planning tool. In my experience, organizations that go beyond broad purposes to treat mission as a thorough description of the business they are currently in—that is, their products and services, customers and clients, and production or delivery technologies—have a far more useful tool at their command. As with the vision, it is essential to distinguish between the detailed internal version, which is intended to make a serious contribution to the strategic management process, and the external version, which is intended to educate and attract public support.

Whereas the vision is intended to be aspirational, inspirational, and expansionary, tending to push a nonprofit into new areas of activity, the mission says clearly what the organization currently is and is not, establishes boundaries for organizational activity, and guards against the tendency to chase opportunities or diversify thoughtlessly. As an organization's vision expands, opportunities to innovate and diversify can arise that put pressure on the mission, and this might force the organization to raise questions, think second thoughts, and calculate the cost of changing the boundaries.

For example, a national association of health product distributors went through the process of linking products and services to two key customers in order to understand its mission for internal planning purposes. The products and services linked to the distributor community, for example, included education and training, information on the changing environment, research, lobbying, the annual trade show and executive education conference, technical assistance publications, and hands-on technical assistance.

A local nonprofit board responsible for overseeing the expenditure of job training monies identified its primary clients as the disadvantaged, the unemployed, welfare recipients, displaced workers, the homeless, the disabled, youth in school and dropouts, adult dropouts, members of families receiving public assistance, parenting youth, food stamp recipients, business and employers, local governments, public secondary and postsecondary educational institutions, and proprietary schools. This list includes two very different customer types: the people receiving services without directly paying—typically called clients in the nonprofit world—and the customers who pay for the services, such as governments and other funding agencies.

This job training board identified the following among its major services and products: job skills and readiness training; needs and interest assessment; referral to education, training, and alternate services; a clearinghouse service; referral to jobs; and customized training for business. The agency provided some services directly but for the most part contracted with other agencies for service delivery.

As part of the mission formulation or updating process, it makes sense to add the identification of the organizational capabilities that appear most essential to carrying out the mission successfully, thereby providing a framework for the analysis of organizational resources later in the strategic management process. For example, the theater company mentioned earlier identified these core competencies: a board that provides strong leadership; a strong managing director who delegates effectively to staff and volunteers; capable directors, actors, and technicians; an adequate facility; adequate equipment; strong plays that attract the audience we want; capable, aggressive marketing; internal management that promotes efficient operations; capable financial planning and management; internal teamwork; and effective internal communication.

Scanning the External Environment

Environmental scanning is basically the process of identifying external conditions and trends that are pertinent to a nonprofit organization's vision and mission, collecting information about those conditions and trends, and analyzing the information to determine its implications. This is not an academic research exercise because such analysis is the richest source of the change challenges—the opportunities, threats, barriers, and problems—that lead to planned organizational change.

A nonprofit organization that is committed to becoming intelligent about the world around it must face two tough problems as it begins its quest: first, the complex world around an organization defies easy understanding and, second, the human mind that sees and interprets it is mysterious, largely unexplored terrain. Leaders and managers with experience in this search have learned a valuable lesson: to look is not necessarily to see and to see is not necessarily to understand. Intelligence gathering and analysis are processes that are anything but simple. The quest is basically a matter of seeing the right phenomena and coming to understand them, but neither objective is easily achieved. The quest involves more art than science; it relies more on human psychology than on technology. Anyone embarking on the journey should understand that delusion and self-deception are always a clear and present danger.

What is the right information to look for in the complex world around us? First and foremost, nonprofits want to see and understand phenomena that are pertinent to their vision, current mission, and existing strategies. They need to look primarily for developments that either offer opportunities—to move toward their vision, to expand or diversity their programming within their mission—or that threaten them in one way. For example, as this is being written, the deep cuts that are almost certain to be made in the National Endowment for the Arts, and perhaps the total elimination of the program, are obviously pertinent to a symphony orchestra like the one we learned about in Chapter Two, as are the changing demographics of the symphony's hometown. Federal legislation aimed at restructuring the labyrinth of funding streams and bureaucracies that make up the national employment and training system obviously merits the close attention of the job training boards discussed earlier in this chapter, as do the local unemployment rate and changes in the local business mix.

In addition to looking for relevance among the trends on the horizon, a nonprofit also should be concerned with their potential impact, urgency, predictability, durability, or permeability. In other words, what is the potential extent of the benefit or the harm promised by an external development, and how soon will the impact be felt? Is the situation part of a trend that is likely to last for some time or is it likely that "this too shall pass?" Is the condition or trend something the nonprofit itself or in league with others might influence? If so, to what extent and how quickly?

Let's take, for example, the women's civic association we met in Chapter Five. The trends toward increasing numbers of women in the workforce and two-career families are obviously very relevant, can be expected to have a tremendous impact on the association, are not immediately urgent, are unlikely to be influenced by any association activity, and are probably permanent. The association would want to shape its own response accordingly, taking the time to think through ways to adapt to a critical but not urgent situation that cannot be influenced to any great extent.

The executive director of the family services agency introduced in Chapter Two has received a signal from his environment in the form of his planning committee's refusal to approve his recommended annual plan and budget, a radical departure from past practice. This occurrence ranks high on the scale of potential impact and urgency and so merits a swift response to avert further erosion of the chief executive–board working relationship. If he looks beyond the immediate event—his rejected budget—in order to understand it more fully, he will find a broader national trend of nonprofit boards demanding to play more assertive, proactive, and meaningful roles in organizational affairs and rejecting the role of passive or worshipful audience for virtuoso chief executives.

Humility is a virtue when making judgments about external phenomena; professional graveyards are filled with once-confident forecasters who deserved to pass from the scene. The fact is, we know little with certainty about much of the world around us and so hedging organizational bets sometimes makes the best sense. We can say that an economic restructuring is well under way as we move toward Drucker's knowledge-based economy, and we can assume that it will probably continue and be durable, but we can say little about the precise details of this dramatic transformation. Where politics and political philosophy are concerned, one cannot bet on stability or project trends far in the future. The American public appears quite fickle these days. What with their volatile moods, who knows what the future holds even a year from now?

So much for the complex world. What about the human mind part of the world-mind interaction? We all know from experience that if it were not for those pesky people, the job of building organizational intelligence would be far easier and much less frustrating. If only machines could do the job! Unfortunately, they never could and never will. When it gears up its people—both board and staff members—to play a productive role in gaining intelligence about the external world, a nonprofit organization must recognize two things from the start. First, people can learn to see and to know more accurately; the skill is teachable, and practice makes better if not perfect. Second, with each human mind that is brought to the task comes a hidden mindset or filter that has a powerful impact on what that mind perceives and knows, as discussed in greater detail in Chapter Five.

Analyzing Stakeholder Relationships

A critical component of environmental scanning that is often overlooked is what I call *stakeholder analysis*. An environment consists not only of economic, demographic, social, and political trends but also of the individuals, groups, organizations, and institutions responsible for those trends. The people with whom it makes sense to build and maintain a relationship because something important is at stake are the nonprofit's stakeholders.

A nonprofit's stakeholders can be the source of change challenges to which it must consider responding. For example, a stakeholder might provide an opportunity by offering financial support or collaboration, might threaten a nonprofit's security through aggressive competition for clients, or might present a barrier to a nonprofit's expansion by rallying opposition.

In addition to serving as a source of strategic issues, stakeholders also play a role later in the strategic management process, when change initiatives are being fashioned. Building a partnership with a key stakeholder may turn out to be a critical part of implementing an initiative. Or a strategy to overcome anticipated stakeholder resistance may be incorporated into an initiative. Stakeholders are gaining importance in a world in which it is increasingly difficult, and often dangerous, for a nonprofit to attempt to go it alone, so paying attention to stakeholders is a serious matter.

It is important for a nonprofit to identify important stakeholders, assess the stakes involved, and to understand the nature of the current relationship with them. Is it close? Distant? Collaborative? Competitive? Hostile? The chamber of commerce board and staff mentioned earlier identified as key stakeholders its members, the regional economic development authority, the city and county government, a historic preservation foundation, and the local board of education, among others. Then the group responsible for stakeholder analysis at their two-day retreat did what I call a quid pro quo analysis of each stakeholder relationship. For example, regarding its relationship with the county government, the chamber wanted a user-friendly government, consolidation of services, and support for a new international trade center. The county wanted information, political support, facilitation, lobbying, support for a city five-hundred auto race. The group determined that the relationship needed work but was improving. Regarding its relationship with the development authority, the chamber wanted an active partnership in local business development efforts. The authority wanted the chamber to provide information, make efforts to improve the business climate, prospect referrals, issue analysis, and action. The relationship was determined to be generally cooperative but also in need of some work, especially in clarifying and integrating roles and objectives.

Every nonprofit organization I have worked with has been amazed at the number of important—that is, high-stakes—relationships to be managed and the lack of time available to devote to the task. As discussed in Chapter Four, one solution is to involve board members in stakeholder relationship management by setting up a standing board committee on external relations. Another is to assign members of a nonprofit's management team to monitor relations with particular stakeholders. A nonsolution is what is known as the squeaky wheel approach—waiting for a problem to develop and then taking action to repair the relationship. More often than not, once the wheel squeaks loudly enough to be heard, permanent damage has been done.

Assessing Organizational Resources

A hardheaded, clear understanding of a nonprofit's resources—including its board, chief executive, staff, finances, political influence, management systems, program performance—is an important source of strategic issues or change challenges that may need to be addressed through the formulation of change initiatives. For example, many nonprofits I have worked with have determined that their board leadership is so deficient that it is a significant deterrent to growth and, therefore, it makes the top list of change challenges to be tackled right away. One community development corporation selected as one of its highest priority issues a financial management system that was so inadequate that funding sources were threatening to cut off funds.

Resource assessment also provides an essential knowledge base for the eventual selection of strategic issues and the formulation of change initiatives. For example, a nonprofit nursing home I am working with is considering expanding along the continuum of care by moving into adult day care and assisted-living services. Its resource analysis at a recent board-staff strategic work session indicated that the core nursing home operations were efficient and effective and provided a solid foundation for expansion, but that the group needed to raise significant funds to fuel any expansion. The group also determined that the board, while dedicated and hardworking, needed to be strengthened significantly before embarking on any expansion. Specifically, the board's membership was not diverse enough, and the board's structure and processes were inadequate to support the kind of creative, in-depth involvement that would take full advantage of the members' skills, experience, and knowledge.

Of course, nonprofits are always limited by the available resources, but this does not mean that they must be trapped. There is frequently a choice: either to live within a particular constraint or to beef up a resource in order to capitalize on an opportunity. For example, a nonprofit two-year educational institution identified as a major change challenge the opportunity to do customized training for local businesses with financial support from federal and state programs. However, it was immediately clear that a successful change initiative aimed at capitalizing on this business opportunity could not be undertaken by the traditional faculty, whose skills and attitudes did not measure up. Having the funds available, this institution hired nontraditional educators with experience in customized training and housed them in a new unit, free of traditional academic constraints. This story has a happy ending: the institution has become a major player in this competitive and lucrative business.

Identifying and Selecting Strategic Issues

The real power of the strategic management process comes from selecting a small number of strategic issues or change challenges—opportunities to move closer to the vision or to resolve problems and barriers hindering forward movement—and then quickly addressing them through change initiatives. Thus, the real test of a nonprofit's seriousness and capability in strategic management is in selecting the highest priority issues and focusing on them rather than becoming involved in shopping lists of wishes and goals. Once the right issues have been chosen, any nonprofit can do the detailed project planning required to produce change initiatives.

Strategic issues come in diverse shapes and sizes and can relate to a wide range of nonprofit activity. The following offers some examples:

• *Clients, customers, programs, and revenues.* There may be an opportunity to address changing client needs or provide a new service to a new customer. There may be a decline in a traditional revenue source, forcing the organization to search for new sources.

• *Image and external relations.* Perhaps the organization needs to build an image that more closely fits its evolving vision and to strengthen membership. Or perhaps work is needed to mend a frayed relationship with a key stakeholder whose support is essential to the implementation of an important new program.

• *Organizational leadership, planning, and management capabilities.* Perhaps the organization needs to upgrade a management system (financial management, for example) because its deficiencies threaten to weaken organizational performance and to consume too much executive time. Or perhaps an internal morale problem is eroding the quality of service delivery or weaknesses in governance are causing frustration and anger among board members.

When Are Issues Strategic?

How can a nonprofit's board, chief executive, and management team decide when an issue is really strategic, thus demanding special attention at a high level, or just operational, something that can be handled through the normal operational planning and management process? Although identifying strategic issues involves more subjective judgment than scientific logic, certain characteristics indicate that the issue is probably a strategic one:

- *It is high stakes.* A strategic issue demands attention because the cost of not dealing with it in the near future is likely to be high in either lost benefits or direct penalties or both. For example, failure to tackle a promising new funding opportunity may result in a fiscal crisis down the road; not responding in a timely fashion to changing member needs may lead to a serious membership decline. Even though the cost of dealing with the issue may not be paid for some years, action is needed now to avert it. This would certainly be the case for the symphony whose audience is greying.

- *It requires intensive attention.* An issue can be so complex and the need for action so pressing that it cannot be left to an organization's routine planning and management process or delegated to a staff person. For example, reaching out to youth and minorities as part of an initiative to build a new symphony audience would certainly not fit the business-as-usual category.

- *It is cross-cutting.* Very often, strategic issues do not fit into any existing organizational operating unit or program. Thus, they can easily fall through the cracks. A program being developed in response to client needs may have no organizational home and not fall into the bailiwick of any member of the management team. Such above-the-line matters as board capability building fall in this category, as often do new products and markets, like the nursing home that wished to move into assisted living.

For example, the health product distributors association discussed earlier in this chapter identified over the course of a one-and-a-half-day board–chief executive retreat a number of issues: a need to rethink the division of its member volunteers into certain market segments in order to respond to the rapid restructuring of the health care field; the need to fashion a clear strategy for its relatively small home health care business; the need to upgrade significantly public understanding of the association; and the opportunity to make the annual trade show a more successful event.

The chamber of commerce concluded over the course of a two-day strategic work session that its cumbersome governance process and structure were major barriers to future growth and that other pressing issues were the chamber's image in the community and the participation of small businesses in chamber affairs. The nonprofit nursing home identified as critical issues opportunities to expand into new areas such as home health care, hospice, an Alzheimer's unit, retirement housing, and assisted living; more effective management of the private pay–Medicaid ratio in the home; the opportunity to add a third home; and the need to create a financial resource development capability and to upgrade board leadership.

Selecting the strategic issues to be addressed during a nonprofit's current planning cycle is another step that lends itself to intensive board-staff deliberation, either as part of a retreat where the issues have been identified, or in a follow-up session for which additional staff analysis has been done to facilitate the selection process. Selection is an indispensable step because the overriding objective of the strategic management process is action and change *in the near term*. Thus, supermarket-style planning, with shopping lists of tantalizing possibilities, does not cut the mustard here. Unfortunately, no nonprofit, no matter how large in membership, staff, or budget, can handle every strategic issue it identifies while continuing to handle its day-to-day activities well.

While going through the selection process, it is important to remember that nonprofits differ greatly from a company like General Motors: they must be quite modest in launching change initiatives to address strategic issues. The challenge for the average nonprofit is to find some time, and perhaps a little money, to deal with two, three, or four serious issues at any given time while continuing to spend 98 percent of its resources on keeping the shop running. It stands to reason, then, that the average nonprofit must choose issues that it can realistically handle. Far from being earthshaking or grandiose, to be manageable the strategic issues must be *chewable bites* that will not overwhelm the nonprofit.

Narrowing the List

Narrowing a list of fifty tantalizing candidates for strategic issue status to four, five, or six chewable bites is more an art than a science. People must spend lots of time around the same table, asking and answering tough questions. Certainly the chief executive and management team are essential players in this selection process; board members can be profitably involved as well, either from the beginning or in a later stage of the selection process.

Logic and common sense can be brought to the selection task if certain key questions are asked, including the following:

- *What is our organization likely to pay in penalties if we do not deal with a particular issue this year?* Penalties typically take the form of direct damage (an eroding relationship, an alienated stakeholder, a budget cut) or a less direct consequence (such as missing a major new grant opportunity or not securing a new market).

- *Is our organization really capable of tackling a particular issue, either alone or in alliance with one or more stakeholders?* Perhaps stronger staff capability must be built or new revenues raised to address a particular issue. What are the odds that the organization can muster the resources that enable it to address the issue?

- *What risks are involved in tackling a particular issue?* Is it politically or technically complex enough to make risk a serious issue? Is it so controversial that by merely tackling it the organization might lose significant support among community supporters or clients? The board, chief executive, and management team may decide that there is no choice but to address certain issues because the penalties for failing to act are so severe. For example, if the group does not move into a new market, another organization surely will, and the opportunity will be lost, perhaps forever. An issue may even threaten a nonprofit's existence, like the nonprofit community development corporation that was threatened with the loss of its grant funding (which would have meant closing its doors within the year), because of its inadequate financial management capability. Upgrading financial management made its strategic issues list without a question.

However, such easy and dramatic decisions do not come an organization's way often. More common, the board, chief executive, and management team must do a balancing job, choosing a small number of issues that promise the greatest organizational benefits, ones assessed as affordable and manageable, and that involve the most favorable ratio of benefits to costs.

Fashioning Change Initiatives

A nonprofit ensures that it is taking action, that is, is actually doing something concrete to address the highest priority change challenges facing it, by building, updating, and managing a change portfolio that consists of what I call *change initiatives*. As already noted, change initiatives are basically action projects aimed at addressing selected strategic issues. Clarifying them is the culminating step in the strategic management process. Interestingly, a nonprofit has already surmounted the highest hurdle when it selects the right strategic issues to be addressed; therein lies the magic of strategic management. No matter how sophisticated the planning, if a nonprofit takes action on lower-priority issues while missing one or more of the biggies it can mean disruption, decline, or even extinction.

Fashioning change initiatives essentially means doing the detailed project planning that most nonprofits are familiar with and do quite well. This is not to say that such planning is a piece of cake. It can be quite demanding, depending on the complexity of the issues being addressed, but it is well within the capability of each of the hundreds of nonprofits with which I am familiar.

Change initiatives are best developed by staff task forces, groups that often involve key stakeholders and sometimes selected board members. The change initiatives should be reviewed in detail by a nonprofit's management team and the board or its planning committee, and eventually formally adopted by the board and—very important—budgeted for. Although the precise form and content of a change initiative will vary depending on the issue being addressed, a typical initiative consists of the following major elements:

- A description of the issues, that is, the needs, problems, or opportunities to be addressed
- The specific objectives to be achieved by the initiative
- The action plan that will achieve the targets, including a schedule of steps and events and assignment of implementation accountability
- The resources required to implement the initiative, including time, money, and political capital

- The sources of required financial support
- The anticipated barriers to implementation

Using All the Change Levers

Noel Tichy (1983) has examined the three paths along which organizational change travels: *the technical,* involving the rational allocation of social and technical resources to achieve stated objectives;
the political, involving the allocation of power; and *the cultural,*
involving the determination of values (that is, the normative glue).
Far from being mutually exclusive, these strands of the strategic
rope are intertwined and difficult to distinguish. Says Tichy,
"Although it is not clear from casual observation what is technical,
what is political, and what is cultural . . . the three strands are there
and they need to be understood and dealt with in order to understand the nature of the organization" (p. 10).

A realistic change initiative must take these three strands into
account in its implementation plan in order to avoid the kind of
myopia that can do change in. For example, let's say that a nonprofit nursing home has impaneled a task force to fashion a change
initiative to take advantage of the opportunity to create a joint venture with a for-profit hospital in home health care. In addition to
meticulously planning the technical and legal strategies, the task
force must take into account likely internal resistance based on a
perceived values conflict. The task force might recognize this problem in its implementation plan by building in several formal opportunities for staff dialogue that focuses on the values issue.

Task forces are effective mechanisms for developing change
initiatives if the task-force process is carefully designed. The
following guidelines are based on hundreds of real-life applications.

- *Task forces should draw staff from different program or functional
areas in the nonprofit.* Because strategic issues significantly affect the
whole organization and because they tend to cut across functions
and organizational divisions, task forces with diverse membership
are essential. An added benefit of such task forces is that they
enhance internal communication and build a stronger internal
culture.

- *They should involve key stakeholders.* Stakeholders can bring critical experience, expertise, and knowledge to the strategy formulation process. In addition, their involvement can strengthen their ties to the organization as well as build their commitment to the eventual implementation of task force recommendations.

- *They must be well led.* Choosing the right task force leaders will help to ensure that the work is accomplished in a complete and timely fashion. Task force leaders should have several important characteristics: a strong understanding of and commitment to the strategy formulation process; good planning and facilitation skills; an ability to relate well to peers; openness to new ideas; and the ability to pay meticulous attention to detail.

- *They must be given a clear, detailed charge.* Because strategic issues can be very different from one another, the strategies to address them can also differ significantly. For example, a task force that must develop a plan for a possible merger with another non-profit will be producing a very different product than one that must fashion a strategy to tap a new revenue source or develop a new product idea to address membership needs. If task forces are to hit the ground running and maintain momentum, they must be given clear, detailed guidance about the job they will perform. In other words, they must know the precise nature of their strategic product, the methodology they are to employ, and the deadlines they are to meet.

- *Constraints must be made clear to them.* It is critical to clarify the constraints under which a task force will work. For example, the board and chief executive might decide that the only acceptable strategy for new expenditures will be one that identifies a new funding source and includes a detailed plan for tapping it. Or they may decide that certain subjects will be off-limits, because of their political sensitivity, perhaps. Whatever the limitations may be, if they are stated at the onset, valuable time will be saved and needless emotion avoided.

- *Their work must be coordinated.* To ensure that the task force process moves forward as planned, it is important that a staff person be assigned to oversee and coordinate the process and that the board regularly reviews progress.

- *They must develop a detailed workplan.* After reviewing their charge at their first meeting, each task force should fashion a detailed workplan to meet its deadlines. The workplan should clearly identify and schedule the tasks to be accomplished and assign specific jobs to each member of the team.

Preparing for Task Force Participation

No matter how well structured the task force process is, its usefulness as a generator of change initiatives can be limited by the skills and predispositions that participants bring to the planning process. Technical skills, such as brainstorming to generate action possibilities or carrying out a cost-benefit analysis to evaluate courses of action, can fairly easily be taught. More challenging is dealing with the deep-seated approaches toward learning in organizations that Chris Argyris (1993) calls *theories in use.* Argyris's research, which my experience supports, indicates that the most popular theory in use is what he calls Model I. Model I "tells individuals to craft their positions, evaluations, and attributions in ways that inhibit inquiries into them and tests of them with others' logic. The consequences of these Model I strategies are likely to be defensiveness, misunderstanding, and self-fulfilling and self-sealing processes" (p. 52).

Ensuring that task force deliberations, and their learning, are characterized by openness and nondefensiveness in the search for solutions will be no small task, in light of the pervasiveness of the Model I theory in use. One practical step is to make task force members aware of the existence of both espoused theories and theories in use and of the two theories-in-use models. Another is to provide opportunities to practice spotting Model I approaches and applying a more open, less defensive approach.

It is also useful to build brainstorming formally into the task force process as a way of opening up the search and stimulating creativity, as Gareth Morgan's research has demonstrated (1988). Morgan documented the importance of "lateral thinking" in promoting creative process. In this regard ensuring cross-functional task force membership can be valuable. Merely ensuring that task force deliberations are not rushed is another way of promoting more open, less defensive deliberations.

The Wide Applicability of Strategic Logic

This chapter has focused on the application of the strategic management logic and methodology in nonprofit organizations. However, as Bryson (1995) has pointed out, strategic planning can be done by subunits of organizations, by consortiums of organizations, by whole communities. In my experience, and that of chief executives and managers with whom I have worked, strategic management can also be a powerful tool for individuals who wish to develop a fuller life and a more successful and fulfilling career.

For example, my decision some fifteen years ago to leave an executive position in higher education for what seemed at the time like the much less secure life of a consultant was the direct result of a confrontation between my expanding vision of what I could be professionally and my current situation as a manager; the conflict was causing so much creative tension that it could not be ignored. My external scan indicated that there was a growing market for consulting, especially in the areas of nonprofit governance and strategy. My internal resource assessment revealed some significant strengths for a consulting career, including an analytical mind, strong writing skills, and considerable self-discipline. However, a major barrier demanded attention: I had a near-pathological self-consciousness that made public speaking almost impossible for me. Thus, my vision drew me to work that demanded frequent public presentations and a powerful stage presence, but my fear of public speaking stood in the way. My decision was to make my fear a top-priority strategic issue, to fashion a change initiative to address it (including going through some psychological counseling and forcing myself to accept speaking engagements), and to implement that initiative on the way to a new professional life.

An Ever-Changing Change Portfolio

It stands to reason that the strategic change initiatives that make up a nonprofit organization's change portfolio will continuously change, as some initiatives are implemented and new initiatives are developed by task forces in response to the identification of new issues at the nonprofit's annual work session. Implemented change initiatives become part of a nonprofit's mainstream operations: board leadership has been upgraded; the assisted-living program has been launched; the high-tech skill training center has been built and is now fully functional; the symphony's community outreach program has been initiated.

But strategies, no matter how well crafted, do not implement themselves. So our attention must move from the planning process to the management of implementation, which is the subject of the following chapter.

In Summary

This chapter described the major phases or steps in the strategic management process: fashioning a strategic framework consisting of values, vision, and mission; scanning the external environment and analyzing stakeholder relationships; assessing organizational resources; identifying and selecting strategic issues; and fashioning change initiatives to address the issues.

Reconciliation of conflicting values is a key purpose of the strategic management process, and the essential differences between vision and mission were pinpointed. Special attention was paid to an important facet of environmental scanning: stakeholder analysis, which is often given short shrift.

Strategic issues tend to involve high stakes, demand intensive attention, and cut across established departments and programs. Selecting the ones to address in any given year is largely a matter of determining the cost of not addressing them and balancing that with the cost of dealing with them. Task forces are an effective vehicle for fashioning change initiatives if they draw their membership from different programs and functional areas, involve key stakeholders, are well led, receive a clear charge, understand the constraints, are monitored and coordinated, and operate according to a detailed workplan.

Implementing Change Initiatives

Coming Attractions

Chapter Eight offers detailed guidance in translating plans into action, focusing on three major issues:

- The icebergs that lie in wait for unwary organizations as they begin their change journey
- Five important ways in which a nonprofit chief executive can support the change process
- Three elements in addition to chief executive leadership that make for a successful change implementation strategy: a special structure and process dedicated to implementation; adequate resources; and strategies for dealing with human resistance

The chapter begins with a fictional example that once again draws on many real-life cases. This time, it's the story of Downtown Church.

Downtown Church: Embarking on the Change Journey

Defying the odds, Downtown Church is well along on its journey of self-generated, directed change. Four months ago, the senior and associate pastors, members of the management team, and several board members spent two days together at the district retreat center on Lake Erie, updating the church's values, vision, and mission, and identifying a number of strategic issues facing this rapidly growing, racially and economically diverse inner-city institution. The list of issues was subsequently winnowed down by an ad hoc committee whose members were selected during the retreat, and planning task forces produced six change initiatives.

Three of the initiatives concerned long-term capacity building: to reorganize Downtown Church's board into three broad governance committees, replacing several traditional administrative committees; to hire a chief operating officer to handle internal administrative functions, thereby freeing up the overextended senior pastor for pastoral and public relations duties; and to put the concept of a cohesive management team into practice. The other three related to programming and marketing: to launch a six-week lecture and discussion series on contemporary moral issues, drawing on prominent community figures as facilitators; to engage in an aggressive image building and marketing campaign aimed at increasing membership; and to start a social group to respond to the needs of a growing number of single members, and to attract a larger share of this growing market.

The task forces took their charges seriously, and the change initiatives were well crafted, detailed, and realistic. They were reviewed carefully by the Downtown Church board and formally accepted. However, although the church had traveled so far so smoothly down the change road, the journey was not over. Some clouds had suddenly appeared on the horizon, and the wind had picked up. The senior pastor had recently sent some signals indicating that, although he accepted intellectually the need for a strong management team and a top internal administrator, he seemed to have something of a martyr complex, enjoyed working himself to the bone, and was nervous about a powerful second-person insulating him from internal affairs.

Furthermore, several long-time members of the congregation, including a number on the board, had become quite vocal about what they perceived as a push toward professional management at the expense of the spiritual values that had drawn them to Downtown Church in the first place. In effect, recent references to the senior pastor as the church's chief executive officer had set their teeth on edge, raising the specter of takeover by a cabal of cold-blooded management types. Some board members who had served faithfully and industriously for years on the soon-to-be disbanded committees were clearly feeling offended, and talk of being "put out to pasture" could be heard in the Downtown Church corridors before and after the Sunday service.

Being on the Alert for Icebergs

Downtown Church's change sea has grown much choppier of late, and smooth sailing is quickly becoming a memory. The glow experienced in the retreat that initiated the journey is growing dimmer by the day, and Downtown Church's change champions have become keenly aware that, no matter how realistic and sophisticated the strategies or far along the process, the gap between plans and action can be quite daunting.

There is nothing unusual about the Downtown Church story; it is all too typical of nonprofits engaged in leading and managing change. The fact is, recognition of need, the best of intentions, and well-crafted plans are only the prerequisites for change; they by no means ensure successful implementation. Planned change is always a fragile process, and the journey is far from over when the plans have been fashioned. As Beckhard and Pritchard (1992) observe: "Most senior managers are comfortable with defining goals and creating strategies to achieve them. Far fewer managers are aware of the need to manage the process of change. Many strategic plans die because of lack of implementation. There is a high correlation between the failure to implement changes and the lack of conscious management of the transitional process" (p. 69).

Several icebergs lurking in the change sea can slow or even stop the change journey. These are day-to-day pressures, unanticipated events, inadequate resources, and human resistance. Figure 8.1 depicts these difficulties in a more graphic form.

Day-to-Day Pressures

The inexorable press of day-to-day events can easily dominate our attention, take every last ounce of energy, and soak up all of our available time, while also making us feel productive, if overworked, and secure. In fact, most nonprofits I have come into contact with are already busy without adding the burden of implementing change initiatives. Staff members are barely keeping up with the myriad demands of running the shop, much less developing it; in-baskets are overflowing, e-mail messages go unread, fax machines spew out reams of paper, the telephone always seems to be ringing

Figure 8.1. Beware of Icebergs!

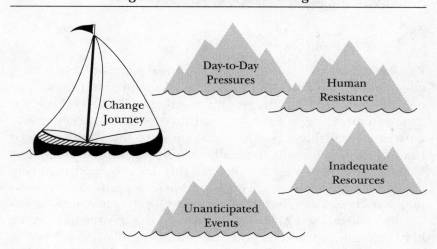

off the hook. In this context, creative change can seem more like a threat than an opportunity.

Unanticipated Events

Unanticipated events can distract us and throw implementation efforts off-schedule. There are always the crises that could not have been prevented by the best of planning. For example, a major daily paper has decided to run a series exposing management deficiencies in a large program, that, to be honest, is somewhat vulnerable, and just lying down and taking it is not a viable response because an expose can cost us our reputation and funding support. There is a chance that we can head them off by meeting with the editorial board and stating our case persuasively; at worst, we can prepare public responses. Similarly, opportunities that cannot be missed often intrude on the best-laid plans. A Ford Foundation program officer has just called to say that if we can produce a top-notch proposal within the next month in alliance with two key stakeholders, we stand a good chance of receiving $500,000 for a pilot program that will firmly establish our place in a growing market. Can we really say, "No thank you, we're sorry, but your opportunity was not included in this year's change portfolio?"

Inadequate Resources

Planned resources—time, money, political support, staff knowledge, and skills—may not be available as planned, setting implementation back if not preventing it entirely. Perhaps the grant proposal intended to fund staff training has been turned down. Earned income that was expected to produce the working capital to fund change has unexpectedly dropped by fifteen percent. A badly leaking roof must be repaired this month, requiring every last cent of the funds that were set aside to support implementation. Four board members whose support for the change initiatives is critical are showing signing of succumbing to pressure from a key stakeholder who feels threatened by the planned changes. Abrupt shifts of fortune are not all that unusual in the world of change.

Human Resistance

Of course, those pesky critters called human beings can surprise us by the depth and tenacity of their resistance to change, even if they seemed to be perfectly happy campers when the change initiatives were fashioned. Indeed, some perceived threats are all too real, taking the form of lost status, reduced income, or personal inability to meet a new challenge. Of course, as discussed in earlier chapters, the workings of the human mind can be mysterious and convoluted and the potential for self-deception—seeing opportunities as problems—often amazingly high.

To the Rescue

To be sure, strong forces present in varying degrees inside and outside nonprofit organizations work against planned, self-directed change, but they need not be insuperable hurdles. Based on my experience in working with hundreds of nonprofits in managing change and on the growing literature (Beckhard and Pritchard, 1992; Bergman, 1996; Dalziel and Schoonover, 1988; Kanter, 1989;

Kirkpatrick, 1985; Lippitt, Langseth, and Mossop, 1985; Mohrman and others, 1989; Tichy, 1983), I address four intertwined elements that, together, form an implementation strategy aimed at making plans reality:

- Strong chief executive leadership backed by a supportive board
- A structure and process dedicated to the implementation of change initiatives
- Adequate resources to fuel implementation
- A strategy explicitly focused on dealing with human resistance

First, let's look at strong chief executive leadership, and all that that entails.

Chief Executive Leadership

A nonprofit's chief executive officer must be its officer in charge of change if change initiatives are ultimately to become organizational practice. Significant planned change happens when the chief executive wants it to, and it almost never happens when he or she does not want it to. As the principal designer, architect, and enabler of planned organizational change, the nonprofit chief executive takes the lead role in producing five outcomes that are indispensable to implementation. These five outcomes will be discussed briefly here and then in more detail later in the chapter:

- Establishing planned change as a clear organizational priority
- Ensuring that planned changes are well managed
- Ensuring that the resources required for implementation are allocated
- Ensuring that staff resistance is dealt with effectively
- Ensuring that the board is aboard the change train

People in organizations care a lot about what their chief executives say and do, especially in times of stress, as during implementation of time-consuming and perhaps nerve-racking change initiatives. To understand the power a chief executive can have during the change process, Americans only need recall the heartening

effect that President Franklin Roosevelt's first inaugural's words—
"The only thing we have to fear is fear itself"—and his subsequent
fireside chats had on millions of Americans during the Great
Depression.

People rightly want to know the answers to some commonsense
questions: Are these changes really necessary and important to our
future, rather than just the latest flavor-of-the-month management
innovation? Does the chief executive really believe in the initiatives? Are they really important to him or her? Does the chief executive really understand what is going on with these initiatives or is
he or she being manipulated by people with a vested interest in the
proposed change? Does he or she really care about what these
changes mean for our day-to-day lives in the organization? People
ask and then look for words and behavior that provide answers to
these questions. Then and only then do they determine their own
commitment to planned changes.

Making It a Priority

One of the most powerful contributions a chief executive can
make to the implementation process is to establish its ideological
legitimacy by communicating on every appropriate occasion the
explicit tie between the nonprofit's strategic framework—its values, vision, and mission—and the planned change initiatives. The
chief executive is in the best position in the organization to speak
authoritatively about the rationality of the planned changes in
terms both of the nonprofit's long-term strategic directions and
the expected benefits from going through the pain of change. Furthermore, if chief executives indicate that they understand the sacrifices that change demands and that they actively sympathize with
their people rather than take their sacrifices for granted, it is
among the best ways to raise morale in times of stress.

One important way in which a chief executive can signal seriousness about planned changes is to devote significant time to visibly leading the implementation process, rather than disappearing
into the inner sanctum after a rousing exhortation, emerging
rarely if at all for periodic boosters. A visibly committed chief executive chairs the meetings of the steering committee that is over-

seeing the implementation activities, stays during the whole meeting, and demonstrates actual knowledge of the details of the implementation strategies. On several occasions I have witnessed management team members exchange knowing glances when a chief executive opens a meeting by reading a prepared formal statement and then exits quickly. The group finds it equally demoralizing when the chief executive cannot answer probing questions about change initiatives without turning to more knowledgeable lieutenants.

Another important way in which a chief executive can add credibility to planned change initiatives is to avoid behavior that obviously contradicts one or more of them. Here are two amusing cases in point.

A large social service agency I worked with had launched an initiative to strengthen internal communication by breaking down formal barriers and consciously fostering informality in interactions. Employees were encouraged to meet face-to-face with those in other departments rather than rely on written or telephone communication. But the chief executive, notorious for her discomfort with people, continued to summon staff to her office for meetings, which she conducted formally, sitting behind her desk rather than in the circle of armchairs that had been purchased for such meetings. Furthermore, she was rarely seen in the corridors, preferring instead the safety of her office. Now, the example is surely not earth shaking, but her behavior without question cast doubt on the priority of the communication initiative.

The second example is more dramatic. The president of a large educational institution I worked with enthusiastically endorsed an initiative to create a new "office of the chief executive." The new strategy would involve the president's focusing on strategic planning, governance, educational program leadership, and on relations with key stakeholders, including the state board of regents. At the same time, his executive vice president would serve as chief operating officer, concentrating on internal operations. The executive vice president, in keeping with this newly clarified internal leadership role, was to chair weekly meetings of the system vice presidents, meetings that had previously been run by the president. But every time this leadership group met with the executive vice president as chair, the president found some way to disrupt the meeting, usually by pulling someone out to answer a question or deal with some obviously manufactured crisis. Furthermore, decisions of the group were routinely second-guessed by the president, who frequently reversed them. The group's structure eventually faded as, ultimately, did the new concept of the office of the chief executive, a victim of contradictory chief executive behavior.

Taking Responsibility for the Management of Change

In keeping with the role of grand designer, the chief executive should take responsibility for ensuring that the change process is well managed. In other words, he or she must see that planned initiatives are realistic and that the implementation process involves clear assignment of accountability, regular monitoring, and rigorous quality control. A tried-and-true approach described in more detail later in this chapter is to create a formal program to manage change with a structure and a process for oversight and operations. The chief executive can take two steps to infuse such a structure and process with the credibility required to play its management role effectively: take an active role in making the change program work as intended (principally by chairing key meetings) and to avoid second-guessing or overturning decisions generated by the program.

Ensuring Adequate Resources

One important step a chief executive can take to ensure that the resources required to implement change initiatives are available is to make sure that they are formally budgeted for during the annual planning cycle. The chief executive can also play an active role in securing grant funding for initiatives, lobbying personally at foundations and other funding sources. The chief executive can also be the guarantor of that most finite of resources, staff time, by protecting the staff from overextending themselves. Perhaps the most important such contribution is not to bombard staff with additional demands made without clear priorities. Merely adding demands willy-nilly is a surefire way to sow the seeds of confusion and kill a staff's enthusiasm for change.

Dealing with Resistance

Addressing the very natural resistance of people to change is discussed later in the chapter. However, in this discussion of the chief executive's role, it is important to remember that the chief executive is a nonprofit's most valuable resource in overcoming resistance, initially by ensuring that resistance is anticipated and planned for. The chief executive can also serve as an inspiration and a model, not only by visibly suffering through the change process himself or herself but also by being willing to share his or her own fears and frailties where change is concerned.

Remember from Chapter Three the department chief executive and second-in-command of the nonprofit financial services organization who were willing to engage in open dialogue with the management team about a controversial reorganization initiative? What impressed the team more than anything else was their leaders' admission of fallibility, their willingness to share candidly the thinking behind the original reorganization decision, their sincere desire to understand the pain that was being caused, and their openness to suggestions for making the reorganization plan more bearable. The two raised morale and strengthened the team's support for change by demonstrating the true humility that is a characteristic of strong leaders.

Other strategies that chief executives can employ to overcome resistance are to choose and reward change champions who will share the burden of leading change; to avoid unwittingly rewarding resistance to or punishing enthusiasm for change; and to avoid overreacting to cries of anguish from resisters.

The squeaky wheel of resistance can sometimes squeak all the more loudly if rewarded with too much attention and sympathy. The chief executive must walk a fine line here, wanting to appear firmly committed to change but also not wanting to appear uncaring and insensitive to the pain involved in implementation. I recall an example that demonstrates the danger in overindulging resistance. The superintendent of one educational institution bent over backwards to assuage the anguish of his chief financial officer, who was obviously horrified by the changes being accomplished and particularly the reform of the budget process, which he perceived as a direct threat to his own status and authority. As with Mr. Chamberlain's policy of appeasement, every attempt to relieve the chief financial officer's discomfort resulted in another demand and a greater willingness to fight the changes publicly. The story's ending is not a happy one. Emboldened by the superintendent's appeasement, the chief financial officer was able to assemble a core group of resisters, who eventually drove the superintendent away, wounded but wiser.

Getting the Board on Board

Finally, a chief executive must ensure that the governing board is appropriately involved in the implementation of change, making full use of it as a resource yet not involving it in too many details. Of course, as discussed in Chapter Seven, an important way to capitalize on the board as a resource while also building understanding and support is to involve the board in fashioning the strategic framework, identifying and selecting strategic issues, and reviewing and adopting change initiatives. After this process, the board should adopt a more distant stance, making policy decisions as required (most important, acting on the budget to support change initiatives) and monitoring the implementation process by relying on regular progress reports from the chief executive. The program should then become an oversight responsibility of one of the board's standing committees, which would keep the full board briefed on its progress, and should be a standing agenda item at full board meetings.

The board can play an important role in establishing the legitimacy of a nonprofit's change program by adopting a formal resolution that establishes the program. Such a resolution might state a commitment to the proactive leadership of change, cite the retreat that began the process of fashioning change initiatives, and explicitly authorize putting the architecture—the organizational units and positions—of the change program in place.

The nonprofit chief executive can also creatively involve board members in ceremonially conferring legitimacy on the change program. For example, the board chair and perhaps other board members might participate in an awards banquet that recognizes task force members for their extraordinary contributions. And a half-hour might also be reserved for a change initiative at every full board meeting, during which time board members are briefed on progress and given an opportunity to ask questions.

At times board members can make a more substantive contribution to the implementation of change initiatives, for example by personally lobbying a funding source for a grant or making contact with key stakeholders whose support is critical to implementation. But once again, the one person responsible for thinking through and facilitating such creative and productive involvement is the officer in charge of change, the chief executive.

"Newstream" Structure and Process

Rosabeth Moss Kanter (1989) has convincingly argued that the implementation of change should be handled through a "newstream" process that is kept separate from "mainstream" operations, so that planned change does not get buried by the relentless pressures of day-to-day operations. "Overall, effective management depends," she observes, "on knowing which streams you're swimming in. What it takes to develop and launch the new is very different from what is acceptable and appropriate for managing the already-established" (p. 202). Many nonprofits have successfully protected change initiatives by creating a formal program—a "strategic change program," for example—intended to serve as a carapace that will keep the planned change process from oozing into daily affairs.

Thus, the strategic change program functions as a kind of organization within the wider organization. It has its own processes and structures dedicated to implementing the initiatives in the change portfolio, which are distinct from the organizational operations described in the annual operational plan and budget. When the chief executive and staff members are involved in the strategic change program, they wear their program hats, never mixing up what they are doing with the nonprofit's daily affairs. For example, when the management team meets as the program steering committee (see the following section for more on this), the agenda never includes items that would appear on the normal management team agenda.

The theory, which I have seen work repeatedly in practice, is that once a planned initiative in the portfolio has been fully implemented, it moves over to the operational side of the organization. Let's take the Downtown Church example that opened this chapter. Once the planned-for chief operating officer has been hired and is fully functioning in the role, this implemented change initiative would find its place in the annual budget and no longer merit the special protection of the strategic change program. Of course, as the years pass, the identification of new strategic issues will result in the addition of new change initiatives to a nonprofit's ever-evolving change portfolio. Therefore, the strategic change program will always be in business, although the items it manages will change in the context of continuing environmental change.

Experience with hundreds of formal strategic change programs has taught me that they deliver important benefits. This kind of formal program helps keep change in a nonprofit's collective consciousness—on the front burner—thereby ensuring that it gets the time and attention that effective implementation requires. It helps build understanding of and support for planned change by giving it a more specific identity, making it a target for board and staff ownership, and providing opportunities for participation in managing change. It enables timely adjustments in change implementation plans in order to respond to changing circumstances. And it promotes accountability and quality control, keeping change on track, on time, and within budget.

Not Managing Can Be Costly

The price of not formally managing change can be high, as I learned a quarter of a century ago when I ran across a dramatic example of change gone awry due to inadequate management. With the impetuousness of youth, I had moved across country without a job. Arriving at my destination, I considered myself lucky to be offered the position of project manager for an ambitious, politically and technically complex, and demanding change initiative that was in the process of being implemented. The project involved the redesign, automation, and integration of the financial management systems of two completely independent organizations. Both were committed to reaping the benefits of advanced technology while realizing the cost savings of consolidation. Included as subsystems were budget preparation, accounting (including developing a cost accounting capability), and financial reporting.

Junior consultants working with little supervision were constantly underfoot (this being the early 1970s, the avant-garde computer types were known by their high-heeled boots and dazzling chains, not to mention their unintelligible jargon), generating mountains of documentation. Several staff task forces were charged to design large pieces of the system, including revenue collection and accounts payable. Their work had before my arrival been somewhat casually coordinated by an overworked management team member who had barely enough time to do his regular job, much less oversee such a complex and costly change effort as this one.

The inevitable result was chaos and near-collapse. As the newcomer on the scene, hired late in the game to serve as overall project manager, I could not make heads or tails of what was going on. Prevailing on a trusted colleague twenty-five hundred miles away, I packaged up a mass of consultant design documentation and sent it to him. The assessment came by telegram a couple of days later: "Nothing makes sense. Please send missing documentation. If documentation complete, only two choices: escape situation quickly or reorganize whole project."

Convinced that the project was a technical abomination quickly heading toward a highly visible disaster that was likely to destroy the careers of many people associated with it—including mine—I was able to convince the higher-ups to stop the project, dismiss the consulting firm, rebid the project, retain another firm, develop detailed project objectives and an implementation plan, and create a structure to provide rigorous coordination and quality control. Eventually, we got back on track but only after hundreds of wasted hours, thousands of wasted dollars, and tremendous anxiety, all because of inadequate implementation planning and structure at the onset.

I was lucky to learn an invaluable lesson about complex project management without having to endure too much pain and suffering. I also learned something about the apparently powerful tendency of people to see what they want to see—to be wishful thinkers—when their vested interests are powerful enough. Early in my tenure there, when I questioned the monstrosity that the project had become, asking penetrating questions about design concepts and system interconnections, the inevitable response was irritation. All I was given was countless reminders about the importance of the project, my relative newness and technical ignorance, and my lack of proper team spirit. Today, I would be more sorely tempted to leave with a parting "A plague on your house!"

Key Change Program Elements

What, then, are the key elements of a nonprofit's strategic change program, in addition to the chief executive officer's serving as an active, hands-on, "officer-in-charge-of-change"? There are five: a program steering committee to direct and oversee the change process; a staff person serving as program coordinator; a master implementation plan to guide and measure progress; task forces to provide hands-on management of implementation; and techniques to enhance the change program's identity. Figure 8.2 depicts the key elements in the program.

Program Steering Committee

Many nonprofits that have successfully implemented change through a formal strategic change program have found that creating a steering committee to direct and oversee the program works well. Always chaired by the chief executive officer, the program steering committee is usually the management team wearing another hat, but sometimes one or more board members are included. The primary purpose of the program steering committee is to serve as the oversight and policy body of the strategic change program. Their activities include the following: overseeing development of, reviewing, and recommending board adoption of the strategic change program comprehensive action plan; overseeing implementation of the action plan; monitoring and reporting progress to the full board; ensuring that any board or wider membership policy decisions (such as revision of by-laws) needed to enable strategic change program implementation are identified

Figure 8.2. The Change Program Structure.

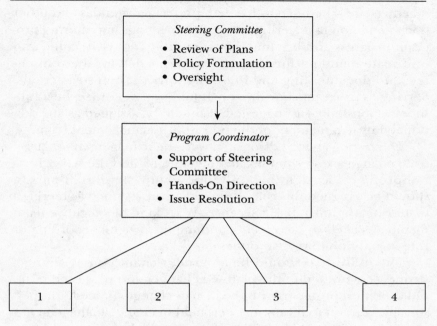

Implementation Task Forces

and made in a timely fashion; allocating the necessary resources to strategic change program implementation; and resolving any policy questions that may arise during implementation.

Program Coordinator

No strategic change program is likely to succeed without staff support. One approach that has worked is to assign one member of the existing management team to wear the hat of the strategic change program coordinator in addition to her regular duties.

The program coordinator is the hands-on executive responsible for day-to-day operation of the program, who ensures that it is on schedule and resolves operational issues as they arise. One of this individual's preeminent responsibilities is to prepare the comprehensive program action plan for steering committee review and adoption. In addition, the program coordinator provides staff support to the steering committee, ensuring that steering committee meetings are scheduled as needed, preparing agendas and other documentation for steering committee meetings, monitoring program progress and briefing the committee regularly, collecting information and performing analysis as needed for the committee, and documenting and following up on committee actions. Serving as program coordinator should not, of course, be a full-time responsibility; as suggested, it should be assigned as an additional duty to a member of the nonprofit's management team.

The responsibilities associated with the management of large-scale change are so complex and demanding and the stakes for a nonprofit are so high that only an executive-level staff person should be assigned this role. It should never assigned as merely a matter of administrative assistance. What kind of executive team member is likely to succeed in handling the program coordinator role in addition to regular duties?

The individual should be an ardent champion of change, strongly committed to the planned changes and possessed of no philosophical problems with the idea of change. Indeed, this person should want to master the new field of change management.

He or she should be highly skilled in, and passionate about, planning and project management. The role cannot be performed adequately by a "big picture" type who has trouble getting down to details, or by a person who finds the management process a bureaucratic irritant.

This individual should have strong written and oral communication skills and possess the kind of executive presence that commands respect and builds confidence and commitment.

It is essential that this person be compatible with the chief executive officer. He or she should be flexible and a virtuoso at juggling complex demands without the threat of a nervous breakdown. And he or she should be an earnest learner, open to acquiring the skills required for successful change management.

The day-to-day relationship of a nonprofit's chief executive and the program coordinator is critical to the coordinator's, and ultimately the program's, success. Thus, access to the chief executive must be easy. Especially in the early days of the program, a number of questions will demand the chief executive's attention. If a program coordinator has trouble getting past the chief executive's secretary, his or her status will quickly decline in the eyes of peers and, of course, program implementation will be set back.

In a very real sense, the most successful program coordinator becomes an alter ego to the chief executive, helping the latter play the leading role in the change program while building a working partnership characterized by strong mutual trust and respect. If the two conflict to a significant degree in personality or style or if they are uncomfortable with each other, the partnership is far less likely to work.

Master Implementation Plan

The comprehensive strategic change program's master implementation plan is the primary vehicle for setting the pace of change, making sure all of the steps involved in implementing targets are well thought through and sequenced appropriately, and monitoring implementation as it moves forward. Developing the plan should be the first and foremost job of the program coordinator, who of course draws on the change initiatives recommended by the task forces in putting it together. The program steering committee should set aside at least a half-day for review and revision of the plan.

The Task Forces

It often makes sense to keep in place the task forces that developed the change initiatives that constitute a nonprofit's change portfolio to serve as hands-on "technical coordinating committees" until the initiatives are fully implemented. The chairs of what are now the implementation task forces report to the program coordinator, who might assemble them periodically for coordinating meetings. Of course, each task force would continue in existence only until its particular change initiative is implemented.

Some Finer Touches

Once the basic strategic change program structure and management processes are firmly in place, the program coordinator and steering committee can experiment with ways to enhance program visibility and credibility. Some simple steps that work well include: developing a program logo that effectively conveys the thrust of the program and an accompanying slogan ("Taking Command of Change," "In the Forefront of Change," for example); providing participants with a three-ring binder with the program logo on the cover to hold the master implementation plan and other program materials; creating special stationery (one of my clients uses a bright red border across the top) that identifies an item as belonging to the program; and holding program meetings in a special "war room" with a blown-up version of the master implementation plan taped to the wall.

The Resource Question

I have already talked about two obvious resources that are critical to the full and timely implementation of planned change initiatives: staff time and money. Also deserving serious consideration during implementation are staff skills, external technical assistance, and a nonprofit's image and political capital.

One result of the implementation of a change initiative can be the hiring of new staff, of course. For example, if a nursing home puts a new home health care business fully into operation it will require more staff to run the program. Similarly, if Downtown Church implements the new office of the chief executive, that will require creating a new position, chief operating officer. But, in my experience, few nonprofits can afford to bring new staff on to manage the implementation of change initiatives and so they are constrained by the values, operating assumptions, and skill levels of their current staff.

This can be a serious constraint when implementing an initiative that demands behavior that the nonprofit's traditional culture has not demanded or even encouraged. There is always the very real danger that the staff will go through the motions without real passion or a deep understanding of the new business directions and demands. In addition, the technical skills and experience required to implement an initiative may be woefully lacking. For example, one educational institution I know was asked to participate in developing a joint venture with a local business-dominated economic development corporation aimed at providing customized training for relocating businesses. But the educational institution's staff found it extremely taxing to communicate with the staff of the economic development corporation, much less with business owners. Although they were smart and capable educators, they used so much jargon and were so formal in their approach to planning and program development that they quickly alienated their potential joint venture partners. The training venture did eventually get off the ground, but it was more a testimony to the commitment and patience of the businesspeople involved than to the willingness of the educational staff to grow and change.

Thorough orientation and training can go far in developing staff skills, but values and fundamental assumptions about the world—those things that make up a nonprofit's culture—are less easily changed and are impervious to quick fixes. Here is another, more poignant story. Fifteen years ago, I met with a senior manager at an old-line industrial firm. Although cash-rich and highly profitable for some years, the company was beginning to experience the traumas associated with global competition, outmoded technology, and an uncompetitive cost structure. It was having tremendous difficulty fostering internal innovation in the face of a hierarchical organizational structure, an authoritarian management style, and the extreme inbreeding that characterizes firms that do not bring in new blood. During our discussion, the manager handed me a copy of a new book then quite the rage on Japanese approaches to management, saying that copies had been distributed far and wide in the firm and that the book should have a real impact. "Too little, too late," I thought to myself on the drive back to my office. "Brain transplants might be the only hope." In fact, the conclusion of this story was bankruptcy and the disappearance of a once-great economic powerhouse.

Elements of a culture can change, of course, just more slowly than technical and political skills. When a proposed change appears to clash with strongly and widely held beliefs and assumptions, a nonprofit is well-advised to assume that more dramatic steps than a training workshop are in order. When the budget can bear the cost, it might make sense when the cultural gap is dramatic to bring in new staff to implement an initiative. But if this is done, it should be anticipated that the newcomers will not necessarily be welcomed with open arms; indeed, they may need some protection. Consultants may also bring missing skills and experience to the implementation process, but if the consultants are not consciously involved in strengthening staff capability, when they leave with their paychecks, the skills will also leave.

In any discussion of resources, time, money, and skills come quickly to mind. But successful implementation of change often depends on other resources: image and political influence are two. A nonprofit's general reputation in its market or service area and the strength of its relationships with key stakeholders are more critical for a proposed change initiative that requires interfacing with the external environment. Creating new board committees or installing a more effective financial management system are internal change targets with little dependence on the wider world. In contrast, launching a new program in a competitive environment may require developing a joint venture partnership, or at least receiving vocal support from key stakeholders whose blessing lends legitimacy to the new venture.

There is a good solution to this problem. When the change program coordinator compiles individual change initiatives into an overall master implementation plan, the coordinator should prepare for review by the steering committee an assessment of the public and political relations requirements of the change initiatives and then develop a detailed plan for satisfying them. Such detailed plans often deal with the following issues:

- *Ways to strengthen the nonprofit's image and reputation.* Vehicles that are frequently used to do this are press releases, an attractive annual report, and speaking engagements at public forums. Such communication should make clear the nonprofit's significant accomplishments and contributions to the wider community.
- *The board and chief executive's roles in strengthening public relations and stakeholder ties.* Often, the board and chief executive can commit to public speaking engagements and other efforts to build ties with high-priority stakeholders.
- *The composition of the board membership itself.* The people on the board should fit the desired (or required) image of the nonprofit, in light of its planned change initiatives.

Dealing with Resistance

People change, and people lead and manage change. Change isn't accomplished by organizations in the abstract or sophisticated change machines. If this were not true, the process of fashioning and implementing change initiatives would be much less complex, less interesting, and less useful. From the first chapter of this book, I have talked about the very normal resistance of people to change—at least to change that affects them directly. Most people I know despise being changed, no matter how laudable its intent. Furthermore, the ability to espouse change in theory while opposing it in practice—without apparently noticing the contradiction—appears to be widespread. Anyone with experience in the change business learns to anticipate resistance and adapt change planning to it as a survival tactic. Thus, no matter how rigorous our thinking, how sophisticated our planning, or how meticulously designed our structures and processes for managing change, it inevitably comes down to people. The successful implementation of planned change depends on their behavior, day after day, in countless situations.

What can change champions—board members, chief executives, and management team members—do to ensure that as many staff as possible participate positively in the change process? To begin, it is important to be aware of the myriad reasons people oppose change and of the nature of their opposition.

A list compiled by Donald Kirkpatrick in *How to Manage Change Effectively* (1985) corresponds with my own experience. Kirkpatrick identifies a number of reasons why people may react negatively to change, including the following: a fear they will lose something personally (such as money, pride, security, freedom, status, good working conditions); a lack of recognition of the need for the change; anticipation that more harm than good will come of it; a lack of respect for the people leading the change effort; little input into the process; a feeling that the planned change is a personal criticism; a fear of additional burdens because of it; and the feeling that the change is coming at a very inconvenient time.

The interesting thing about this list is its dependence on feelings, attitudes, and perceptions rather than on objective phenomena. What the person being asked to change or to participate in the change effort perceives is what really matters; the intent and motivations of a particular change champion are not. So in dealing with resistance, it is essential to understand the mindsets that help to shape perceptions of reality and to take them into account when fashioning implementation strategies. It naturally follows that open, two-way communication is an indispensable element in any change process.

Mindsets can be very well-defined and extremely resistant to alteration. For example, it should have been obvious to the manager mentioned earlier that the chances of his colleagues adapting Japanese management methods and styles merely because they had read a book were infinitesimal in that authoritarian and hierarchical culture. Such fundamental mental shifts are not produced merely by exposing people to the literature!

Long-lasting change that affects fundamental values and mental models—change that involves significant aspects of organizational culture—is likely to require an intensive transformational effort that must be measured in months and years, not days. This is not to say that planned change at variance in important ways with a nonprofit's prevalent culture cannot take place until the cultural transformation has been completed, that is, until there is wide adoption of values, beliefs, and worldviews friendlier to, and more consonant, with the new direction. However, such changes are likely to arouse fierce opposition and to entail more than their share of pain and suffering. And since cultural change is a demanding, long-term process that does not fit into an annual planning cycle, it can be expected to encounter resistance for some time. This resistance should be anticipated and planned for, while the longer-term transformational effort—such as an intensive values identification and explication process led by the chief executive and involving countless small-group sessions—is completed.

To ensure that resistance to change initiatives is kept within bounds so that implementation can go forward, nonprofits can take six practical steps:

1. Make absolutely clear the ties of planned changes to organizational values, vision, and mission.
2. Build ownership of change initiatives.
3. Keep the change program realistic in scope and pace.

4. Maximize individual benefit and minimize loss.
5. Reward cooperation while not rewarding resistance.
6. Communicate, communicate, communicate.

Of course, taking these steps will be to no avail unless there is strong chief executive commitment and visible, aggressive leadership; the importance of this was already discussed earlier.

Making the Tie to Values, Vision, and Mission

A nonprofit's evolving strategic framework provides legitimacy for organizational activities, inspires loyalty, and motivates effort (Bennis, 1989; Covey, 1989; De Pree, 1989; O'Toole, 1995; Senge, 1990). Understanding and sharing values and the individual elements of the vision and mission can sustain morale when times get tough, providing a light at the end of the tunnel of change. As Senge observed, "Visions are exhilarating. They create the spark, the excitement that lifts an organization out of the mundane" (p. 208).

One of the most powerful ways to create an environment conducive to implementing change is to keep values, vision, and mission at the forefront of the change effort, on everyone's mind and at the head of everyone's list. It is also important to link specific change initiatives to particular facets of the strategic framework in order to strengthen their legitimacy and foster a sense of ownership. I have found that the most effective way to keep the strategic framework at the forefront of organizational change is for the chief executive personally to talk about the planned changes in the context of the values, vision, and mission, thereby providing planned changes a philosophical context and deeper meaning. In carrying out this responsibility, oral communication should take place as frequently and in as many forums as feasible. Written communication, although less effective, is another way to get the message out.

A few years ago, I witnessed the chief executive and management team of a large regulatory agency creatively and enthusiastically perform the critical task of keeping first things first. As a prelude to a retreat at which vision, mission, and strategic issues were to be explored by some one hundred assembled managers from all over the United States, the chief executive and five senior managers formed a panel to describe what appeared to be the core values motivating and guiding the agency. After each value had been articulated, the panel members, without rehearsal, reflected on its meaning from their different perspectives. Retreat participants were invited to question and challenge panel members. What an inspiring kick-off this proved to be! It gave the organization's values their proper leading role in change, demonstrated their various facets, and invited new interpretations. The deeper understanding that was gained from this creative form of communication could not have been achieved through distribution of a written values statement.

Building Ownership

When individuals feel like owners of change initiatives, rather than mere foot soldiers carrying out commands from above, they are more likely to accept planned changes and be willing to do their part in implementing the changes. The feeling of ownership is created by participation. The strength of the feeling depends on the extent, depth, and meaningfulness of the participation. If an individual's participation is shallow, basically cosmetic, and low impact, then the feeling of ownership is likely to be weak and fleeting. But if the participation is generative rather than interactive, producing impacts that are obviously important to the nonprofit, then the feeling of ownership will be stronger.

For example, a staff member might be asked to participate in a brainstorming group in a retreat setting to fashion a detailed vision statement. This might be followed by serving on the task force created to refine the rough vision for eventual review by the management team and board planning committee. Even better, this contributor might be involved in a task force to fashion a change initiative aimed at translating an important aspect of the vision into practice and even continue on the task force in order to coordinate implementation.

When someone is invited into an obviously important process from the beginning, producing a vision rather than merely reacting to someone's version of it, and involved over an extended period in the vision development process and the translation of that vision into a concrete change initiative, he or she will almost surely feel considerable ownership of the change initiative that ultimately emerges. In contrast, think of the participant who merely serves on an ad hoc committee to review or comment on a draft vision. Creators, in my experience, always feel more like owners than reactors.

Wider participation also spices up the strategic stew of ideas. The more diverse the participation, the more ideas likely to be generated. Reflecting on their experience in large-scale change management at the World Bank, Lippitt, Langseth, and Mossop (1985) observe that participation "creates more and newer ideas for change than can be generated by management, staff experts, or outside consultants" (p. 149).

Carefully Pacing Change

Planned change should never be allowed to threaten the integrity of ongoing programs and services or to cause so much anxiety that morale and performance are damaged. Such pathology can be prevented if change initiatives put realistic demands on the nonprofits that implement them. One way to ensure that this happens is to require that the task forces charged to produce the strategy go through a rigorous process involving comprehensive assessment of costs and resources (for more on this see Chapter Seven) and that the management team carefully reviews the initiatives to ensure that their implementation is affordable in both time and money.

The change program coordinator can also guard against organizational overextension when preparing the comprehensive master implementation plan, making sure that events are paced so as to avoid unnecessary pressure. Furthermore, during the implementation process, the program steering committee should be alert for signs of stress and strain and take action to adjust the schedule to avoid stretching people too thinly.

Increasing the Winners

People tend to resist change when they perceive a possible personal loss. As Kirkpatrick (1985) points out, perceived personal loss can feel just as bad as real loss, whether of status, money, pride, authority, or something else.

I was recently told by a knowledgeable, loyal, energetic board member in a nonprofit that was reorganizing the board's committee structure and upgrading its leadership role that she no longer "felt like an important part of what's going on" and thought that things "have passed me by." I begged to differ, yet I was impressed by the depth of her feeling and its influence on her view of the impending reorganization.

Even real gains can feel like losses, depending on one's perspective. For example, I have frequently witnessed board members lament the loss of a detailed monthly financial report, even though they neither needed the detail for their governance work nor even understood all of the report, and to feel shortchanged by the streamlined new report, even though it contained precisely the level of detail they needed. It sometimes seems as if a giant mass of paper serves as a kind of security blanket and that without it board members may feel vaguely less well informed and unsettled, without knowing exactly why. The feeling that change makes one a loser in some way rather than a winner is sure to blunt enthusiasm for change or even to turn a person into an active opponent, regardless of the real merits of the case.

Once again, the chief executive and management team can take some practical steps to expand the pool of winners while keeping the number of losers to a minimum. First, it is important to anticipate losses, asking in reference to each change initiative which people might really lose something or might be likely to feel a loss. This can be done both by the task forces that fashion the change initiatives and by the steering committees that reviews the recommended initiatives. When perceived losses will not involve any real loss (for example, a title change may sound like a demotion but actually involve increased responsibility and authority), clear communication aimed at fostering a realistic understanding of the planned change can avert a potential problem. Of course, when personal consultation is required, this can be a time-consuming solution; still, the cost may be far outweighed by the benefit of a happy, supportive follower.

Sometimes change does involve real losses. In these cases, sensitivity in dealing with those who will suffer loss can help minimize the damage. In no event should a loss be allowed to catch the loser off-guard, embarrassing or humiliating him or her publicly. And there may be opportunities to blunt the impact of a loss by offering a compensating benefit, which may not totally make up for the loss but at least assuage the pain. Several years ago, a nonprofit social services agency went through an extensive reorganization. It was faced with the challenge of moving a widely respected and well-loved man in his early fifties from the directorship of a highly visible community development program. The question was never whether, but how, because he had clearly demonstrated that he could not meet the growing demands of the job.

The chief executive spent hours coming up with a strategy to effect this essential change without unnecessarily wounding, much less humiliating, this man, who deserved their respect and affection and whose opposition, by the way, would have seriously set back the change program. (Being humane is seldom entirely altruistic, of course.) First, the chief executive spent a lot of time talking with the man, explaining why the move was necessary. Second, he found a less demanding but still visible and important job for him in one of the agency's four community centers, where his skills could be put to excellent use. Third, the chief executive collaborated with him to come up with a public rationale for the move that was calculated to preserve his dignity. Thus, hours and hours of time and energy were spent, but they were well worth the effort for both ethical and programmatic reasons.

Offering Rewards

There are all kinds of ways to reward staff members for their active cooperation in implementing change initiatives. Few nonprofits are in a position to provide financial incentives, but some can, and doing so does make a difference. For example, an educational institution involved in a wide-ranging change program provided incentive pay to faculty who served on committees and task forces. Instead of direct payment, a nonprofit might finance travel for people involved in leading implementation, for example, to visit the site of a program to understand its operational dynamics or to attend a pertinent conference.

Providing staff with opportunities for professional growth through meaningful, challenging participation helps to compensate for the pain and suffering involved in implementing change, as do different kinds of public recognition. Frequent access to the chief executive is a potent form of recognition. For example, some nonprofit chief executives hear oral presentations of implementation task force reports in their personal conference rooms, sometimes followed by a reception. Awards may be handed out by the chief executive for service "above and beyond the call of duty" during ceremonial occasions. One association I worked with beautifully staged such an occasion. Change program participants were recognized individually, presented with handsome engraved paperweights, and thanked personally by the chief executive for their contributions.

I talked earlier in this chapter about the importance of not encouraging resistance to the implementation of change by being too responsive to resisters. The chief executive must do a balancing act, without any scientific guidelines to follow, on the one hand dealing with legitimate concerns, and on the other being careful not to reward laziness, wrongheadedness, or obvious disloyalty. "My nonprofit, right or wrong" is too far at one end of the spectrum, but allowing people themselves to determine when and how they will support planned change is too far at the other. As is so often true, the balance is struck somewhere in the middle. Common sense is the primary guide.

Communicating

Finally, successful implementation of change—that is, planned initiatives that are implemented fully, in a timely fashion, within budget, and without undue pain and suffering—depends on communication, and lots and lots of it. Indeed, there cannot be too much communication; at least, I have never seen it happen.

It is through communication that understanding of the change program itself is fostered, laying a foundation of participation and cooperation. Lippitt, Langseth, and Mossop (1985), drawing on their experience in managing change at the World Bank, observe that, "To help the people involved in a change process, there should be a minimum of professional 'gobbledygook'; but, when necessary, everyone should be able to share a common language for describing elements of the process, personnel, and procedures" (p. 151).

As the change process moves forward and the inevitable stresses and strains of carrying out the change while also holding a full-time job begin to take their toll, frequent, open, two-way communication can help to smooth the way. Kirkpatrick (1985) calls communication "the second key to successful change." He points out that it means "more than 'telling'; it means 'creating understanding" (p. 118). He goes on to say that understanding is only achieved through effective two-way communication. But there are barriers to accomplishing this challenging task.

The staff working in the trenches almost always take heart from knowing to the extent feasible what is going on in the change program, whether or not the information can be of use to them in carrying out their responsibilities. Sharing information creates a sense of unity and shared burden; it provides perspective; it enhances morale. These are compelling reasons to communicate as widely and as often as possible, through publications and face-to-face meetings. Whoever dares to advise that information be shared on a need-to-know basis is revealing fundamental ignorance about the change process and offering foolish, potentially harmful advice.

Two-way communication, between the chief executive and management team on the one hand and the staff on the front lines of change on the other, for example, can produce two valuable benefits. The input from those actually carrying out the changes can be used to make necessary adjustments to the master implementation plan, adjusting both the content and pace of change to avert organizational overload and avoid unnecessary staff pain. Open two-way communication can also serve a therapeutic purpose, acting as a pressure valve as nonprofit leaders take the time to listen and discuss the concerns, anxieties, and problems that staff on the front lines are grappling with.

In Summary

This chapter began with a look at some of the dangerous icebergs lurking within the sea of change: the pressures of daily events, unanticipated events, the failure to generate adequate resources, and human resistance. Four key elements in successfully bypassing these icebergs were discussed: strong chief executive leadership backed by a supportive board; a structure and a process dedicated to the implementation of change; adequate resources; and a strategy for overcoming human resistance.

Chief executives can make planned change a high priority, ensure that the change process is well managed, see that the required resources are allocated, ensure that staff resistance is dealt with, and keep the board committed. They can help to establish the legitimacy of the change effort by pointing out the tie to values, vision, and mission; they can devote significant time to visible leadership of the implementation process; and they can avoid behavior that contradicts the desired changes. The chief executive can also guarantee that resistance is anticipated and planned for and personally get involved, participating visibly in the change process itself, sharing some of the pain and suffering, and sharing personal fears openly with others.

With a chief executive at the head, a strategic change program that involves a structure for policy oversight and coordination of implementation can protect planned changes from the demands of day-to-day operations. The program should include a steering committee to oversee and guide the process, a program coordinator to provide essential support, a master implementation plan to tie planned initiatives together and schedule them realistically, and implementation task forces to play a hands-on role in the process.

In addition to time and money, resources necessary to support the implementation of change initiatives include the skills and attitudes of the people involved and the image and political influence of the nonprofit. Six steps can be taken to deal with staff resistance to change: linking the changes to a nonprofit's values, vision, and mission; building ownership of the initiatives; keeping the change program realistic in scope and pace; maximizing individual benefits and minimizing loss; rewarding cooperation; and communicating effectively.

Making Innovation Work

Coming Attractions

Chapter Nine concludes this book with two final discussions:

- A summary of the 3CAP approach to leading and managing change
- Practical guidance for putting 3CAP into practice

A Clear Choice in Today's World

These are exciting times filled with opportunities for nonprofits to refine, improve, and expand the increasingly important services they are providing in America and other societies around the world. But these are also challenging times, fraught with peril for all nonprofit organizations, and especially threatening for those that fail to develop the capacity to lead and manage their own change. Since the world around us will not oblige us by changing more slowly or less dramatically—indeed, the extent and pace of change show every sign of continuing to escalate—nonprofits must make a critical choice. Exercising self-determination, they can choose to take the initiative in leading and managing their own change. The only other choice is to be changed by the forces around them. Not changing is to choose the victim's role, bringing with it sure pain and possible extinction.

3CAP as a Powerful Tool

The preeminent outcome of a nonprofit's applying the 3CAP approach to leading and managing change is customers and clients who are better served and, ultimately, an improved society. This social benefit is realized through a nonprofit's conscious, systematic investment in its own change so as to capitalize on opportunities to move toward its vision and minimize barriers and threats blocking progress toward its vision. In a nutshell, 3CAP involves a nonprofit's developing and managing a portfolio of change initiatives or projects that continually evolve as new initiatives are added and existing ones implemented. Creating and managing this portfolio successfully depends on a nonprofit's developing three critical capacities:

- *Leadership,* principally the leadership of the chief executive officer and the board
- *Innovation,* essentially a matter of building and marrying creative capacity to a planning process capable of using it to produce change initiatives
- *Implementation* of the change initiatives

I do not claim that the 3CAP approach is a full-fledged system that alone can meet all of the change leadership and management needs of all nonprofits. I do not claim the 3CAP approach has the capacity to forecast in any detail what the future will bring, much less exert a significant measure of control over external events. But I do confidently claim—based on my twenty-five years of experience and my reading of the literature—that by putting the 3CAP approach into practice, a nonprofit organization can significantly influence the content, impact, and pace of its own change. The 3CAP approach can make change more productive and less disruptive and ensure that opportunities are seized and threats and problems dealt with.

Although the 3CAP approach can significantly strengthen a nonprofit's self-determination in a challenging world, applying 3CAP is not likely to be a pain-free experience. On the contrary, where important change is concerned the adage "No pain, no gain" generally holds true. In fact, the odds are stacked against implementing significant, self-generated change. Most people, myself included, do not welcome or celebrate changing themselves, and since nonprofit organizations are above all else groups of people, they do not change easily.

Human beings resist change for many reasons, both conscious and subconscious, both rational and irrational. Planned change can jangle a nerve or threaten very real loss. It almost always makes life more complicated. In addition to human resistance, a nonprofit's planned change can be thrown off course by a failure to come up with the resources required to implement it, by the inexorable press of day-to-day events, and by unanticipated environmental change.

Organizational change can take many shapes and forms. It can be largely external in focus, having to do with influencing external conditions and events, image building and public relations, managing stakeholder relationships, and responding to changing needs and demands through new services and delivery mechanisms. It can be more internal in focus, having to do with strengthening leadership, planning and management capacities, structures, and processes. It can vary in scope, depth, impact, complexity, and cost. There is no hard and fast distinction between so-called strategic and operational change; precise definitions would serve no useful purpose. The annual operational planning and budget preparation process can produce significant planned change through the normal organizational channels. However, one of the most important decisions that a board, chief executive, and management team must make in leading change is to determine when issues involve such complexity and high stakes that they must be managed "above the line" as part of the nonprofit's strategic change portfolio.

Leadership

Leadership ensures that the innovation and implementation capacities are developed and work as intended. Organizational leadership sees that structures and processes are designed, directs and orchestrates their operation, supplies the required resources, builds understanding and support for change, and neutralizes resistance. Leadership is basically the result of a close board-staff partnership, but the chief executive, because of the full-time nature of the position, has practical control of rewards and punishments, and operational authority and is clearly the senior partner and leading change champion. If a chief executive is deeply opposed to change or lacks the knowledge and skills to lead it and does not wish to develop them, change is not likely to occur.

Effective chief executive leadership of change in today's wild and woolly world entails far more than persuading the troops to go along and taking firm command of the administrative functions of a nonprofit. Chief executive leadership in turbulent times requires taking primary accountability for producing five outcomes essential for effective change:

- Building a nonprofit's unity and cohesion by seeing that clear values, vision, and mission statements are fashioned and taking the lead in building commitment to them through communication and behavior that reinforce them
- A coherent organizational design that ensures that the key elements in the organization—board, management team, budget process—produce the required results and are well integrated
- Organizational stability and security, through maintaining effective external relations, behaving in a fashion that builds credibility and trust, and pacing change so that it is not needlessly punishing and disruptive
- An organization that is innovation-friendly, principally through building a culture that welcomes and nurtures creative behavior and a planning process that makes use of creativity to produce change initiatives
- And empowered people, through the design of processes that enable them to exercise significant influence and to build stronger skills and a culture that prizes diversity in styles, skills, and opinions

In addition to having strong technical skills in such essential areas as communication, planning, and financial management, a chief executive committed to strong leadership of change must develop three key attributes that have to do with one's character and psychological make-up and more often than not demand significant personal change and growth:

- *True humility.* Based on the belief that one is not the end-all, be-all of existence but, rather, a part of a universe that is governed by certain God-given values, true humility frees a person from the need to strive for perfection or to be right and preserve face at all costs. True humility fosters the self-confidence that makes it possible to develop and treasure strength in close associates without feeling threatened. True humility also inspires the trust and confidence of others.

- *Realistic self-knowledge.* Seeing the world objectively requires a kind of self-understanding that can only come from an inner journey to understand one's own strong emotions. If not uncovered and understood, these emotions can cause a person to interpret external events through distorting lens.

- *Courage.* Courage comes from a strong spiritual life, which steels a person to defend fundamental values against assault and makes possible the often terrifying inner journey in search of the self-knowledge.

Nonprofit boards are a rich but largely untapped resource. For a nonprofit board to be an active partner with the chief executive in the change process, it must evolve beyond its role as an appreciative audience for staff-produced documents. The old view of a nonprofit board sees it as the pinnacle of the organizational pyramid toward which staff-produced information flows. In the more contemporary view, it is an organization within the nonprofit organization that plays an important if not exclusive role in producing such bottom-line results as updated values, vision, and mission statements.

Leading boards take clear accountability for designing their governance work and the structure and processes for doing it. They demand governance processes that enable them to contribute to a nonprofit's directions and performance, principally by making full use of their members' knowledge, experience, talents, expertise, and connections. Leading boards also take accountability for their composition, regularly renewing their membership through a detailed profile of desired qualifications and attributes. They rigorously monitor their own performance against standards that they themselves have set.

Innovation

Innovation is the process of generating change initiatives consisting of intended change targets and implementation plans. Innovation can take the form of incremental adjustments to existing programs, at one end of the change spectrum, to dramatic shifts in vision and direction at the other. The only point of innovating is to deploy a nonprofit's resources, including its experience and expertise, in order to achieve its vision as fully as feasible, in light of environmental opportunities and constraints. Serious innovation is not about pie-in-the-sky wish lists or tilting at windmills. The point is to produce as much benefit as possible under the circumstances: to do it, not indulge in wishful thinking about it.

A nonprofit's innovative capacity develops from two key subcapacities: creativity and planning. Creativity generates the possibilities for innovation; planning selects from among the possibilities and translates them into feasible change initiatives. Through much of human history, creativity has been thought of as a largely mysterious, divinely inspired capacity, the stuff of geniuses. But in the twentieth century, advances in psychoanalytical and cognitive psychology and in neurophysiology have brought much of the landscape of creativity into sharper relief, although ample territory remains unilluminated.

Organizational creative capacity depends on the creative capacity of the individuals in the organization. One way to expand their creative capacity is to help people overcome the barriers to creative expression that reside in the subconscious and, hence, often go unrecognized and unaddressed. Traveling this path is likely to lead to dramatic growth in creative capacity, but it requires in-depth work that few nonprofits will want to undertake. More practical are educational and training programs and planning and management processes that stimulate creative growth, such as planning retreats that employ brainstorming techniques to come up with ideas for change initiatives.

Because of its penchant for neatness and control, traditional short-range and long-range planning are weak tools for innovation. Because strategic long-range planning has a tendency to describe in great detail what a nonprofit is already doing and then to project the present three or five years into an essentially unpredictable future, it has produced scant innovation, instead filling shelves with little-consulted tomes and deforesting much of America. However, a fairly recent variation on the strategic planning theme—strategic management—has proved to be a more reliable mechanism for translating creativity into practical change initiatives. The strategic management process focuses on identifying and selecting strategic issues in the context of a nonprofit's external environment and its internal strengths and weaknesses.

Strategic issues are significant opportunities available to move toward a nonprofit's vision as well as the important barriers standing in the way of realizing the vision. I use the term *strategic* to identify issues that are so complex and involve such high stakes that they cannot be trusted to the business-as-usual operational planning process. They demand more intense attention or do not fit into an organizational unit or program or both. Strategic management works when the highest priority issues are selected. The point is not to miss the opportunities that promise the greatest benefit or the problems that are likely to produce the greatest damage.

If planned correctly, a retreat that brings together the board, the chief executive, and the management team can be a powerful way of kicking off the strategic management process while making full use of the board as a resource. A carefully designed retreat can produce such important results as updated values, vision, and mission statements; a scan of external trends and conditions; an assessment of organizational strengths and weaknesses; and the identification of strategic issues. Using brainstorming techniques can ensure a free-ranging exploration of issues while also building feelings of ownership and enthusiasm through participation.

Implementation

Plans do not implement themselves, no matter how well crafted they are. In fact, for those inclined to display bumper stickers, one that reads, "Planned changes tend not to happen" would understate the case. No wonder so many people feel disillusioned, and even cynical, about planning, often having put in countless hours to little effect.

The icebergs that lie in the sea of change can easily throw the ship of implementation off its course, or destroy it altogether. Four of the most important icebergs are the following:

- Day-to-day pressures that tend to consume virtually all available money, time, and attention

- Unanticipated events that throw a monkey wrench into the change machine
- Inadequate resources, including money and time and staff skills as well
- And that old bugaboo, human resistance to change

Although the perils along the change journey are all too real, over the past couple of decades we have learned a great deal about managing the implementation of change, and we have some strong tools to keep the change ship afloat: a nonprofit's chief executive seriously taking on the role of officer in charge of change; creating a special change program that dedicates structure and process to implementation of change initiatives; providing the resources required for full and timely implementation of initiatives; and fashioning and carrying out a detailed strategy for dealing with staff resistance.

If the chief executive does not visibly and aggressively lead and support a change program, it will almost certainly fail. People in organizations watch their chief executive's behavior carefully to determine what the real priorities of the organization are, rather than merely buying into the stated party line. Through active participation, the chief executive confirms the importance of a change program. The chief executive also makes sure that the board is on board before embarking on the implementation journey.

Perhaps the most effective way to keep a change effort from being overwhelmed by the inexorable press of day-to-day concerns and operations is to create a special structure and process dedicated to the implementation of change initiatives. Headed by the chief executive, this change program should include a steering committee to establish policies and oversee performance, a program coordinator to provide hands-on direction and technical assistance, and task forces to carry out implementation plans. By giving the change effort organizational form in this way, a nonprofit can prevent its disappearing from the collective consciousness while also giving it status and credibility.

As already discussed, there are many reasons why people in organizations oppose change, some subconscious and hence unrecognized, others quite conscious and sensible. The fact is, people sometimes lose status and occasionally even jobs because of

change. Also, taking on new responsibilities can cause considerable mental anguish, especially when one's self-esteem is linked to
doing the old job well. Some tried-and-true ways to decrease staff
resistance and build support include:

- Explicitly clarifying the link between the planned change and
  the values, vision, and mission
- Building a sense of staff ownership of the change initiatives
  through active participation in both creating and implementing them
- Making sure that losses are kept to a minimum and that
  benefits are maximized
- Rewarding cooperation and not blessing resistance
- Making sure that everyone knows what is going on all of
  the time through constant, open communication

So What Now?

Having made it through the first eight chapters of this book, readers will naturally ask, "What do I do next?" Just understanding the
three key capacities and their interrelationships is not sufficient to
undertake the journey of building change leadership capacity successfully. Lots of planning, commitment, determination, and tenacity—and a large dollop of common sense—are required for the
journey. To help the reader and his or her nonprofit get under way,
I would like to conclude the book with some practical commonsense suggestions for putting the 3CAP approach into practice. In
doing so, I will briefly address one exclusive board leadership
responsibility, but I will concentrate at greater length on the role
of the preeminent change champion in every nonprofit, the chief
executive, working in partnership with his or her board.

First, the whole leadership team—board, chief executive, and
senior managers—must remember that there is no painless way to
put 3CAP into practice while also running the shop. Furthermore,
the job cannot be accomplished overnight. Developing the three
capacities to lead change effectively involves implementing complex change while handling all the myriad operational details of
running a nonprofit, as well as other issues that demand immediate attention. In the real world, we cannot blithely shut down a

nonprofit's operations for six months while retooling for 3CAP, as a factory might do, and so a demanding juggling act is called for.

Let's take, for example, Inner City Hospital, an eighty-year-old municipal treasure that has managed to serve a large percentage of the poor in its community while also conducting nationally significant research, providing excellent education for medical residents, and building a top-notch trauma center. Despite its stellar record of research and service, Inner City is on the brink of financial disaster. The county government subsidy has been cut in half; the middle class has almost completely deserted the hospital's primary market area; an antiquated physical plant that contributes to elevated costs desperately needs upgrading; and lower-cost delivery systems are nipping at Inner City's heels.

Fortunately, the Inner City board and the chief executive are in the midst of merger talks that promise to keep Inner City afloat. But there are a thousand and one details that must be worked out in the coming months before Inner City Hospital becomes part of the new managed care corporation. While carrying out this survival strategy, are the board and chief executive likely to put the merger discussions completely aside to make room for the development of the 3CAP approach? Not unless they want to risk their sanity being questioned! However, in a world of dizzying change, Inner City Hospital cannot afford *not* to strengthen its ongoing capacity to lead and manage change. So, how to balance these needs becomes the $64,000 question.

Inner City Hospital is not an extraordinary case these days. Rather, it is a common-enough example of a nonprofit under stress that will have a difficult time dealing with capacity building in the midst of other changes. Indeed, I can think of countless real-life examples: a nonprofit contemporary art center simultaneously struggling to balance a budget stretched to the limit, turn around falling membership and attendance, and trying to find a new director; an employment and training agency cutting back staff dramatically due to federal budget cuts while attempting to respond to new federal workforce development legislation that can only be seen through a glass darkly; a nonprofit nursing home attempting to cope with slashes in Medicaid reimbursement without giving up its mission to the poor and going 100 percent in the private pay direction; a community development corporation in danger of losing a huge grant that is its financial life blood because its accounting system cannot generate the required reports. And on and on and on.

Is it even possible to tackle the application of the 3CAP approach in organizations facing so much stress? The answer is clearly yes, but only if the nonprofit incorporates two key elements in its 3CAP development strategy. First, 3CAP must be carefully paced so that operational integrity is not threatened and other top priorities, such as Inner City Hospital's completing the merger process, are not jeopardized. Second, implementing 3CAP must involve as much top-down leadership as bottom-up participation, and probably much more in the early stages. The term "top-down" is not so politically correct these days, but if the head is not actively engaged in guiding the development of 3CAP, you can expect to see lots of legs getting tangled and feet getting stepped on.

The Board's Chief Responsibility

Above all else, the successful development of the three capacities at the heart of the 3CAP approach to change leadership depends on having the right chief executive in place, a task that only the board is capable of performing. If a nonprofit board is engaged in recruiting a new chief executive, there are some practical ways to determine whether candidates for the job are capable of applying the 3CAP approach.

The board can look for evidence of successful change leadership experience, through reference checking and the examination of pertinent documentation, such as articles reporting such experience.

The board can conduct an in-depth interview of leading candidates, inquiring about candidates' philosophy, techniques, and experience in the realm of change leadership.

Most nonprofits already have a chief executive in place, and in this situation the board might rely on negotiation, evaluation, and counseling in carrying out its responsibility. When the commitment is made to implement a 3CAP approach to leading change, it would make sense for the board and the chief executive to engage in an intensive dialogue, exploring in detail the kind of chief executive leadership required in building the three key capacities. Once the expectations of the chief executive are clarified, a candid evaluation of the chief executive's capabilities, focusing on an assessment of past experience, is in order. Ideally, the board does not sit back in judgment of the chief executive; rather, the chief executive is a willing and even ardent participant in this exercise. Both strong and weak points will naturally emerge if the assessment process is undertaken seriously, and the two parties must decide how to deal with the important weaknesses that are identified.

I once worked with a chief executive who headed a widely respected nonprofit that operated a state-of-the-art nursing home and provided several other services, including home care. Highly trained, technically top-notch, and intellectually nimble, she ran a very centralized operation with a thin veneer of participatory management. Her controlling style and authoritarian approach resulted in a planning process that brooked little free discussion, much less serious questioning of the direction she established. She would not have welcomed or promoted a freer, more creative planning process; only her board could have identified this weakness and worked with her to remedy it.

Most people can change in very important ways if they really want to. I have witnessed incredible transformations over the years that have made me somewhat of an optimist, at least where the potential to change is concerned. But there will always be people, chief executives included, to whom changing will not seem worth the pain and effort. On the verge of taking on the tremendous challenge of applying the 3CAP approach, a board confronting a chief executive who is unwilling to change a style or approach that is likely to jeopardize the 3CAP effort has only one real choice: change the chief executive's mind or ask that chief executive to leave.

Is it unrealistic to expect most nonprofit boards to take this responsibility to heart and carry it out fully? Unfortunately, I believe it is, based on my experience. Nevertheless, a board that is prepared to play a leading governance role would find no serious technical barriers to this negotiation and evaluation process. As is usually the case, the barriers would most likely be interpersonal—the board worrying that it might threaten or insult its chief executive.

The Chief Executive with Board Support

The chief executive who is committed to building the nonprofit's capacity to lead and manage change should take three critical steps early in the process:

1. Take responsibility for developing his or her own change leadership skills and attributes
2. See that a change program, with a special structure and process, is established to deal with the application of the 3CAP approach in the context of other organizational change
3. Employ the principle of first-things-first-but-too-much-never in building the change leadership capacities

Chapter Three offered some practical advice to chief executives who are committed to developing the skills and attributes most important to leading and managing change. There are no simple recipes for developing such fundamental attributes as true humility, realistic self-knowledge, and the courage that draws on solid spiritual underpinnings. The way is never direct or easy when the matter of core values and character are at issue. The indispensable first step is realistic self-assessment, followed by frank dialogue with trusted colleagues and friends and eventually with the board. Once developmental needs are recognized, the next step is to commit to working on them, even if such a dramatic and usually threatening step as counseling is required.

Let's look at the illness of depression, for example. Depression is said to be a common phenomenon in these challenging times, especially among high-achieving people such as chief executives, who tend to judge themselves by extraordinarily high standards and are frequently harshly self-critical. In today's changing world, with its growing complexity, accelerating change, increasing competitiveness, and declining job security, people who are accustomed to being in command may take some serious blows to their self-esteem and consequently suffer from depression. Fortunately, depression is recognized as a real and treatable malady that frequently responds to the appropriate medication. Therefore, one of the wisest moves that a perfectionist chief executive might make these days is to be alert for signs of depression and to seek medical help if they are spotted.

Chapter Eight described in detail how to establish a change leadership and management program with a structure and process that are kept separate from day-to-day management. It is imperative that such a program be established as one of the earliest steps in developing the change leadership capacities involved in the 3CAP approach, which otherwise would likely be buried by an avalanche of daily demands and inevitable crises. Not only will putting the change program in place early in the 3CAP process ensure that the changes involved in developing the approach are planned, funded, and managed in an orderly fashion, the program will also enable a nonprofit to manage all significant change efforts, including developing 3CAP, concurrently.

The change program process will allow the nonprofit to determine what developments will take place during the coming year in the key 3CAP components: board and chief executive leadership; innovation (creativity and planning process); and change implementation. And the annual change master plan generated by the program will include the other changes not directly related to 3CAP. For example, the board, chief executive, and management team might identify at a two-day planning retreat two 3CAP-related changes that need to be addressed during the coming year, along with such changes as responding to new funding legislation, developing a new product, and attracting a new membership group. By dealing with all significant planned changes together, a nonprofit can ensure that the time, money, energy, and other resources required to deal with them during the same year can be allocated.

The first-things-first rule dictates that higher-stakes issues be dealt with first, while those that can wait are addressed later on. Taking the Inner City Hospital example, the merger talks would obviously be the highest priority change initiative because the institution's very survival is involved. But the institution might concurrently move ahead to develop higher priority facets of the 3CAP approach, such as upgrading the strategic planning process to make it more innovation-focused and clarifying leadership roles and structures of the board.

The extent and pace of the annual 3CAP-related change initiatives would, through the change program structure, be determined in the context of other essential changes, such as a new financial management system or the hospital's merger process, so as not to jeopardize them. Thus, it might make good sense to build a strategic management process over a three-year period, with incremental enhancements being implemented yearly, for example, rather than biting off such a large piece of change in a single year that it causes more harm than good. Staff creativity training might be seen as an ongoing, rather leisurely paced process that involves discussions in staff meetings, semiannual two-day training sessions, the circulation of reading materials, and in-service training through participation in an upgraded planning process. A more dramatic approach to creative capacity building—launching an intensive week of training in the midst of all kinds of other organizational pressures, for example—might be so counterproductive that it actually sets back the cause of creativity rather than advancing it.

In Summary

This chapter summarized the message of this book: nonprofits of all shapes and sizes, no matter what their business—from an all-volunteer community theater with a $30,000 budget to a three thousand–employee hospital with a $1.2 billion budget—can put the principles and tools of the 3CAP approach to use in designing and leading their own change. In today's challenging world, no nonprofit can afford *not* to build the capacities that are critical for leading change. Fortunately, any nonprofit can make practical use of the 3CAP approach without investing in exotic or expensive technology. It is a low-tech, commonsensical, people-oriented approach. Nor does the application of 3CAP demand that a nonprofit transform itself overnight; incremental capacity building is not only possible but, in the real world, often the only viable course of action. Putting 3CAP into practice requires above all else the following:

- A strong board, chief executive, and management team committed to developing the capacities essential for leading change
- A master plan that puts the changes involved in the 3CAP approach in the context of other organizational changes
- The willingness, fortitude, and tenacity to endure the frustrations and pain and suffering that inevitably accompany any

serious individual or organizational growth, to allocate the resources required to support the growth, and to avoid the siren song of quick fixes and cheap solutions
- Flexibility that allows for creative adjustment of strategies, plans, and schedules as needed, without becoming demoralized or being thrown into disarray

Taking firm command of change in a nonprofit, exercising a significant degree of organizational self-determination, is not only possible but essential if nonprofits around the world are to maintain and expand their capacity to address economic and social issues, thus making our world a more livable place. The 3CAP approach brings such self-determination within reach of any nonprofit, whatever it does and wherever it does it.